GOD THE SON

GOD THE SON

Twenty things everyone should know
about Jesus

Don K. Clements

Metokos Press
Narrows, VA 24124

Published by Metokos Press Inc., committed to providing materials easily accessible to the average reader while at the same time presenting biblical truth from within the framework of biblical and confessional churches of Reformed and Presbyterian heritage. Visit us on the web at *www.metokospress.com*.

Cover design by Chip Evans, Walker-Atlanta, Atlanta, GA.

Printed in the United States by Lightning Source, LaVergne, TN.

ISBN 978-0-9742331-9-2

Contents

Those who know me will smile when they read these words, but they are important for everyone to know. Don Clements is not a theologian. So if you are looking for another theological analysis of the person and work of Jesus, you've come to the wrong place. That is not the purpose of this book.

While I am not a theologian, I am a preacher, and at times, an evangelist. This book is drawn from that part of my life. I have made up a list of twenty things I believe people need to understand about Jesus. There are probably a number of items included in other works about Jesus that have been left out here. I'm sorry about that. At the end of the day, I could only use twenty items, and these are the ones I picked.

Why twenty? Why not a David Letterman "Top Ten List"? Well, there are way more than ten important things for Christians to know about Jesus. Why not twenty-five? After all, the football and basketball polls seem to think that's the right number. Well, I picked twenty for a very practical reason. One of the uses of this book will be as part of the curriculum in the Ruling Elder Training Academy (www.RulingElder.com), and that curriculum is set up to have ten lessons per course. So I needed a number that would fit easily in ten lessons—two chapters per week equals twenty chapters for ten lessons. (I wasn't a math major for a year and a half of college for nothing!)

One other thing is worth mentioning at this point—you'll notice it soon enough. I consistently refer to Jesus as Jesus, or as Jesus the Messiah, and seldom as Christ. It's a pet peeve of mine—probably because I was a Hebrew linguist in the Navy, and also took lots of language classes both in my M.Div. and D.Min. studies. As you may know, "Christ" is the English translation for the Greek *Christos,* which is the Greek translation for the Hebrew *Mesheach*, which comes into English as "Messiah." I see the theme of Messiah as a crucial one (it's on the list of twenty, you'll notice). It seems to me that when Jesus lived, he was referred to as "Jesus the Messiah," which got translated from the Greek into English as Jesus Christ. But that sounds to me too much like a first and last name—and that is as far from the truth as can be. I would be a little happier with the consistency of "Jesus the Messiah," but after more than five hundred years of the printing of Bibles in English, it's probably too late to campaign for a change. So I just call him Jesus!

Most of the work in this book is original. In my need to make a strict publication date, I decided to use material taken from several sermons from sources outside my own writing. In each case, full credit is given at the beginning of the chapter. I make no apology for that. I've read a lot of books about Jesus over the years, and for the most part they were pretty boring, not the kind of thing you want to read for morning devotions. I hope that this sermonic and evangelistic material will not be that.

If what I am is a preacher and an evangelist, then sermons are my tools. This means that you will find in this book something you don't find in many books. I make specific application of the primary issue (doctrine, if you will) discussed in each chapter to people as individuals and as the church. You might want to keep a set of steel-toed boots handy just in case I step on your toes!

My prayer is that God would bless the reading of this book, that at least a few people would come to know Jesus better—and what a wonderful blessing it would be if a few hearts were changed from spiritual stone to living, Jesus-loving flesh. Pray with me for that, would you please?

Acknowledgements

Special thanks to the Radforfd (Virginia) Church Plant Bible Study who let me use these 20 items on them as a trial run during the winter-spring of 2009.

Narrows, Virginia
May 2007

Don Clements has made a long, winding trip from Navy enlisted man to college debater and back to the Navy, retiring as a chaplain, then on to mountain pastor, evangelist and now author. In the journey, he has seen many places and many sides of life. As in his previous works, he has drawn richly on this background.

Although he claims that these books are written primarily for "the many people (but especially 'guys') in churches who do not regularly read books about 'church stuff,'" they are much more, as this volume shows.

It is, of course, theology written for those who disavow the term and what they imagine it entails. Even more, as the Presbyterian community abandons our Catechisms and produces legacy members armed only with a few "biblical stories" and "sword drill" verses, it both fills in the blanks and opens wide the doors of scripture.

And for those of us who do remember parts of the Catechisms and the covenantal structure of scripture,

Don's insights and non-churchy writing throws fresh, new light on key points, helping us see them in newer (and, often, fuller) ways. In short, this book is a significant resource for the entire Body of Christ...

God The Son is remarkably clear of theological jargon and long on concise explication of key scriptures. It encourages and feeds readers. Chapter 17 on the Great Commandments ("Learning about Love from Dale Earnhardt.") alone is worth the cost – in money and reading time.

I challenge you to read this book and remain unchanged.

Bob Brame
Stanardsville, Virginia
April, 2009

Chapter One
Incarnation – "I and the Father Are One"

The apostle John is known as the great evangelist. I can give testimony to his power as an evangelist—I personally came to faith in Jesus while reading John's Gospel. As far as I am concerned, if you want to learn about Jesus, you start with the Gospel of John.

Much of the first chapter of the gospel is really the story about a different John, John the Baptizer. As he relates this story, the apostle is forced to introduce Jesus at least briefly because it was John the Baptizer's purpose to become a witness to Jesus. So obviously the apostle had to say something about Jesus. Here are the first eighteen verses of John chapter 1:

> ¹In the beginning was the Word, and the Word was with God, and the Word was God. ²He was in the beginning with God. ³All things were made through him, and without him was not any thing made that was made. ⁴In him was life, and the life was the light of men. ⁵The light shines in the darkness, and the darkness has not overcome it.
>
> ⁶There was a man sent from God, whose name was John. ⁷He came as a witness, to bear witness about the light, that all might believe through him. ⁸He was not the light, but came to bear witness about the light.

⁹The true light, which enlightens everyone, was coming into the world. ¹⁰He was in the world, and the world was made through him, yet the world did not know him. ¹¹He came to his own, and his own people did not receive him. ¹²But to all who did receive him, who believed in his name, he gave the right to become children of God ¹³who were born, not of blood nor of the will of the flesh nor of the will of man, but of God.

¹⁴And the Word became flesh and dwelt among us, and we have seen his glory, glory as of the only Son from the Father, full of grace and truth. ¹⁵(John bore witness about him, and cried out, "This was he of whom I said, 'He who comes after me ranks before me, because he was before me'") ¹⁶And from his fullness we have all received, grace upon grace. ¹⁷For the law was given through Moses; grace and truth came through Jesus Christ. ¹⁸No one has ever seen God; the only God, who is at the Father's side, he has made him known.

These first eighteen verses of chapter 1 are all the apostle says at this point. Those verses are filled with statements that are difficult to grasp because they tell us things that go beyond our human, natural understanding.

"In the beginning was the Word, and the Word was with God, and the Word was God." It's obvious that the apostle John is using "Word" to refer to Jesus. In verse 14 he says, *"The Word became flesh and dwelt among us, and we have seen his glory, glory as of the only Son from the Father."*

The apostle is telling us that this "Word" he is talking about is the "only Son from the Father"—Jesus, God the Son.

Back to that first verse, and let's substitute "Jesus" for "Word" and read it again. "In the beginning was Jesus and Jesus was with God and Jesus was God." We need to understand three crucial things in that verse.

In the beginning was Jesus. Jesus was there at the beginning. What might that beginning be? Where else do we read in the Bible about "the beginning"? Why, in Genesis 1, verses 1 and 2, of course:

> [1]*In the beginning, God created the heavens and the earth. *[2]*The earth was without form and void, and darkness was over the face of the deep. And the Spirit of God was hovering over the face of the waters.*

Interesting, isn't it? Genesis 1 talks about God and about the Spirit of God. So where is God the Son? Well, Moses didn't tell us. Because as God revealed his Word to Moses in that special revelation way to ensure that it was God's own Word and without error, God did not reveal much about Jesus at the outset. As we read the Old Testament, we have to dig deep to see Jesus—but he was there. John told us so.

"In the beginning was the Word." That's at the very beginning. Jesus existed as early as God, and as early as the Holy Spirit. This great triune God has always existed in three Persons—and they were all there at creation.

The apostle Paul recognized Jesus had a role in creation. Look at Colossians 1:16–17: *"For by him all things were created, in heaven and on earth, visible and invisible, whether thrones or dominions or rulers or authorities—all things were created through him and for him. [17]And he is before all things, and in him all things hold together."*

Not too hard to understand, is it? By Jesus, all things were created. All things (and Paul lists the categories) were created through him and for him, and Jesus is "before" all things. In other words, Jesus existed even before creation because Jesus is part of the triune God, who has existed forever.

In the first chapter of my work titled *God the Holy Spirit,* I deal with the issue of the Trinity at great length. It's worth restating part of that chapter here as it relates to Jesus:

So, what does the Bible teach is the best way to understand the Holy Trinity? Well, let's look at the very best definition one can find—from the Westminster Shorter Catechism Question 6: "How many persons are there in the Godhead? There are three persons in the Godhead; the Father, the Son, and the Holy Spirit; and these three are one God, the same in substance, equal in power and glory."

First, let's focus on the concept of each member of the Trinity being a "person." What constitutes "personhood"? Nearly everyone would acknowledge that a person has a mind that can process knowledge, has a will to decide when to act or not to act, has emotions and feelings, and has the ability to communicate with other persons.

So, God the Father is a person. He's not a cow, he's not the sun, he's not the wind, he's not just an idea or theory (all of which are gods of different groups of people). No, he is a person. Admittedly, he is quite different from persons such as you and me, because as our young children learn in the children's catechism: "God is a Spirit and doesn't have a body like man." You see, having a body is not part of "personhood." It is certainly a part of being a human person, but not the concept of "personhood."

God the Son, Jesus, is also a person. Before Jesus took on human form on the night we now celebrate as Christmas, he didn't have a body. He was part of the eternal Trinity—and he was then a spirit—just like God the Father.

However, ever since the incarnation, ever since Jesus came to earth to take on human form to become both truly God and truly man, Jesus has been a person with a human body! Even now, since the resurrection, he still has a body. It is no longer identical to a human body—the Bible calls it a "spiritual body"—but it's enough like a human body that we'll have no trouble recognizing any other humans we may know when we see them in heaven in their spiritual bodies.

So, what do we know so far from John chapter 1? We know that Jesus is part of the Trinity, the part that carries the name "God the Son." We know that he has existed as long as God the Father has existed, which is to say forever, eternally. There was never a time that Jesus did not exist, and we know that not only was he "with" God, we know he "was" God.

We know that he "became flesh and dwelt among us" (verse 10), and that presents a problem. You see, the crucial matter that we must understand right from the beginning—that Jesus is both human and divine—is not just *our* problem. It has been a problem for human beings always. It was a *big* problem for the Jews living at the time Jesus lived. John gives us just a hint of that in verse 11 of chapter 1: *"He came to his own, and his own people did not receive him."*

Now we must turn—as I will do just as often as possible throughout this work—and see what Jesus himself has to say about this problem, about how to understand the tension people feel when they learn that Jesus is both human and divine at the same time. Jesus speaks to that issue most clearly in an encounter he had one day when some Jews got so upset over this issue that they were about to kill him. John the apostle relates the encounter in John 10, verses 31–39:

> *31The Jews picked up stones again to stone him. 32Jesus answered them, "I have shown you many good works from the Father; for which of them are you going to stone me?" 33The Jews answered him, "It is*

not for a good work that we are going to stone you but for blasphemy, because you, being a man, make yourself God." [34]Jesus answered them, "Is it not written in your Law, 'I said, you are gods'? [35]If he called them gods to whom the word of God came— and Scripture cannot be broken—[36]do you say of him whom the Father consecrated and sent into the world, 'You are blaspheming,' because I said, 'I am the Son of God'? [37]If I am not doing the works of my Father, then do not believe me; [38]but if I do them, even though you do not believe me, believe the works, that you may know and understand that the Father is in me and I am in the Father." [39]Again they sought to arrest him, but he escaped from their hands.

Let's begin by trying to understand why the Jews were so angry. There are lots of different types of anger, and we need to figure out which one this was.

For many people, anger comes when their sense of justice is challenged. You see this with your children all the time. They scream, "It's not fair. Johnny got to do it; why can't I?" Or, "Mary did the same thing. Why isn't she being punished?"

Children aren't the only ones who express anger at their sense of injustice. Lots of adults get angry when they don't get what they think they deserve, especially when it involves job selection or promotions. Many people—especially those who are self-centered—express anger over what they sense as injustice.

For other people, anger comes quickly when they are told something that causes them grief. There is an interesting process that just about everyone goes through when told that a loved one has died—especially when the news is unexpected. Usually they begin with denial—claming that the news couldn't possibly be true.

The second stage of grief is anger. Once the reality of the news sinks in, most people burst out in anger. Sometimes the anger comes almost immediately if they just sort of skip through the denial stage.

Once as a Navy chaplain, I had to inform a young man that his sister, who was a sailor assigned to the ship that I served as senior chaplain, had been killed earlier that day in an auto accident. The young man, who was sitting down, suddenly stood up and took a swing at me. Understanding the frequency of anger responses to grief, I had the presence of mind to duck.

There are times when we hear something that goes against all our normal, rational thinking and we strike out in anger at the closest object. Often that is the person bringing us the information—you know, the "don't kill the messenger" syndrome.

There is a sense in which both of these sources of anger are present in this incident in John chapter 10. It's pretty clear right in verse 31 that the Pharisees are angry about something. *"The Jews picked up stones again to stone him."* What is it that brought on this extreme level of anger?

Well, Jesus has been around for a few months by this time and the Pharisees have heard him say some things that were hard for them to swallow. In John 6:42 Jesus said, *"I have come down from heaven."* When challenged by the Pharisees about his claim to be the "light of the world," Jesus had responded in John 8:18: *"I am the one who bears witness about myself, and the Father who sent me bears witness about me."* When the Jews responded by asking him where his Father was, Jesus scolded them in verse 19: *"You know neither me nor my Father. If you knew me, you would know my Father also."*

Then in an incident that immediately preceded the passage we are considering, Jesus just came right out and said—in words that no one could misunderstand—that he, Jesus, was in fact God. In verse 30, he said, *"I and the Father are one"*!

This is the statement that precipitates the violent reaction on the part of Jesus' adversaries in verse 31, as they pick up stones with which they intend to kill him. Certainly that qualifies as anger, but even in the face of this mortal threat, Jesus answers in verse 32, *"I have shown you many good works from the Father; for which of them are you going to stone me?"*

Finally, the Pharisees reveal the real source of their anger. It's there in verse 33. *"It is not for a good work that we are going to stone you but for blasphemy, because you, being a man, make yourself God."* The situation dramatically presents the problem that every human being has when

9

being confronted with the truth that Jesus of Nazareth is both God and man.

Sometimes he refers to himself as the "Son of man"—stressing his human nature. That's not a big problem to most people. After all, the Pharisees have seen Jesus around. Here he is again, standing in front of them, obviously a man. He speaks. He breathes. He walks. He exhibits all the common characteristics of humanity. Yet he says, *"I and the Father are one,"* and the Pharisees actually understand what he means.

He is saying that he and the one and only true God—the God of Abraham, Isaac, and Jacob—the God of Moses and David—the God of Israel—their God—Jesus says that he and this God are one. They are the same.

This is not the first time Jesus has tried to explain who he was to the Pharisees. Back in chapter 5 of John's Gospel, we find this in verse 18: *"This was why the Jews were seeking all the more to kill him, because not only was he breaking the Sabbath, but he was even calling God his own Father, making himself equal with God."* Jesus had added some fuel to that fire by saying in verse 23, *"all (should) honor the Son, just as they honor the Father . . . who sent him."*

In the minds of his adversaries, the Pharisees, for one who is so obviously a man to claim to be God—to be equal with God the Father, to deserve the same honor as the one and only true God—this could not possibly be true.

Therefore, such a claim was the rankest blasphemy and instilled great passions of anger.

This explains why they became so angry with Jesus for saying that he was the Son of God. His response there in verse 34 is magnificent. He is quoting from Psalm 82:6, which reads: "*I said, 'You are gods, sons of the Most High, all of you . . . .'*" The word translated "gods" in this psalm is *elohim,* which can also be translated as "judges" or "rulers" or "leaders." Even as early as the writing of the psalms, God was teaching his people that they were all "adopted"—children—they were his true family.

Jesus continues in verses 35 and 36. "*If he called them gods to whom the word of God came—and Scripture cannot be broken—do you say of him whom the Father consecrated and sent into the world, 'You are blaspheming,' because I said, 'I am the Son of God'?*"

The fact that there is this God-related element in all men, even the wicked men of whom Psalm 82 was speaking, should be sufficient evidence to show that the incarnation of Jesus is not a contradiction or impossibility. (By the way, that fancy word "incarnation" I just used is the technical language that the theologians use when they speak of God the Son becoming man, taking on a human form.)

Even so, Jesus is not claiming something totally irrational, like a square being a circle. In fact, the claim back in verse 30, "*I and the Father are one*" is not only rational, it is possible—in which case it would not necessarily be blasphemy. But the Pharisees cannot accept that.

Jesus doesn't give up easily. In verses 37 and 38, he tries to get them to look at more evidence. *"If I am not doing the works of my Father, then do not believe me; but if I do them, even though you do not believe me, believe the works, that you may know and understand that the Father is in me and I am in the Father."*

Look, you stubborn, hardheaded Pharisees—if you can't believe me, then believe the miracles I have been performing month after month right in front of your face. Surely, I must be in the Father and the Father in me. In other words, I must have a divine nature, just like God, or else I couldn't be performing all these miracles.

The fact that the Pharisees still did not admit the logic of his reply but instead (there in verse 39) *"sought to arrest him, but he escaped from their hands"* is, of course, not evidence against the reasonableness of the doctrine of the incarnation. The Pharisees' disbelief is simply a sin against God, which results in their rejection of the claims of Jesus.

The Pharisees' anger comes from several sources. There is, first of all, a sense of loss—of grief —in the thought of accepting Jesus' logic. If Jesus is the Son of God, then they have not been teaching truth in their interpretation of the Scriptures, and the people don't have to keep every single detail of the law to be in a right relationship with God. To take away the truth of their tradition is more than they can bear—and they respond with anger.

There is also the aspect that their anger was a result of their false sense of justice. It just wasn't fair that God would send his Son to earth to be the Messiah at this time. This would mean that they no longer had the supreme religious authority. They would have to submit to the authority of the Messiah—the Bread of Life—the Light of the World—the True Shepherd. Their selfishness blocked their ability to recognize the truth.

But basically, their anger—as ultimately all anger is— was based on unbelief. When you boil it down to basics, folks, *all* anger is a result of not fully trusting—not really believing—God and his Word. (See James 1:19-21.)

Now let me remind you, for those of you who read the Preface to this book, that my purpose is not only to teach you the twenty most important truths (doctrines, if you will) about Jesus. As valuable as that purpose is, I am going to go further. Since I told you I am not a theologian but rather a preacher and evangelist, I'm going to do some application of these truths.

When it comes to the Pharisees rejecting the truth that Jesus is God the Son, let me tell you that you and I are frequently no better than those Pharisees. You and I (while we might be reluctant to admit it—and we certainly try very hard not to show it) reject the truth that Jesus is indeed God the Son in much the same ways.

Many times, we are not even aware that we are rejecting Jesus. Of course, we don't openly show anger by striking out at Him. Oh no, we're much too civilized for that. Rather, we show our rejection with the well-known form we call the cold shoulder.

You know how it is when you are really angry with people. Instead of throwing something to try to kill them, or yelling and screaming at them, you just ignore them. Sometimes you will not speak to them for days or weeks or, in some cases, even months and years. This is still anger even though it is a silent form.

We selfishly express our silent anger toward Jesus when we demand our own idea of justice instead of taking God at his Word and understanding that there is only one justice in the world—the justice that demands perfection in order to be in a right relationship with God. That perfection occurred only once in all of human history, in the person of Jesus, God the Son. (We'll take a closer look at that truth in another chapter.)

Without bowing before his authority and putting all of our trust in him and in him alone, we can't—in fact, no one in the world can—ever be in a right relationship with God or ever hope to attain to eternal life in heaven.

We also express our silent anger when we are asked to lose our self-righteousness and our self-satisfaction, or when we refuse to put to death our sinful nature. We don't want to lose our sins. We are very attached to them, just as the Pharisees were very attached to their belief system. We certainly don't want to be told that in order to have true faith in Jesus, we have to repent of our sins. You see, we not only have to say we're sorry about them, we also have to turn away from them, to put them to death. And we are so comfortable with our sinful nature, that it grieves us to have to put it away.

Of course, we are silently angry because at the very basic level, we don't believe God. We fail to take the promises of God at face value. We feel *we* must take action to make things right. We can't just leave it in *his* hands. It's as if we don't think God is wise enough, and powerful enough, and sovereign enough to handle our problems.

If only you and I could trust and believe God and his Word in all things—without anger. We would then be able to bow down in worship and adoration, graciously accepting his justice. We would be eager to repent of our sins and to put all of our trust and faith only in Jesus.

The doctrine of the incarnation is at the very heart of our salvation. You see, Jesus is indeed God the Son. He is God; he is divine—just as he told us in his own words. Jesus had to be God the Son or there would have been no incarnation, no Christmas—and no Easter. As God's one and only, unique son—the God/man—Jesus was born, lived a sinless life, and died in our place to pay the penalty for sin that you and I could never pay. Because we are not perfect, and perfection is the demand for entrance into heaven, we need Jesus to pay the penalty that we are helpless to afford.

Jesus as a man—as fully human as you and I—was perfect. He was able to live a perfect, sinless, spotless life, without blemish, and thus he could earn entrance into eternal life in heaven. His perfection became ours in the great transaction on the cross (another item on our top twenty list) as his righteousness was imputed to us. At the same time, he gave his life as an atonement for our sins (another top twenty), paying the immense price that provides our access to a right relationship with God.

So, my appeal to you today is . . . quit giving Jesus the cold shoulder. Quit refusing to communicate with him. Read the Bible and offer deep, sincere prayers. Meditate. Be fully reconciled to him. Put your trust in Jesus, God the Son. Recognize that he deserves all your worship and adoration. Quite frankly, unless and until you do, you probably won't understand much else in this book!

F irst, we need to define the fancy theological term that I am using for the chapter title. I usually will go out of my way *not* to use these kinds of fancy terms, but occasionally they are essential. The Merriam-Webster's dictionary that I keep on my computer desktop as a search engine defines "theophany" this way: "a visible manifestation of a deity." In order to make this fit the biblical definition, I would add a word or two, change one word, and say that a theophany is "a visible and audible manifestation of God."

Even before we look at some illustrations of theophanies, let me clear up the difference between a theophany and a type. A theophany is something visible and audible, that speaks as and for God. A type is something that we can look at to learn something about God—but is clearly himself or itself not God.

Moses was a type of Jesus, especially in his prophetic mode. The ram caught in the thicket for the sacrifice by Abraham and his son Isaac is a type of Jesus on the cross (as are many of the Old Testament sacrifices). A theophany, however, is much different. It is an actual appearance of God. An example is the pillar of smoke by day and pillar of fire by night that led the Israelites through the desert.

Now immediately we have a problem with this definition, because we are told many times in the Bible that you and I— human beings in general—are not able to see God, and certainly being "visible" means it is something we see. Here are just a few of the verses that teach this basic truth:

Exodus 33:20: *"But,"* he said, *"you cannot see my face, for man shall not see me and live."*

John 4:24: *"God is spirit, and those who worship him must worship in spirit and truth."*

1 Timothy 6:16: *". . . who alone has immortality, who dwells in unapproachable light, whom no one has ever seen or can see. To him be honor and eternal dominion. Amen."*

1 John 4:12: *"No one has ever seen God . . . ."*

So we are logically left with the understanding that any theophanies we find in the Bible are not "visible" manifestations of God the Father, for that would be contrary to the teaching of the Bible. But then, what are they? Sometimes they are nonhuman appearances. The burning bush that spoke to Moses is the classic example of that. Sometimes they are angelic forms who clearly represent God but are not specifically defined other than as representatives who speak for God. The angel who speaks to Abraham and Sarah in Genesis 18:1–19:1 fits that bill, as does the angel standing at the top of Jacob's ladder in Genesis 28. They clearly speak as if they were God, and they are worshiped as if they were God, but we know nothing more definitive about them.

There are several theophanies in the Old Testament that we have no trouble at all identifying as Jesus. In each of these cases, there is identification that this is someone special, *"the*

Angel of the Lord." Sometimes Jesus appears as a theophany in a vision; sometimes he seems to appear in real life. Either way, it doesn't change who the theophany is, nor does it change the value of what's being taught. Since visions are one of the normal ways God communicates his Word of Truth in the Old Testament, the vision is just as valuable for us as a "real" appearance.

I want to look at four theophanies referred to as "the Angel of the Lord" and examine some ways that we can identify them as pre-incarnation appearances of Jesus. We will also apply some truths from these incidents to our lives today.

The first is the appearance of the Angel of the Lord to Sarah's handmaid, Hagar. The story is told in Genesis 16, verses 7–15:

The angel of the Lord found her by a spring of water in the wilderness, the spring on the way to Shur. [8]And he said, "Hagar, servant of Sarai, where have you come from and where are you going?" She said, "I am fleeing from my mistress Sarai." [9]The angel of the Lord said to her, "Return to your mistress and submit to her." [10]The angel of the Lord also said to her, "I will surely multiply your offspring so that they cannot be numbered for multitude." [11]And the angel of the Lord said to her, "Behold, you are pregnant and shall bear a son. You shall call his name Ishmael, because the Lord has listened to your affliction. [12]He shall be a wild donkey of a man, his hand against everyone and everyone's hand against him, and he shall dwell over against all his kinsmen." [13]So she called the name of the Lord who spoke to her, "You are a God of *seeing," for she said, "Truly here I have seen him who looks after me." ¹⁴Therefore the well was called Beer-lahai-roi; it lies between Kadesh and Bered. ¹⁵And Hagar bore Abram a son, and Abram called the name of his son, whom Hagar bore, Ishmael. ¹⁶Abram was eighty-six years old when Hagar bore Ishmael to Abram.*

Note a couple things about this incident. Notice how this angel is referred to as *"the angel of the Lord."* Note, too, that it was easy for Hagar to identify this angel as being God himself.

What can we learn about the angel? Well, he certainly had prophetic abilities—telling her not only that she was expecting a child, but also identifying the child, naming the child, and telling of the future life of the child. It looks like this is an appearance of God the Son fulfilling his prophetic role, doesn't it?

The next incident of a theophany is in Genesis 32:22–32:

The same night he arose and took his two wives, his two female servants, and his eleven children, and crossed the ford of the Jabbok. ²³He took them and sent them across the stream, and everything else that he had. ²⁴And Jacob was left alone. And a man wrestled with him until the breaking of the day. ²⁵When the man saw that he did not prevail against Jacob, he touched his hip socket, and Jacob's hip was put out of joint as he wrestled with him. ²⁶Then he said, "Let me go, for the day has broken." But Jacob said, "I will not let you go unless you bless me." ²⁷And he said to him, "What is your name?" And he said, "Jacob." ²⁸Then he said, "Your name shall no longer be called Jacob, but Israel, for you have striven with God and *with men, and have prevailed." ²⁹Then Jacob asked him, "Please tell me your name." But he said, "Why is it that you ask my name?" And there he blessed him. ³⁰So Jacob called the name of the place Peniel, saying, "For I have seen God face to face, and yet my life has been delivered." ³¹The sun rose upon him as he passed Peniel, limping because of his hip. ³³Therefore to this day the people of Israel do not eat the sinew of the thigh that is on the hip socket, because he touched the socket of Jacob's hip on the sinew of the thigh.*

This Scripture vividly records this battle for Jacob's soul. Our text tells us that a man wrestled with Jacob all night long. Some commentators have suggested that Jacob's battle within himself was so great that it took the form simply of a dream of wrestling with a man. But Jacob's own testimony, and the name he gave to the ford in the river, give us the real truth. He called the place Peniel, which means "the face of God," and he said there in verse 30: *"For I have seen God face to face, and yet my life has been delivered."*

In reality, his new life was just beginning. As the crucial night of encounter ended, Jacob was crippled in the socket of his thigh—the hip, if you will. Jacob would not let God go until he blessed him. That was his greatest need from childhood. The Lord's response was to give him a new name. He was no longer Jacob, the "one who grabs the heels," but now Israel, "God strives." That's the issue of the new man emerging in the old Jacob. God had and would always do the striving with, for, and on behalf of him and his descendents, who, spiritually speaking, include you and me.

God was the only one whom Jacob could not manipulate. He gave the blessing for which Jacob longed because it is God's nature to bless. Jacob did nothing to deserve or earn it. In fact, all through his life up to that night, he had done just about everything he could to negate it. Now he had a limp that would remind him that God not only touched his hip, but the secret places of his heart.

'When morning came, it was the beginning of a new life. We meet a totally new Jacob, now called Israel. After that night, his new name reminded him that God had striven with him and now would strive for him. The willful manipulator had become willing to be molded by God. From that time on, we see compassion, gentleness, openness and receptivity in Israel. He didn't have to work at being loved any longer. He was blessed.

After the wrestling match was finished and the sun had lifted the veil of night, Israel looked up and saw Esau coming. The Scripture makes no mention of a spasm of panic in Israel this time. The wrestling with the Lord had accomplished a transformation. Israel had allowed God to bless him, and then he was free to receive a blessing from Esau.

We are amazed that Jacob, now Israel, asked for the name of the one with whom he was wrestling. He pleads in verse 29: *"Please tell me your name!"* God's response was a question to end all Israel's questions: *"Why is it that you ask my name?"* Why indeed! After all the times God had intervened for him and spoken to him, he should have known. But willfulness not only has a short fuse, it also has a short memory. Jacob wanted to be sure. He knew that this was the crucial encounter of his life and he did not want it to pass, leaving him unblessed again.

Jacob asked for the name of the man who wrestled with him and never got it. You and I know the end of the story so we know his name. Since God the Father is a spirit and does not have a body like a man, it couldn't have been him. However, that is not true of God the Son. Jesus not only took on the form of a human permanently on the night of his birth at Bethlehem, from time to time in the Old Testament he would make appearances in bodily form. This is one of them. This is clearly an appearance of Jesus, the Son of God—long before he was ever given that name.

What is it like to wrestle with God? It is a struggle with the past and a battle over who will be in charge of the future. God wants to make us willing to seek him and to do his will—not by our own strength, but depending on his strength for our results. A combination of fear, guilt, and a life of manipulation caused Jacob to resist God's presence and power in his life.

Do you know what that is like? Have you ever relived the past with each failure marching before your mind's eye? Have you ever been awakened in a panic in the middle of the night and gone to the mat with the Lord with restless worry? Then you know, as I do, what it's like to have God battle for control of your will until you allow him to forgive the past and take charge of the future.

The third incident of a theophany comes from the life of Joshua and involves the invasion of the town of Jericho. There is a famous song taken from this Bible story, called "Joshua Fought the Battle of Jericho." As we look carefully at this passage, we will soon learn that we should change the title of the song to "Jesus Fought the Battle of Jericho." Look at Joshua 5:13–6:5:

When Joshua was by Jericho, he lifted up his eyes and looked, and behold, a man was standing before him with his drawn sword in his hand. And Joshua went to him and said to him, "Are you for us, or for our adversaries?" [14]And he said, "No; but I am the commander of the army of the Lord. Now I have come." And Joshua fell on his face to the earth and worshiped and said to him, "What does my lord say to his servant?" [15]And the commander of the Lord's army said to Joshua, "Take off your sandals from your feet, for the place where you are standing is holy." And Joshua did so.

[1]Now Jericho was shut up inside and outside because of the people of Israel. None went out, and none came in. [2]And the Lord said to Joshua, "See, I have given Jericho into your hand, with its king and mighty men of valor. [3]You shall march around the city, all the men of war going around the city once. Thus shall you do for six days. [4]Seven priests shall bear seven trumpets of rams' horns before the ark. On the seventh day you shall march around the city seven times, and the priests shall blow the trumpets. [5]And when they make a long blast with the ram's horn, when you hear the sound of the trumpet, then all the people shall shout with a great shout, and the wall of the city will fall down flat, and the people shall go up, everyone straight before him."

The years of wandering were over. Moses was dead. The Lord who had parted the Red Sea to lead Israel out of Egypt had also parted the Jordan River to lead them into the Promised Land. The manna had ceased. They were now to live on the land God had given them.

As Joshua looked up at the walls and towers of Jericho, the charge that God had given him rang in his heart. It is contained in chapter 1 of this same book, at verses 5 and 9:

> *No man shall be able to stand before you all the days of your life. Just as I was with Moses, so I will be with you. I will not leave you or forsake you. . . . [9]Have I not commanded you? Be strong and courageous. Do not be frightened, and do not be dismayed, for the Lord your God is with you wherever you go."*

Joshua had the pledge of God's presence and the charge to keep God's commandments. What strategy should he now follow? How was Jericho to be assaulted? As Joshua pondered this question, he was startled to see a warrior confronting him with a drawn sword, there in the first verse of our text, chapter 5, verse 13. Joshua's hand went to his own sword as he advanced to challenge the stranger: *"Are you for us, or for our adversaries?"*

The stranger didn't answer the question directly, but instead spoke those wonderful words in verse 14: *"No; but I am the commander of the army of the Lord. Now I have come."*

Joshua fell on his face. He knew immediately he was speaking to the Lord. Continuing in verse 14, *"What does my lord say to his servant?"* At the burning bush in Sinai, God had told Moses to take off his sandals. Now he told Joshua to do the same thing (verse 15): *"Take off your sandals from your feet, for the place where you are standing is holy."*

The Lord had promised to be with Joshua. He now revealed his presence to him. The Lord came bearing the sword as the Commander, not simply of the armies of Israel but of the hosts of heaven. The commander of Israel, named Joshua, met his Supreme Commander, named Jesus.

You see, here is yet another pre-incarnate appearance of Jesus, this time as the Supreme Commander. This is clearly a picture of Jesus in the Old Testament. He has come to carry out his own will and his own plan, and he spoke to Joshua to instruct him in the divine strategy by which Jericho would be taken. To put it simply, Jesus fought the battle of Jericho!

You and I fight spiritual battles every day. In those battles, we must recognize that we do not battle alone. For one thing, we have a whole army supporting us, our brothers and sisters in Christ—our family, our friends, our church. Everyone who is a Christian is a part of our army, providing both support and defense. If you feel like you are fighting your battles all by yourself, it might be because you don't spend enough time with God's people. Get to know them. Let them get to know you. Find ways of mutual encouragement and support. A Christian, like any soldier, cannot fight a war by himself; he needs help.

Not only do we have a whole army of people supporting us, we have a backup force of angels. They are with us even though we cannot see them, helping us to battle our spiritual enemies. But even better than having an army made up of other Christians and of angels, we have Jesus leading us into battle. By the presence and power of his Holy Spirit, he is with us wherever and whenever we enter our spiritual battles.

The question is, then, how do you relate to your Supreme Commander? If his role is to lead you into battle, what is your role? Well, certainly, we better know what his battle plan is. He told Joshua to have all the armed men march around the city for six days, and then on the seventh day to march around the city seven times. Everyone was to make a great battle cry and the walls would come tumbling down—a very specific and very easy-to-understand battle plan. You and I need to know the plan he has set out for us in our Christian lives, the plan he gives in the Scriptures.

Perhaps the reason you lose so many spiritual battles is because you are not studying the battle plan in the Bible. There are enough details in the Bible about the plan that you may *never* be able to study it thoroughly. If you just listen to a few war stories each month, you can't win a battle. To win spiritual battles, you must read and study the battle plan daily so that you know it well.

Our Supreme Commander wants us to work like a group of soldiers in the army. Joshua could not walk out and take Jericho on his own. As great a leader as he was, he still needed the army. You and I are certainly not on the spiritual level that Joshua was. So even more, we need to be part of an army, working together as a group.

Can you imagine what an army would be like if the soldiers never drilled, never studied together, or never learned how to work together? Can you imagine if they just showed up for the battle? That's absurd, of course. It is just as absurd for a Christian to think he or she can go into spiritual battles every day without group training. That's why we need to be part of a church, to be involved in small groups and Bible studies, attend Sunday school classes, and regularly worship with other Christians.

One more thing the Supreme Commander wants is instant obedience. When a young man or woman goes off to boot camp, one of the most important things he or she is taught is to obey instantly. New soldiers learn to trust their leaders and to follow their commands because when you get into battle, you don't have time to think. In battle you barely have time to react, and your leaders are there to tell you what to do so you can win the battle.

Now in real life, in the Army, Navy, Air Force, or Marines, the leaders are fallible—sinners like you and me. They do not provide perfect leadership, and you have to use some discernment in following their orders. But in our spiritual warfare, Jesus is our leader, and he provides the kind of perfect leadership we really need. So without question, without hesitation, he deserves and should get our instant obedience.

In summary, our basic lesson is this: *God's people never go to war alone.* We have a battle plan we can study in the Bible. We go into battle as a unit, a team made up of other Christians; and we go into battle with Jesus as our Supreme Commander, ready to give him instant obedience.

The final appearance or theophany of Jesus in the Old Testament comes in the night visions of Zechariah, and it is one of my favorites. It takes place in the fourth vision, which is usually titled "Joshua Before the Angel of the Lord." The text is Zechariah 3:1–10.

Then he showed me Joshua the high priest standing before the angel of the Lord, and Satan standing at his right hand to accuse him. [2]And the Lord said to Satan, "The Lord rebuke you, O Satan! The Lord who has chosen Jerusalem rebuke you! Is not this a brand plucked from the fire?" [3]Now Joshua was standing before the angel, clothed with filthy garments. [4]And the angel said to those who were standing before him, "Remove the filthy garments from him." And to him he said, "Behold, I have taken your iniquity away from you, and I will clothe you with pure vestments." [5]And I said, "Let them put a clean turban on his head." So they put a clean turban on his head and clothed him with garments. And the angel of the Lord was standing by.

[6]And the angel of the Lord solemnly assured Joshua, [7]"Thus says the Lord of hosts: If you will walk in my ways and keep my charge, then you shall rule my house and have charge of my courts, and I will give you the right of access among those who are standing here. [8]Hear now, O Joshua the high priest, you and your friends who sit before you, for they are men who are a sign: behold, I will bring my servant the Branch. [9]For behold, on the stone that I have set before Joshua, on a single stone with seven eyes, I will engrave its inscription, declares the Lord of hosts, and I will remove the iniquity of this land in a single day. [10]In that day, declares the Lord of hosts, every

one of you will invite his neighbor to come under his vine and under his fig tree."

While this vision is filled with great teaching, especially about the nature and the completeness of the cleansing that Jesus provides for his people, we will concentrate our examination on what is going on with the Angel of the Lord.

What is the picture Zechariah sees in verse 1? At first glance, the picture seems rather dull and boring compared with some of the beautiful pictures in other visions. It looks like there are three people standing around, apparently without any background. There is Joshua, the high priest. There is the Angel of the Lord and there is Satan. My, my—it seems like Satan is always around where he isn't wanted, and here he is right in the middle of one of Zechariah's beautiful night visions. But as we look more closely into the vision, the background that at first was out of focus becomes clear to us and we see a truly amazing sight. The stage that had seemed to contain only the three lead characters now appears to be filled with other characters, and sets.

Let's start at verse four: *"The angel* [that's the Angel of the Lord] *said to those who were standing before him . . . "* Now, just who are *"those who were standing before him"*? There seem to be quite a few of them, and they are seen to be serving the Angel of the Lord. Down in verse 7, we find these same characters at the end of the verse, *" . . . and I will give you a place among these standing here."* This group of characters is standing by the house, by the courts of the Angel of the Lord.

Actually, these characters are none other than the cherubim who dwell in the Holy of Holies, that inner sanctuary in the temple. They are always hovering, ready at any time to do the will of the Lord. Ezekiel describes these characters for us in chapter 10 of his prophecy. He shows that they are not merely statues in the Holy of Holies, but living creatures. Ezekiel tells us they were winged creatures with features both animal and human. Each had four faces—one each of a man, a lion, an ox, and an eagle.

We frequently find the cherubim spoken of in conjunction with some similar characters, the seraphim. We find them in the prophetical books of the Bible, and their service, their mission, is always rendered immediately to God. This gives us solid evidence that "the Angel of the Lord" in this vision is indeed Jesus.

We won't take time to examine everything that is going on in this vision other than to say that when we look closely at Joshua the high priest, we find him standing in the very presence of the Lord on the Day of Atonement. He is covered in garments that are as filthy as can be. In fact, they are covered with dung, and the problem is just how does Joshua get cleaned up? He needs more than just a quick Marine shower. How will he be thoroughly cleaned so he can remain in the presence of God?

Let's remind ourselves right now that if God sets out to do something, he will do it completely. He will do it thoroughly. As we look at verse 4, we find that Joshua does not take care of the problem of his filth. We as individuals do not have the ability to cleanse ourselves. In other words, you and I can do nothing about our sin. We are utterly helpless to take care of the problem of our sin and pollution that would separate us from God. God must do it for us. And so in verse 4, it is the Angel of the Lord speaking to the cherubim about Joshua, saying, "Take off these filthy clothes." You see, God does this cleansing himself. The removal of the garments symbolizes God's taking away our iniquity, our sins. "See, I have taken away your sin," says the Angel of the Lord.

Again, please understand, it is God who takes our sins away. We can't do it. Paul writes, "one who sins is a slave to sin" (Rom. 6:16ff). No matter how hard any one of us tries to do good, to keep even the moral law of God, it is impossible to do so by ourselves. We are all sinners. We are all filthy because of our sins. Only God can remove our filthy garments. It is only by God's sovereign grace that we may be cleansed.

How does this cleansing come about for you and for me? It is by the blood of Jesus Christ, spilled at Calvary, that we are cleansed, and no other way. Do we have any questions about this fact? Do we not know it so clearly? Jesus Christ, who was perfect—who had no filth whatsoever—had to die so that our sin, our pollution, our filth could be washed away in his blood. Oh, what a great promise, what a great act this was, Jesus Christ—the sinless—dying for the sinner.

You see, the cleansing of God does not stop with stripping us of our filthy garments. He doesn't leave us to run around naked. Rather, he clothes us with other garments. He clothes us, in fact, with festal garments. This change of raiment mentioned in verse 4 is quite clearly a change into the garments that are to be worn by the high priest on his entering the Holy of

Holies on the Day of Atonement. And what does this white robe represent? It represents the righteousness of Jesus Christ. If we are truly cleansed of our sin, then we must be re-clothed with the righteousness of Jesus Christ.

In many evangelical churches in the world today, this very, very important point either has been forgotten or is being purposely ignored. However, it must not be ignored by you and by me because this re-clothing in the righteousness of Christ is a must. It is essential to our salvation; it is essential to our justification. Without being re-clothed in the righteousness of Christ, we cannot call ourselves Christians.

Can you see it? We have not only been justified by the blood of Christ, we have also been made righteous. We have not only had our dirty clothes stripped off us, but we have been re-clothed in the righteousness of Christ. Romans 4:25 says, *"He was delivered over to death for our sins, and was raised to life for our righteousness."* You see, the work of Jesus Christ does not stop with paying the penalty for our sins. Jesus Christ was raised again for our righteousness so that God the Father might look out at us and see us—not naked, but as he sees his very own Son. Our cleansing is complete. It takes the filth off us, and it re-clothes us in clean garments, in the righteousness of Jesus Christ.

Well, there's a bunch more really good stuff in Zechariah 3, but at least we can see for now that Jesus does in fact appear during the days of Old Testament Israel. When he appears in the books of the Old Testament, whether in a vision or in person, he gives us a pre-incarnate glimpse of who he is and what great work he will be doing once he comes as a baby in the New Testament, and does an eternal work in our lives.

Some people say all you need to know about Jesus you can find in the New Testament. In these first two chapters, I think we have disproved that theory. In the next chapter, we'll examine some of the great Old Testament prophecies about the coming of the Messiah.

Chapter Three
Messiah – "What the Old Testament Tells Us to Expect About Jesus"

When one looks at the Old Testament and seeks to find all of the messianic passages (that is, ones that speak about the coming of the Messiah, who we know is named Jesus), one could literally take all day—or to be more precise, he could take all year. In fact, there have been many doctoral dissertations and major books written on this topic. I think we can afford to spend a few pages on the topic in this book.

In all honesty, I must tell you that the Old Testament writers did not use the term Messiah, or more technically "the Anointed One," until the time of Daniel. So we can't go to the search engines, plug in "Messiah," and pop out a list. But we certainly know that by the time Jesus began his ministry, there was a very clear understanding among the Jews about the Scriptures' promise of a Messiah. In telling his brother Simon Peter about his first encounter with Jesus, the Apostle Andrew says in John 1:41, *"We have found the Messiah!"*

Even the Samarian woman Jesus met at the well (someone who would not be considered a great scholar of the Old Testament) was able to say with relative ease in John 4:25, *"I know that Messiah is coming. . . . When he comes, he will tell us all things."* As you know, Jesus immediately identifies himself to the woman as this promised Messiah.

Several Old Testament prophecies are so important they will be covered in chapters of their own. The virgin birth foretold in Isaiah 7, Moses' prediction that Jesus would be the great prophet, and the suffering of Jesus predicted in Isaiah 53 (which becomes part of his work as a priest) are a few of these important prophecies. Other examples are the kingship of Jesus over the world as foretold in Psalm 2, and Daniel's and Zechariah's prophecies about the return of Jesus.

These passages about the future work of God's Son, who we now know was the promised Messiah, are so important they end up being essential items on our "top twenty list." That ought to tell you something in and of itself. The Old Testament is literally filled with prophecy and prediction about Jesus. This means a Christian who reads only the New Testament is going to miss a lot of good stuff about Jesus and about God's plan for the world centered on the work of Jesus. If you are of this mindset, perhaps as we hit some of the highlights in these passages, you will have your interest piqued enough to read the Old Testament books from which they come.

We begin our study of what to expect about Jesus from the messianic passages with some of the predictions in the books of Moses, the Pentateuch, the first five books of the Old Testament. The first prediction we see is the one of the snake as the eternal enemy of the Messiah. We find that in Genesis 3:15, God speaks to the snake that tempted Adam and Eve and warns him, *"I will put enmity between you and the woman, and between your offspring and her offspring; he shall bruise your head, and you shall bruise his heel."*

Clearly, the snake is symbolic for Satan. His ultimate doom is fulfilled in Revelation 20:2, *"And he seized the dragon, that ancient serpent, who is the devil and Satan, and bound him for a thousand years. . . . "* Looking back at the verse in Genesis, who do you suppose is the "he" who will bruise the head of the serpent and have his heel bruised in return?

In context, "he" refers to the seed of the woman, but in the larger context, the New Testament explains in several places that this is the very first prediction of the work of Jesus himself: Romans 16:20: *"The God of peace will soon crush Satan under your feet. The grace of our Lord Jesus Christ be with you."* Hebrews 2:14: *"Since therefore the children share in flesh and blood, he himself likewise partook of the same things, that through death he might destroy the one who has the power of death, that is, the devil. . . . "* No doubts left about that interpretation.

The next prophecy from Moses also concerns the seed of the woman. The promise of the blessing that will come through him to all mankind is seen in Genesis 22:18: *"and in your offspring shall all the nations of the earth be blessed, because you have obeyed my voice."* The blessing of all the nations is the heart of the promises of the covenant of grace. (See my book *God the Father* for details on this covenant.) The promise of blessing here in Genesis 22, as well as all the promises of the covenant, come to fulfillment when Jesus gives up his life as an atonement for sin. Notice the extent of the blessing as explained in John 3:16, *"For God so loved the world, that he gave his only Son, that whoever believes in him should not perish but have eternal life."* The extent of the blessing is worldwide; it is to *"whoever believes."* Surely this fulfills the *"all the nations"* prophecy of Genesis 22.

The next prophecy I want to look at is not always highlighted in such summaries as this one. It comes from Jacob's blessing to his son Judah in Genesis 49:10: *"The scepter shall not depart from Judah, nor the ruler's staff from between his feet, until tribute comes to him; and to him shall be the obedience of the peoples."* In this translation (ESV), the scepter is the sign of authority of a ruler who comes from the tribe of Judah. He will ultimately receive tribute and obedience from the people. (This is the theme we will discuss at length in the chapter titled "I'm the King of the World," based on Psalm 2.) Many other translations such as the New King James Version render the phrase *"until tribute comes to him"* as *"until Shiloh comes."* This makes it more specifically messianic, pointing to the Savior, if one sees Shiloh as a reference to the Messiah, Jesus.

Either way, it is the scepter that I want you to notice. The meaning is expanded in 2 Samuel 7:16, in the midst of the expanded revelation of the covenant of grace to David: *"And your house and your kingdom shall be made sure forever before me. Your throne shall be established forever."'* The promise of the scepter, the sign of authority, sees its New Testament fulfillment described in Luke 2:14 when the angels sing, *"Glory to God in the highest, and on earth peace among those with whom he is pleased!"* This peace of which the angels sing is, of course, the final peace that comes only through Jesus, the messianic ruler.

Moses tells us of the next messianic prophecy in a most unusual way—through the mouth of a donkey, in the famous Balaam story in Numbers. Balaam says in Numbers 24:17, *"I see him, but not now; I behold him, but not near: a star shall come out of Jacob, and a scepter shall rise out of Israel; it shall crush the forehead of Moab and break down all the sons of Sheth."* There's the scepter again, but I want to focus on this star coming out of Jacob. The star, you see, is the one that caused the famous visit of the Magi, or kings, or wise men (whichever translation you prefer) in the wonderful story   in Matthew 2:1-12:

> *Now after Jesus was born in Bethlehem of Judea in the days of Herod the king, behold, wise men from the east came to Jerusalem, [2]saying, "Where is he who has been born king of the Jews? For we saw his star when it rose and have come to worship him." [3]When Herod the king heard this, he was troubled, and all Jerusalem with him; [4]and assembling all the chief priests and scribes of the people, he inquired of them where the Christ was to be born. [5]They told him, "In Bethlehem of Judea, for so it is written by the prophet: [6]'And you, O Bethlehem, in the land of Judah, are by no means least among the rulers of Judah; for from you shall come a ruler who will shepherd my people Israel.'"*
>
> *[7]Then Herod summoned the wise men secretly and ascertained from them what time the star had appeared. [8]And he sent them to Bethlehem, saying, "Go and search diligently for the child, and when you have found him, bring me word, that I too may come and worship him." [9]After listening to the king, they went on their way. And*

behold, the star that they had seen when it rose went before them until it came to rest over the place where the child was. ¹⁰When they saw the star, they rejoiced exceedingly with great joy. ¹¹And going into the house they saw the child with Mary his mother, and they fell down and worshiped him. Then, opening their treasures, they offered him gifts, gold and frankincense and myrrh. ¹²And being warned in a dream not to return to Herod, they departed to their own country by another way.

Look at verse 2 of Matthew 2. The wise men say they *"saw his star."* How did these men, who obviously were some kind of practitioners of divination in the lands far to the east of Israel (most likely Babylon or Persia), know it was the Messiah's star? It's obvious they had not read the Old Testament because they had to ask Herod where the birth took place. Had they known the Hebrew Scriptures, they would have already known it was Bethlehem. How did these guys, who probably came from a much larger group of magi, figure this out?

We are not given an explicit answer to that question (as is so often the case in the Bible), but Matthew gives us some pretty good hints. These guys were looking for (they said in verse 2) *"the King of the Jews."* When we read Matthew's entire gospel, we find him stressing the legitimate genealogy of Jesus by placing it at the very beginning of the gospel. Jesus is presented there as the descendant of Abraham, then of Judah, and finally of David, Israel's greatest king. At the end of the gospel, what do we see written by Pilate summarizing why Jesus had been put to death? *"This is Jesus, the King of the Jews."* In God's providence, these wise men had heard of this prophecy. I think all the clues in Matthew's gospel lead us to the source of that information.

If you read Daniel carefully, you find that Daniel, a Hebrew captive of noble blood, was taken to Babylon where he had a long and distinguished life of public service under both Babylonian and, later, Persian kings. He was a faithful servant of Israel's God. Intriguingly, the Bible records that he was also appointed (perhaps unwillingly) to be in charge of all of Babylon's wise men. That must have included the diviners and sorcerers. Although he may not have been a revered leader of this group, is it not likely that Daniel's writings were preserved among at least a few archivists, as was their custom?

So here are wise men who know at least something about a newborn king of the Jews, and they come to fulfill the promise of Balaam's donkey. Tell me God doesn't have a sense of humor!

Let's turn our attention now to the Psalms and see how many of them can be given the honor of inclusion in the list of messianic psalms. Of course, many people have their own lists. I have tried to combine several of these, and here is a list (probably not complete) of psalms that have something or other to do with the Messiah: 2, 8, 16, 17, 19, 20, 22, 31, 41, 45, 49, 55, 65, 67, 68, 72, 94, 95, 96, 97, 98, 109, 110, 118, and 132. Obviously some of these are more important than others. For instance, we'll take a whole chapter to work through Psalm 2. But first, let's look briefly at a few of them.

Psalm 16 contains what has to be the Old Testament's greatest teaching of the Messiah's ultimate resurrection. To put it another way, if you are a preacher looking for a different text to preach next Easter, try Psalm 16, especially verses 9 through 11: *"Therefore my heart is glad, and my whole being rejoices; my flesh also dwells secure. [10]For you will not abandon my soul to Sheol, or let your holy one see corruption. [11]You make known to me the path of life; in your presence there is fullness of joy; at your right hand are pleasures forevermore."*

We see here the common pattern of Old Testament writers—in this case, David—who refer to their own personal experiences but also, in a prophetic way, refer to Jesus. Clearly, Jesus is the *"holy one"* of verse 10. If there is one point that the Easter story tells us, it is that when the women rolled back the stone that first Easter morning there was no body in the grave. That's what Easter is all about—Jesus' body was gone. He was no longer dead. He was alive!

There appear to be two things worth noting about the Old Testament's teaching about the resurrection. The first is that the people of God (known as Israel) in the Old Testament did not focus on resurrection in the same way Christians do today. While you and I celebrate Easter as a holiday that focuses on hope for the future (Peter refers to Jesus' resurrection from the dead as the *"living hope."*), Israel had a different hope. All of their future hope, all of their desire, and nearly all of their prophetic writings focused on the hope of the coming Messiah. They could look back to their starting point in the Exodus from Egypt and recall how graciously God had dealt with them. But they were constantly looking forward to the day when all of the promises of God would be fulfilled in the coming of the Holy One of Israel—the Messiah—the Lamb of God—the Savior.

Today, having read the New Testament, we look forward to Jesus' *second* coming.

The second thing worth noting is the unique connection David makes here in Psalm 16 between the resurrection and heaven. Too often on Easter, we focus so much on the historical fact of the resurrection of Jesus that we overlook the results of the resurrection. Psalm 16 points us to the wonderful result that first Jesus, and then at a later date you and me (in our resurrection bodies), will spend eternity in heaven. Look at verse 11 of the psalm. *"You make known to me the path of life; in your presence there is fullness of joy; at your right hand are pleasures forevermore."* Do you see the emphasis there? Being in the presence of God is to dwell in heaven. Being in heaven means you and I, everyone who believes in Jesus, will share in his resurrection, will enjoy *"eternal pleasures"* forever. I think even a lay preacher could find an Easter sermon in that text!

Next, we want to look at Psalm 22. I am writing this chapter just five days after the devastation caused on the Gulf Coast of the United States by Hurricane Katrina. Many people are saying this may be the worst human disaster, certainly in the United States, but perhaps in the world. We are just beginning to learn about the level of suffering. Psalm 22, in its prediction of the Messiah's suffering on the cross, teaches us the answer to the question that is always on the lips of people going through great tragedy or personal crises, "Where is God when I suffer?"

The bottom line is that there is no logical answer to that classic question. When someone you love is in the midst of suffering from disease or trauma, you don't simply need a logical argument that God exists. You need a practical answer to the question. The heart of the answer is that God himself is with us, actually sharing our suffering.

We may not understand many things about God, but one thing we can never say is that God has no idea what suffering is. At the cross, we discover a God whose suffering went beyond anything we can imagine. Jesus, the Messiah, suffered the horrors of hell. He was completely abandoned by his Father in heaven, and cried out, as recorded in Matthew 27:46, *"Eli, Eli, lema sabachthani?"* That is, *"My God, my God, why have you forsaken me?"* Those are, you see, the very words of Psalm 22. Now, how in the world could David prophesy in this psalm that Jesus would say this? How could he in Old Testament times see Jesus so clearly? How could he know that Jesus would suffer just as he had?

Well, even before Jesus came to earth and took the world's pain upon himself, God shared in the suffering of his people. For example, after a description of the oppression that God's people were enduring because of their sins, Judges 10:16 tells us, *"So they put away the foreign gods from among them and served the Lord, and he became impatient over the misery of Israel."* Do you see that? Their pain was his pain, and he couldn't stand it anymore. Just like you, he felt impatience. Old Testament, New Testament, in our lives today—there is no doubt about it. Jesus shares in our suffering.

One final messianic psalm we will examine is Psalm 72. I almost didn't include this psalm because it deals with an issue that greatly divides Christians today, the level of involvement in the affairs of government. I come from the "old school" presbyterian view that says the work of the church is spiritual, and that the church as an institution should not get involved in human governmental issues other than "humble petition" at times that could clearly be "cases extraordinary," in the words of the Westminster Confession of Faith, Chapter XXXI Section 4:

> Synods and councils are to handle, or conclude nothing, but that which is ecclesiastical: and are not to intermeddle with civil affairs which concern the commonwealth, unless by way of humble petition in cases extraordinary; or, by way of advice, for satisfaction of conscience, if they be thereunto required by the civil magistrate.

Yet Christians, as individual citizens, must be involved in all spheres of life, and so we must be concerned about our civil magistrates (or in American terminology, our elected officials). Psalm 72 gives us some sound advice to follow as it describes the Messiah Jesus as the perfect King, and thus the model for all human leaders.

Psalm 72 is, in its total, a prayer of blessing for the new king in Israel, but is at the same time a prayer of blessing for the eternal King Jesus. The psalm describes a wise and good ruler who will benefit not only the king's own nation, but all the nations of the world. At the center of this vision are ideas such as justice and righteousness.

I want to examine just a few of the verses and principles in the psalm. In verse 1, the author is identified as Solomon, so we know these words (inspired by God, of course) come from the wisest of all human rulers. *"Give the king your justice, O*

God, and your righteousness to the royal son!" Justice and righteousness must be the hallmarks of any human magistrate. Happily, we have no space to examine the failings of human magistrates today.

Next, we are told in verse 7 that the king should also promote prosperity and peace. *"In his days may the righteous flourish, and peace abound, till the moon be no more!"* Interestingly, the NIV leaves out the word *"peace"* and simply says that "prosperity will abound." This is not a work that can deal with exegetical differences such as this, but suffice it to say that while the NIV chose to leave out the concept of peace, prosperity is worthless without peace. But notice the point—the emphasis is on the application toward human governments. They should be concerned with prosperity. It is part of their mandate to encourage economies to flourish.

Now, that's easy enough to say when we live in a free economy as we do in America. Those who can do well economically can actually flourish. But even in free economy settings, you still have poor people, and the psalmists won't let the king or human governors forsake the poor. This message is in verses 12 through 14: *"For he delivers the needy when he calls, the poor and him who has no helper. [13]He has pity on the weak and the needy, and saves the lives of the needy. [14]From oppression and violence he redeems their life, and precious is their blood in his sight."* One of the paramount responsibilities for government leaders is to care for the needy and protect the defenseless. When governments become self-serving, it is the poor, the needy, and the defenseless who are victimized. We need human leaders who reflect the ideals of Psalm 72, who recognize the primary importance of justice and righteousness.

We need leaders who recognize their responsibility to create an economy that allows people to flourish and will take care of the poor and needy in a way that would be honoring to God.

Let's move now to the Prophets, where we find many more messianic passages. The largest number of them is found in Isaiah, so much so that he has been called the "Old Testament evangelist." We are all familiar with the multiple prophecies in Isaiah concerning the names of the Messiah, such as:

> *Therefore the Lord himself will give you a sign. Behold, the virgin shall conceive and bear a son, and shall call his name Immanuel. (Isa. 7:14)*

> *For to us a child is born, to us a son is given; and the government shall be upon his shoulder, and his name shall be called Wonderful Counselor, Mighty God, Everlasting Father, Prince of Peace. (Isa. 9:6)*

But Isaiah has much more to say. In 9:1–2 we read, *"But there will be no gloom for her who was in anguish. In the former time he brought into contempt the land of Zebulun and the land of Naphtali, but in the latter time he has made glorious the way of the sea, the land beyond the Jordan, Galilee of the nations. [2]The people who walked in darkness have seen a great light; those who dwelt in a land of deep darkness, on them has light shined."* Of course, this is the exact verse that Matthew uses (4:14–16) to identify the route that Jesus took on his very first ministry trip.

In Isaiah 28:16, we see the first mention in the Old Testament of the connection of faith and the Messiah.

"Therefore thus says the Lord God, 'Behold, I am the one who has laid as a foundation in Zion, a stone, a tested stone, a precious cornerstone, of a sure foundation: Whoever believes will not be in haste'." Isaiah is telling us that all who trust in the Messiah will not be anxious or confused (i.e., "in haste"), which, of course, is the assurance we find in our faith in Jesus.

The next important prophecy from Isaiah we will look at here (we will deal in a later chapter with the great Suffering Servant message of Isaiah 53) comes in 61:1–2: *"The Spirit of the Lord God is upon me, because the Lord has anointed me to bring good news to the poor; he has sent me to bind up the brokenhearted, to proclaim liberty to the captives, and the opening of the prison to those who are bound; ²to proclaim the year of the Lord's favor, and the day of vengeance of our God; to comfort all who mourn . . . ."* Luke tells us (4:16) that when Jesus spoke his first words of ministry in the synagogue in Nazareth at the beginning of his ministry, he opened the scroll of Isaiah and read these very words from 61:1–2, and then said to all the worshipers, *"Today this Scripture has been fulfilled in your hearing"* (Luke 4:21). This, after a brief conversation, resulted in him being run out of town!

Other prophets spoke of the coming Messiah, of course. Daniel did so in the famous verses in 9:24–27:

"Seventy weeks are decreed about your people and your holy city, to finish the transgression, to put an end to sin, and to atone for iniquity, to bring in everlasting righteousness, to seal both vision and prophet, and to anoint a most holy place. ²⁵Know therefore and understand that from the going out of the word to restore

and build Jerusalem to the coming of an anointed one, a prince, there shall be seven weeks. Then for sixty-two weeks it shall be built again with squares and moat, but in a troubled time. [26]And after the sixty-two weeks, an anointed one shall be cut off and shall have nothing. And the people of the prince who is to come shall destroy the city and the sanctuary. Its end shall come with a flood, and to the end there shall be war. Desolations are decreed. [27]And he shall make a strong covenant with many for one week, and for half of the week he shall put an end to sacrifice and offering. And on the wing of abominations shall come one who makes desolate, until the decreed end is poured out on the desolator."

People have many different interpretations of when and how this prophecy will be fulfilled, but there is no difference among them on one thing—the "anointed one" Daniel spoke of is none other than the Messiah, Jesus. In fact, the literal translation of Messiah is "anointed one."

Among the minor prophets, there are several significant prophecies from Zechariah. The first is 9:9–10: *"Rejoice greatly, O daughter of Zion! Shout aloud, O daughter of Jerusalem! Behold, your king is coming to you; righteous and having salvation is he, humble and mounted on a donkey, on a colt, the foal of a donkey. [10]I will cut off the chariot from Ephraim and the war horse from Jerusalem; and the battle bow shall be cut off, and he shall speak peace to the nations; his rule shall be from sea to sea, and from the River to the ends of the earth."* This, of course, is the great "triumphal entry" prophecy of Palm Sunday.

Although there are many, many more, the last one we will look at is Zechariah 11:12–13. *"Then I said to them, 'If it seems good to you, give me my wages; but if not, keep them.' And they weighed out as my wages thirty pieces of silver.* [13]*Then the Lord said to me, 'Throw it to the potter'— the lordly price at which I was priced by them. So I took the thirty pieces of silver and threw them into the house of the Lord, to the potter."* The *"I"* at the beginning of verse 12 is none other than *"the shepherd of the flock, doomed to be slaughtered by the sheep traders"* (verse 7). The thirty pieces of silver is apparently the going price to buy and sell a slave. Interestingly, Judas took that amount from the Jewish officials, indicating what he felt the life of Jesus was worth. Then, the throwing of them on the floor of the temple (verse 13) is fulfilled by Judas, as reported in Matthew 27.

One is constantly awed by the ability of so many Old Testament authors—even under the guidance of the Holy Spirit—to put so much into the Scriptures of Israel about their coming Messiah. My own awe is overcome only by my sadness that so few of the Israelites—from the days of Jesus until today—have failed to recognize him as the promised Messiah. Perhaps the best application we can make from this chapter is our need to pray fervently for what Paul requested in Romans 10:1: *"Brothers, my heart's desire and prayer to God for them is that they may be saved."*

Chapter Four
Virgin Birth – "I Just Can't Be Pregnant"

It should go without saying that the two most important days in the Christian year are Christmas and Easter. Statistics—and this is not just in America, but around the world—show that attendance in church on those two special holidays is up by large percentage points. This is especially true in the mainline churches that tend to be less biblically oriented than evangelical churches. Why are Christmas and Easter so important? Well, my suggestion is that they are the celebration of the two greatest miracles in the life of Jesus: the incarnation (that theological word we talked about in Chapter One) as it takes form in the virgin birth, and the resurrection. The two holidays commemorate bookend pinnacles of a life filled with many other miracles. (Remember in Chapter One how Jesus tried to convince his enemies that he was God because of the miracles he was able to perform?) If there is anything that brings unity among Bible-believing, evangelical Christians, it is a consistent belief in the miracles of the life of Jesus—especially the miracles of the virgin birth and the resurrection.

There seems to me to be a growing and significant difference between the current celebrations of these two great holidays of the Christian church. On Easter, just about every single evangelical preacher focuses his sermon on the miracle of the resurrection. But when it comes to Christmas, there is not that same singular focus. In fact, over the 35 years that I have been actively involved in preaching and ministry, there seems to be less and less emphasis on the miracle of the virgin birth and more and more stress on the far less-important (yet completely true) aspects of Christmas such as love and peace and giving.

It is a great concern to me that this trend continues to expand. I believe it is part of a great slippage of commitment to biblical truth, one that sooner or later will result in the downplaying of the resurrection on Easter—just as there has already been a downplaying of the virgin birth at Christmas. When *that* happens, the evangelical church will begin to disappear. I say that because without a full commitment to the inerrancy of the Bible, which must include a complete and unwavering belief in the miracles of Jesus' life, one cannot be an evangelical Christian.

Why is the virgin birth so important? Well, there are a number of things one can rightly say about it and what it means to us even today, but in order to remain within the design of this book, I will limit our discussion to just three. I will focus most of our discussion on one of the two New Testament accounts that explain the virgin birth—looking primarily at Luke 1:26-38.

In the sixth month the angel Gabriel was sent from God to a city of Galilee named Nazareth, [27]to a virgin betrothed to a man whose name was Joseph, of the house of David. And the virgin's name was Mary. [28]And he came to her and said, "Greetings, O favored one, the Lord is with you!" [29]But she was greatly troubled at the saying, and tried to discern what sort of greeting this might be. [30]And the angel said to her, "Do not be afraid, Mary, for you have found favor with God. [31]And behold, you will conceive in your womb and bear a son, and you shall call his name Jesus. [32]He will be great and will be called the Son of the Most High. And the Lord God will give to him the throne of his father David, [33]and he will reign over the house of Jacob forever, and of his kingdom there will be no end."

[34]And Mary said to the angel, "How will this be, since I am a virgin?"

[35]And the angel answered her, "The Holy Spirit will come upon you, and the power of the Most High will overshadow you; therefore the child to be born will be called holy — the Son of God. [36]And behold, your relative Elizabeth in her old age has also conceived a son, and this is the sixth month with her who was called barren. [37]For nothing will be impossible with God." [38]And Mary said, "Behold, I am the servant of the Lord; let it be to me according to your word." And the angel departed from her.

The first thing we can learn from this text is that, because of the virgin birth of Jesus, we can have good reason to accept the inspiration and inerrancy of the Bible. Let that sink in for a minute. We know that Jesus *was* born of a virgin; therefore, we *can* believe and accept the Bible as the Word of God. One of the principal methods by which human beings can examine any writing and be able to determine that it is or isn't the Word of God is by seeing whether or not those events that are prophesied in them actually take place. The fulfillment of prophecy is one of the surest ways to know whether a book is from God or merely from man. Only those things that God himself prophesies can be assured of taking place.

Let's for a moment turn back to the Old Testament, to chapter 7 of Isaiah, to see exactly what it is that the prophet Isaiah predicted. Normally I would just read the Old Testament prophetic verse in question, and then explain its New Testament fulfillment. However, this verse, Isaiah 7:14, demands a much deeper understanding of its Old Testament background—thus enabling us to see its importance in the New Testament.

On this occasion, we find Isaiah speaking to Ahaz, the king of Judah, who had refused up to this point to seek the truth of God's providential care over his people. What is at issue here is Ahaz's refusal to look to God for a sign. The date is 735 B.C. The situation is a desperate bid by the northern kingdom, Israel, and her neighbor Syria, to unite against the huge army of their mutual arch-enemy Assyria (which later became part of Babylon). However, the southern kingdom, Judah, has already cut a political alliance with Assyria. So Israel and Syria are planning to invade Judah, remove the king (who is the one in the lineage of David, God's anointed king), and put their own man on the throne to force Judah to join their side. The story line is contained in Isaiah 7:1–13:

In the days of Ahaz the son of Jotham, son of Uzziah, king of Judah, Rezin the king of Syria and Pekah the son of Remaliah the king of Israel came up to Jerusalem to wage war against it, but could not yet mount an attack against it. [2]When the house of David was told, "Syria is in league with Ephraim," the heart of Ahaz and the heart of his people shook as the trees of the forest shake before the wind. [3]And the Lord said to Isaiah, "Go out to meet Ahaz, you and Shear-jashub your son, at the end of the conduit of the upper pool on the highway to the Washer's Field. [4]And say to him, "Be careful, be quiet, do not fear, and do not let your heart be faint because of these two smoldering stumps of firebrands, at the fierce anger of Rezin and Syria and the son of Remaliah. [5]Because Syria, with Ephraim and the son of Remaliah, has devised evil against you, saying, [6]"Let us go up against Judah and terrify it, and let us conquer it for ourselves, and set up the son of Tabeel as king in the midst of it," [7]thus says the Lord God: "'It shall not stand, and it shall not come to pass. [8]For the head of Syria is Damascus, and the head of Damascus is Rezin. (Within sixty-five years, Ephraim will be broken to pieces so that it will no longer be a people.) [9]" "And the head of Ephraim is Samaria, and the head of Samaria is the son of Remaliah. If you are not firm in faith, you will not be firm at all."'

[10]Again the Lord spoke to Ahaz, [11]"Ask a sign of the Lord your God; let it be deep as Sheol or high as heaven." [12]But Ahaz said, "I will not ask, and I will not put the Lord to the test." [13]And he said, "Hear then, O house of David! Is it too little for you to weary men, that you weary my God also?"

As the story opens, we see two people—the prophet Isaiah and a guy named Ahaz, the king of Judah. Ahaz is out inspecting the waterworks surrounding the city of Jerusalem, a pretty normal thing for a king to be doing prior to an expected assault on his city. He wants to make sure everything is ready to fend off the attack. The names of all these people are not important, and actually the location of the events is not ultimately important although it is interesting that a number of years later, the leading general is in Assyria's army (remember, Assyria is Judah's political ally right now). What is important to see and to understand in this incident is that this prophecy from Isaiah shows the never-ending conflict between God's anointed and a usurper. We must see this truth as a picture of the conflict between the true king, the Messiah, and a false king, the unbelieving world.

With this background, we see the prophet Isaiah is trying to tell the king that he's worrying about the wrong thing. Instead of worrying about the material defenses around the city, he should be concerned about his relationship with God. He must stop worrying about secular, political things, and he must demonstrate his faith in the God who called him to be the king.

When you stop to think about it, this is the same choice that you and I always face. Do we depend on our worldly situation— our own strength, our family situation, or financial situation, or job situation? Or do we depend on the grace, mercy, and providence of God? Keep that question handy. We're going to get back to it soon.

Well, what is Ahaz' decision? What is his choice? The world . . . or the grace, mercy, and providence of God? Apparently he has chosen the ways of the world. That's why he's worried about the coming attack and he's out inspecting his worldly defenses. Isaiah is trying to make Ahaz's decision clear to him, and to do so, he uses a classic teaching technique—an object lesson.

This object lesson happens to be the prophet's own son, whom we see there in verse 3 is named She-ar-jasub. You see,

Isaiah puts this boy with this strange name right in front of Ahaz in order to get his attention. In Hebrew, She-ar-jashub means, "a remnant will return." Isaiah is trying to get Ahaz to see that God is going to win, no matter what. He wants Ahaz to know that the true people of God will always survive, will always prevail. A remnant will always return, will always believe in and have faith in God. So to expand on this object lesson, there beginning in verse 7 and going through the middle of verse 9, Isaiah gives Ahaz a very clear explanation of what God wants him to understand.

> ". . . thus says the Lord God: "It shall not stand, and it shall not come to pass. ⁸For the head of Syria is Damascus, and the head of Damascus is Rezin. (Within sixty-five years Ephraim will be broken to pieces so that it will no longer be a people.) And the head of Ephraim is Samaria, and the head of Samaria is the son of Remaliah."

Do you see it, my friends? God is telling Ahaz, through the prophet, that these perceived enemies are nobodies. In fact, one of them will disappear from the face of the earth in just 65 more years. You don't have to fear the world, Ahaz! But Ahaz still doesn't get it. Given the choice between the grace, mercy, and providence of God and the enemies of God—Ahaz continues to make the wrong choice. As the prophet explains in the last half of verse 9, he does not stand firm. *"If you are not firm in faith, you will not be firm at all."* In other words, if your heart is not set in faith and worship of God, then you have no faith at all and will not have the grace, mercy, and providence of God to protect you.

A lot of people in the world today are just like Ahaz. They listen to the Word of God and they look at the world all around them, then they refuse to believe God's Word. They concentrate all of their efforts, all of their resources, all of their attention, all of their worries, on the world . . . and refuse to trust God. Instead of choosing the Messiah, they chose the Messiah's enemies.

Confronted with the stubbornness and hard-heartedness of Ahaz, Isaiah still does not give up. He makes one more try at breaking through Ahaz's denial and unbelief there in verse 11. He explains to Ahaz that God will demonstrate through a miraculous, visible sign that he, the great and powerful, the one and only true God of the universe, should be trusted. He even offers to allow Ahaz to pick whatever sign he wants. Look at verses 10 and 11. *"Again the Lord spoke to Ahaz, ¹¹'Ask a sign of the Lord your God; let it be deep as Sheol or high as heaven.'"*

Wouldn't you like that? Wouldn't it be wonderful if God were to say to you through a true prophet that he would send you a sign—something visible so you could understand and believe that God was in control of all things? A sign so you could really believe in God. We'll see in a moment that this is exactly what God offers to us!

So, after all of Isaiah's efforts, what does Ahaz do? He cops out. Verse 12: *"But Ahaz said, 'I will not ask, and I will not put the Lord to the test.'"* He is so afraid of asking for a sign that might result in his having to trust God, he refuses to ask for *any* sign. His heart is so hardened that he refuses the miraculous offer the prophet presents him. No breaking through *his* spiritual defenses—no sir-ree, Bob!

Is that what you would do if you were given the same opportunity? Let me tell you, if you want to place a bet on how people would respond today, the oddsmakers in Nevada would give you about twenty to one against accepting God's offer through the prophet. You see, that's about the percentage of people in America today who are evangelical, Bible-believing, trusting-in-Jesus Christians —about one in twenty.

Oh sure, about one out of three Americans go to church with some regularity. But if you were to confront most of them with the truth of the Word of God as Isaiah is confronting Ahaz in this chapter, they would respond in exactly the same way. They would not fully open their hearts to God and put the full trust of their whole lives in his hands.

So, in the face of this final rejection of God by Ahaz and in light of the promises of God, what does Isaiah do? He does what all true Christian ministers still do today. He begins preaching the truth about Jesus! Look at verses 13 and 14 again. *"And he said, 'Hear then, O house of David! Is it too little for you to weary men, that you weary my God also? Therefore the Lord himself will give you a sign. Behold, the virgin shall conceive and bear a son, and shall call his name Immanuel.'"* Even though Ahaz turns down the promise of a sign, even though the world today still rejects the promise of a sign, God gives the sign anyway. Now do you see how important this sign really is, yet even today?

The prophecy of Isaiah was that a certain virgin would bear a son—a most unusual prophecy because it countered the biological fact of normal human procreation. That son would be called by a very special name—Immanuel (God with us). Of course, in the near term, over 700 years before the birth of Jesus, Israel rejected the sign. You see, Isaiah uttered this prophecy in the eighth century before the birth of Jesus at Bethlehem. More than 700 years passed before something happened that confirmed this prophecy. Yet confirmed it was. The whole point of this text from chapter 1 of Luke's Gospel is to confirm the events foretold by Isaiah. The angel Gabriel came to announce the great news that Mary, (no doubt) a virgin, would bear a child who would be the Son of God. In other words, he would be *"God with us."* He would be the incarnate second person of the Trinity.

There is a somewhat parallel account of the birth of Jesus over in chapter 1 of Matthew's gospel. In verses 20–23, we find an angel of the Lord speaking to Joseph, the husband-to-be of Mary. *"But as he considered these things, behold, an angel of the Lord appeared to him in a dream, saying, "Joseph, son of David, do not fear to take Mary as your wife, for that which is conceived in her is from the Holy Spirit. [21]She will bear a son, and you shall call his name Jesus, for he will save his people from their sins." [22]All this took place to fulfill what the Lord had spoken by the prophet: [23]"Behold, the virgin shall conceive and bear a son, and they shall call his name Immanuel, (which means, God with us)."*

Back in those days, while it was acceptable for a betrothed couple to engage in sex, certainly Joseph knew that he and Mary had not done so. By Jewish law, Joseph could have returned Mary to her parents and broken the engagement once everyone knew she was "with child." But that was not in God's plan. God's providential plan for Jesus included being raised in Joseph's house, so Joseph would also have to understand about the miracle of the virgin birth.

Not only does this passage in Matthew verify beyond a doubt that the birth of Jesus was in fact fulfillment of Isaiah's prophecy, it also helps us understand the answer to the question that many people have as to why the prophetic name *"Immanuel"* did not become Jesus' actual name. After the time of the prophecy of Isaiah, the predominant thought, which was highlighted by Daniel and kept before the people of God, was that they were to expect a Messiah, who would be God himself, as the name Immanuel used in the prophecy implies. However, when the event finally takes place 700+ years later, the prophecy becomes fulfilled and the emphasis is shifted. The people were no longer to keep looking for the Messiah. They were no longer to look for the one who would be "God with them." Instead, he was, in fact, come; he was with them now. So God's angel, speaking to Joseph in the account from Matthew, explained that the name would be the one he would carry during his life on earth. It would be one that would more closely describe the mission he was to carry out among men. And so he was named Jesus, which means, "The Lord is salvation." In other words, the emphasis now shifted from expected prophecy to the fact of fulfilled salvation through the Son of God.

The birth of Jesus (the savior of men) did in fact fulfill the prophecy of Isaiah, and thus gave us a solid piece of evidence by which we can know that his prophecies were completely accurate. By applying these same criteria to all the books in the Bible, we are able to conclude that the Bible is indeed the Word of God. (Of course, there is a whole separate book in the Presbyterian Primer series, titled *Biblical Interpretation*, and a separate course on www.rulingelder.com that deals with those issues in great depth.)

Let's turn our attention now to a second thing that the miracle of the virgin birth means to us today. By it, we have overwhelming evidence of the power and sovereignty of God. It is clear from this text in Luke's Gospel that this birth could not come about in any other way than through the power of God.

Now, what do you think any young girl who was indeed a virgin, who had in no human way been susceptible to pregnancy, would she say if someone—angel or not—told her that she was going to have a baby? I think the words we find in verse 24 of our text in Luke 1 are just about what we would expect, right? *"And Mary said to the angel, 'How will this be, since I am a virgin?'"* Or to put it in today's vernacular, "But I just can't be pregnant!"

I'm not sure we should accuse Mary of doubting what the angel was telling her. She simply knew that children could only be conceived as the result of the normal act of procreation, and she had never had sex of any kind. So as far as she was concerned, it was not possible for her to be pregnant. But the angel explains things pretty well to her there in verse 35. *"The Holy Spirit will come upon you, and the power of the Most High will overshadow you; therefore the child to be born will be called holy—the Son of God."* We really need to understand what this verse is teaching us. The virgin birth did not come about as the result of a normal, sexual union. Rather it was the result of the miraculous action of the third person of the triune God, God the Holy Spirit.

This in no way implies that there was any physical contact between the Holy Spirit and Mary. That wouldn't be possible. The Holy Spirit is not a physical being; he's a spirit and doesn't have a body like a man's body. Indeed, what is being implied here is that this birth would happen completely without *any* natural, human form of procreation. To boil it down to its basics, the virgin birth was the result of a miracle and nothing less.

We don't expect miracles today, do we? At least we don't sit around and wait for one all the time. It's not that they don't happen, but they are not anticipated as a normal course of action. The Bible tells us that Mary herself was a little dubious at first about the idea of a miracle. At least the angel Gabriel sensed that she was doubtful, for right away—in verse 36—he gives her an example of another recent miracle that she could check out for herself. *"And behold, your relative Elizabeth in her old age has also conceived a son, and this is the sixth month with her who was called barren."* Apparently, Mary had not visited with her cousin Elizabeth for some time and didn't know that she was going to have a baby even though she was well past the age of menopause. This is much like the miracle of Abraham and Sarah having a child, even though Sarah also had been well past child-rearing age.

So we see here in Luke chapter 1 that the virgin birth came about as the result of a real miracle, and nothing less. This gives us more solid evidence that God has great power and that what he wants done in this world will certainly be done, even if it takes a miracle! We can understand without any doubt the words of the angel in verse 37, *"For nothing will be impossible with God."*

There's a good lesson for us personally in that statement, isn't there? Is there something in your life today that you feel might be impossible? I know I've got a couple of thoughts in that regard myself . . . about things that I wish would happen but that I can't see any solution for in the future. Even though I see things this way, I still know that if God wants them to happen—in fact, if God wants anything to happen (notice I said if *God* wants it, not if *I* want it)—they will surely happen. With God, nothing is impossible. Even if it is something that is contrary to nature, it will happen and can happen through a miracle.

If the fact that we have evidence for the inspiration of the Bible and we have evidence for the sovereign power of God are not enough, there is yet a third reason why the virgin birth is so important. In many ways, I believe this is the most important reason that the virgin birth has real application to our lives today. It goes right to the heart of why Jesus was born. Jesus was born so he could die! It is as simple as that. His death on the cross was the only way that you or I could gain eternal life.

There had to be something very special about his death. In order for his death to be special, his life had to be special, and this is the prime importance of the virgin birth. As a result of the virgin birth, Jesus was born sinless, lived a perfect life (see Hebrews 4:15), and was able to be the perfect, unblemished sacrifice to suffer the penalty for the sins of men when he died at Calvary.

We already know that all human beings are sinners, right? The basic verse that teaches us this is Romans 3:23: *"For all have sinned and fall short of the glory of God."* In Romans chapter 5, the teaching about original sin is more specific, in verses 15–19: *"But the free gift is not like the trespass. For if many died through one man's trespass, much more have the grace of God and the free gift by the grace of that one man Jesus Christ abounded for many. [16]And the free gift is not like the result of that one man's sin. For the judgment following one trespass brought condemnation, but the free gift following many trespasses brought justification. [17]If, because of one man's trespass, death reigned through that one man, much more will those who receive the abundance of grace and the free gift of righteousness reign in life through the one man Jesus Christ. [18]Therefore, as one trespass led to condemnation for all men, so one act of righteousness leads to justification and life for all men. [19]For as by the one man's disobedience the many were made sinners, so by the one man's obedience the many will be made righteous."*

While Paul's overall purpose in this passage is to explain justification, in order to do so he has to explain original sin. Look at those emphases: verse 15 says, "*many died through one man's trespass*"; verse 17 reiterates, "*because of one man's trespass, death reigned through that one man . . .*"; verse 19 again tells us, "*by the one man's disobedience the many were made sinners.*" Not much doubt about Paul's teaching. We are all sinners because of the original sin of Adam. Every human being is in the same condition, except one.

We find the essence of this idea of the sinlessness of Jesus also in verse 35 of our text in Luke chapter 1. *"Therefore the child to be born will be called holy."* I like the use of the "therefore" in this clause. What it means is that Jesus was born as the result of a miracle that we call the virgin birth in order that he could be called holy. In other words, we understand from the angel's announcement that this child was to be completely holy, without sin.

There has never been before, nor will there ever be again, another child about which that very same thing could be said. Only Jesus was, and is, and will be a completely holy, sinless human being. Throughout the New Testament, we find reference to the sinlessness of Jesus. Jesus himself confronted his enemies with the challenge, saying as he did in John 8:46, *"Which one of you convicts me of sin?"* Peter expresses the same thought in 1 Peter 2:21–22, where he writes, *"For to this you have been called, because [the Messiah] also suffered for you, leaving you an example, so that you might follow in his steps. [22]He committed no sin, neither was deceit found in his mouth."* We find this same teaching about the sinlessness of Jesus in at least three or four other passages in the New Testament.

The spotless lamb, without blemish, was required for the Passover. The words "without blemish" constantly recur in the description of the sacrifice, which clearly pointed toward the atonement accomplished by Jesus. So we can see from the Bible that the sinlessness of Jesus is not merely a personal characteristic but also an attribute that is absolutely essential to the substitutionary death he accomplished on the cross at Calvary.

Now . . . how does the sinlessness of Jesus, which is the result of the virgin birth and which is an essential fact of the atonement, apply to you and me today? Well, it can only apply to us if the atonement applies to us. In other words, it applies only if we have faith in Jesus as our substitute on the cross of Calvary where *we* deserved to die for our own sins. It applies to us only if we confess that it is through the death of the child who was born on Christmas day that we can know the forgiveness of our sins this day and know the joy of eternal life. God requires that there be no forgiveness of sins for anyone unless a totally sinless person pays the penalty price of death on the other person's behalf.

This is the real message of Christmas. This is the central teaching of Christianity. While others may make other emphases during Christmas sermons, a true Christian knows there is no peace other than the peace that comes through the finished work of Jesus. A true Christian knows there is no true love other than the love that God has shown us through sending his Son. A true Christian knows that there is no giving that compares to the priceless gift of God's one and only, unique Son. That Son wasn't a baby who needs us to bring gifts to him—but was himself the gracious gift of God the Father. God gave his one and only Son so that as he died, we could live forever.

If you have ever gone through a Christmas period without knowing the real meaning of the virgin birth, *do not* let another one go by without confessing that you know the saving purpose of Jesus' birth and death and that its real meaning applies to you. If you have ever gone through a Christmas without knowing the meaning of the gift of the Christ Child in your own life as the personal sacrifice for every one of your own sins, *do not* let Christmas go by this year without turning to Jesus and asking him into your heart.

If you, as many (if not most) of you reading this book have done, already have come to a saving knowledge of Jesus, let the meaning of the virgin birth have a new effect in your life too. Remember that through it we can have assurance of the power and sovereignty of God in the world and particularly in our own lives. We can know that his Word, which tells us the Christmas story—or to use our fancy doctrinal word, the doctrine of the incarnation—is not just a myth, but is indeed the truth from God himself. Use this Word—call on this all-powerful Lord—to help you communicate to someone else, someone you dearly love, the necessity of the virgin birth and all that comes with it, so that it might take root in his or her heart this very year.

A s I started to work on this chapter I googled the word "modeling" and came up with dozens and dozens of different categories of meanings. Of course, the world of runway models such as Naomi Campbell, Claudia Schiffer (and for you old guys like me, Christy Brinkley) had all the top sites. Then the paths went every which way: software models, chemistry models, warfare and security threat models, computer graphic models, corporate models, dinosaur models, and on and on and on. I quit after page 15.

What I did not find is what I have always believed was the *numero uno* model, the top of all top-ten list categories of modeling. That type of example is the effect an adult can have on a child—particularly the effect a parent can have on his or her own child.

While I was a Navy chaplain I spent a number of years working in what we then called family studies—trying to figure out what was really going on in families when dad was gone for long periods of time (as sailors are prone to do even in peacetime). My longest deployment away from my family was nine months (although we broke up that time by having Esther and the girls fly to Southern Europe for a three-week vacation in the middle of that time).

In today's environment of reduced forces, it is not uncommon to see twelve- and fourteen-month deployments, including both moms and dads being away from their families. While my work was primarily to study the effects of a missing father, I can only guess how much worse things must be with a missing mother. For our purposes in this chapter, however, we will focus on the missing father figure.

One thing we discovered in our Navy studies is that in homes where the father was gone a lot—when there was no father figure at home to be a model for the male children (boys)—there tended to be many more discipline and personality problems with these boys. To exacerbate the situation, there were very few other men around of the same age as their fathers. So the boys would just find another male figure to model, usually a youth just slightly older than they were, and more often than not these would not be particularly good role models.

Teenage girls, and even more commonly pre-teenage girls, also are very impressionable and subject to modeling influences. My wife and I raised three girls, and we would occasionally take them to contemporary Christian music concerts. I vividly recall an Amy Grant concert (this was in the "early Amy" days). You could not believe the crush of the mob of young girls crowding around the stage—trying to get a good look at her, or for some, even to touch her.

More recently, I watched very young girls in the congregation I served as pastor when Brittney Spears came along. Even in the "early Brittany" stage (when she was being presented as the epitome of a "good girl"), these young fans would wear clothes just like hers, exposing their navels—at age eight! They would emulate the way she walked, her facial expressions, the whole package.

Modeling is somehow just built in to our human condition. I have no training in child psychology, but I don't think I need any to recognize that this issue of proper modeling is absolutely essential to the development of young children. It seems to me that the modeling issue is at the very heart of controversies such as whether or not "life-committed" homosexual couples should be allowed to adopt children. Since they would be modeling what is consistently considered by evangelical Christians as an aberrant lifestyle, it makes sense to me that Christians would organize to oppose such adoptions. The rights of the children to have proper, God-intended role models in the home take a far higher priority than any so-called "gay rights."

Now it should come as no surprise to those of us who are Bible-believing Christians that the world's psychological community has concluded that modeling is important in raising children. All they have done is uncover, in what they call "nature," a plain and simple biblical truth. It is the truth we will examine as our theme in this chapter as we look at Philippians 2 and some related verses in order to study the issue of the humiliation of Jesus.

The plain, simple theme that we will find is this: each and every Christian should earnestly seek to model the humility of Jesus. For, you see, Jesus was a perfect role model. Particularly in this area of humility, the Scriptures call on us to model ourselves after him.

Perhaps it seems a bit strange to you after looking at the prophecies of Jesus prior to his birth, and then looking at the Christmas story and the nature of his virgin birth, that the very first thing we turn to is his humiliation, his leaving his divine home and coming to earth as a mere human. Why not look at his great teachings, the parables, and such? Why not look at his confrontations with the Jewish religious leaders of his day? Why not look at the training, the "discipleship" of his disciples? Well, it was explained at the outset that we couldn't cover everything, but all these issues, which many call the "prophetic ministry" of Jesus, ultimately need to be understood in light of Jesus' humiliation. Let me explain what I mean.

It is my assumption that people react with different levels of belief and especially with different levels of application depending on the source of the information they receive. For instance, if a peer, someone just like you—human, sinful by nature, limited in both knowledge and skills—were to tell you something they wanted you to believe and to apply to your life, you might or you might not agree with them. Your ultimate reaction would depend greatly on your relationship to the teacher. Does he know and understand you, and your culture, and your life situation? Does he know firsthand what he's talking about because "he's been there." Is he able to show you clearly how his teaching applies to you? If those things all come together, there is a halfway decent chance you will believe and apply that truth.

Now, let's go to the other extreme. Suppose the one telling you the truth they wanted you to believe and apply to your life was God himself. You had no doubts whatsoever that this word was coming directly from God. How would you react? Well, if you use the framework of those Christian denominations and faith groups that believe that God still reveals truth today—that he still speaks directly to Christians today—you would expect a tremendously higher percentage of belief and obedience, wouldn't you? If God were really speaking to you and me, would we not just immediately fall down and worship, then get up and do exactly what he wanted us to do?

What do you suppose the results would be of a sociological study of the level of belief and obedience between Christians today who believe in continuing revelation, and those who believe that the canon is closed (that God no longer speaks directly to us, but rather everything he wants us to believe and to do is found in the Bible)? Why, there would be no difference at all! There may be a slight veneer of holiness on the outside of the continuing revelation group, but a closer examination of the lives of both groups would show just about exactly the same thing. Both groups would give evidence of true belief (I'm not questioning that for even a second), but also evidence of the same leftover effects of original sin. The ongoing struggle of sin would be present in every Christian's life. Everyone still needs to grow spiritually.

So if there is no significant difference whether you hear a biblical truth from another human being just like you, or whether you hear it as direct revelation from God, then what's left? Where is there hope for deep, spiritual transformation? Well, it is that very question that the Reverend Michael Sharrett asks in the subtitle to his new work, *Watching Over the Heart* (Narrows, VA: 2005, Metokos Press). His answer is, overwhelmingly, that spiritual growth comes when truth comes in the context of the work of Jesus in our lives. You take the divinity, the God nature of Jesus, and add to it the humanity, the human nature of Jesus, and you have a synergy through which the Holy Spirit can and does bring about spiritual growth. Let me put it to you more simply. The humiliation of Jesus, the fact that Jesus as God also became human by a choice he made, as well as the process by which that dual nature came about, makes all the difference in the world.

Let's go to the heart of the event, the transaction where all of this takes place. It's told to us in Philippians, chapter 2, verses 1–11. This passage has been known throughout the centuries as the Kenosis passage.

So if there is any encouragement in Christ, any comfort from love, any participation in the Spirit, any affection and sympathy, [2]complete my joy by being of the same mind, having the same love, being in full accord and of one mind. [3]Do nothing from rivalry or conceit, but in humility count others more significant than yourselves. [4]Let each of you look not only to his own interests, but also to the interests of others. [5]Have this mind among yourselves, which is yours in Christ Jesus, [6]who, though he was in the form of God, did not count equality with God a thing to be grasped, [7]but made himself nothing, taking the form of a servant, being born in the likeness of men. And being found in human form, [8]he humbled himself by becoming obedient to the point of death, even death on a cross. [9]Therefore God has highly exalted him and bestowed on him the name that is above every name, [10]so that at the name of Jesus every knee should bow, in heaven and on earth and under the earth, [11]and every tongue confess that Jesus Christ is Lord, to the glory of God the Father.

I hope each of you reading this work will recognize this passage and, in fact, have the good fortune to recall that it is a passage about which you have heard a lot of sermons preached. This would tell me that you were raised in a fine, strong Bible-believing church. These verses are *that* important a passage of Scripture.

As you may have noticed, the text is really a sermon that Paul is preaching to the folks at Philippi and surrounding cities who would have heard the letter read in their services. It will also apply to us as well—something that can't be avoided.

The underlying theological truth about the work of Jesus, which is known as his humiliation, holds this whole thing together. The first thing that should jump off the page of Philippians 2 is that every Christian—every true child of God— should seek to have the same attitude of humility that Jesus had. In other words, we should "model" our lives after Jesus. Now in order to model ourselves after Jesus' humility, we have to understand what it was really all about.

To begin with, the humility of Jesus involves what we call the incarnation. We have already looked at this concept in Chapters One and Four. Jesus' humility is part and parcel of his becoming a human being. That's what Paul means in verse 7, when he writes that Jesus *"made himself nothing, taking the form of a servant, being born in the likeness of men."*

Some Christians—particularly the more pietistic or fundamentalist ones—have for many years taught that being a human being was not such a good deal. They suggest that what we need to do is to stop being so human and start being more "Christ-like." You've heard that before, haven't you? Well, I don't know about you, but for myself, I can't really do all that well at being "Christ-like." Most people who know me would say that fundamentalism is not one of my strong suits. And frankly, I don't think that being that sort of fundamentalist is true of very many Christians in the world today anyway. What is really needed is not for us to be more God-like (which is to say, to be more Jesus-divine-nature-like), but rather what is needed is for us to be more human (which is to say, to be more Jesus-human-nature-like). A lot of people miss that emphasis in the Bible.

Let's be careful here to be sure we all understand what it means to be Jesus-human-nature-like. It's not the same thing as being simply more human. Robert Schuller has picked up this theme. He writes in his best-selling book on self-esteem that "God is trying . . . to build a society of human beings who live out the golden rule" (Robert Shuller, *Self-Esteem*, Word Press, Waco, TX, 1982, p. 135). But I'm afraid it's not so much what Schuller says, it's what he does not—ever—say. He all but ignores the effect of sin. You see, Jesus was a perfect human because he did not sin whatsoever—but you and I don't have the ability to do that. Our sin is always getting in the way of our being more and more perfectly human.

I think verses 2 and 3 of this passage help us to see what true humanness is all about (as contrasted with sinful humanness). Paul is there encouraging us to be *"of the same mind, having the same love, being in full accord and of one mind. ³Do nothing from rivalry or conceit, but in humility count others more significant than yourselves."* You see, that's what being human is all about, caring for others, putting others above yourself, never putting yourself first. Paul is emphasizing that we are not to have *self*-esteem, as Schuller does, but rather *other*-esteem.

If Jesus had wanted to emphasize self-esteem, he would have just stayed in his divine nature. In taking on human nature, however, he took on the role of a servant, Paul tells us, thus emphasizing other-esteem. That's what true humanness is. That's the type of humility for which we should strive.

Another thing that the humility of Jesus involves besides humanness is suffering. The end of verse 7 tells us that he *"made himself nothing, taking the form of a servant, being born in the likeness of men."* I'm convinced that when Paul talks about Jesus' role as a servant, he is trying to have us understand that humility involves suffering. Those who know the Old Testament Scriptures as well as Paul knew them would immediately make the connection between "servant" and "suffering." What is it that Isaiah wrote in 53:3, the famous "Suffering Servant" passage? *"He was despised and rejected by men; a man of sorrows, and acquainted with grief; and as one from whom men hide their faces he was despised, and we esteemed him not."* We will be spending an entire chapter a bit later dealing with how Jesus suffered on this earth, but what I want to do now is to take some time to be sure we all see how it is that *we* are to "model" ourselves after Jesus in our own suffering.

I'm afraid this is another area where some Christians have gone overboard in the past. I remember a number of years ago when I first lived in the Philippines. (I hate to tell you how many years ago that was, but back then Ferdinand Marcos had not yet become president. He probably was worth only a couple thousand pesos and his wife only had three pairs of shoes.) Anyway, one Good Friday I went to see a ceremony that was taking place in the village near our Navy communications station in San Miguel on the coast of the South China Sea.

Each year during Holy Week, a number of young Filipino men would start walking from Manila, the capital city, to their home village. They carried large crosses, the size of the cross on which Jesus died. They wore only sandals and a very small loincloth. They would eat no food and take only water mixed with vinegar. They would walk, carrying this large wooden cross, a distance of between 40 and 50 miles. The men in the ceremony I witnessed were from San Miguel, 45 miles from Manila. There were dozens of young men participating in this drama, walking to nearly every small town.

If the walk wasn't bad enough, when they got to their village, which they always timed for midday on Good Friday, they would begin to walk on their knees—or crawl—the last mile. From the outskirts of town toward the town center, down a dirt road, they dragged the crosses behind them. Each would be carrying a leather strap or thong that had pieces of glass or metal, or both, attached firmly in the leather. They would use these thongs with the sharp pieces projecting from them to beat themselves on their backs in regular motions as they walked or crawled.

They continued this activity until they arrived in front of an altar, where a religious ceremony was held to "celebrate" Good Friday. The year I watched the ceremony, one of the young men became so very weak about 500 yards from the finish line that he had to be taken to a hospital. I learned that he died several days later. During all of this ceremony, the people who were lining the main street in town at least ten deep, and who lined the road from Manila all the way, just stood silently and watched. There was no cheering, no celebrating, just the vicarious participation in the suffering taking place in front of their very eyes.

It is my understanding that these ceremonies still take place in the Philippines—although the government has sought to crack down on the practice. The people do it now with less publicity, and only a few insiders know the actual route and final village. Some Filipinos practice their brand of Roman Catholicism this way, at least as far as "suffering" is understood.

I believe you will agree with me (and I wasn't even a Christian at the time I saw all this) that this was a totally useless display of religious zeal and fervor. That is *not* what Jesus meant by suffering. The suffering of Jesus, which you and I are to model in our lives, is simply to live our lives as human beings in a fallen world. You see, if there had been no sin, there would be no suffering. So sharing in the sufferings of Jesus is simply seeking to live a Christian life in this world of sin.

We suffer when loved ones die. We suffer pain from injury and disease. We suffer when we are wrongly accused because of our testimony for the Lord. We suffer when we or our loved ones are deeply affected by natural disasters such as this year's major hurricanes. We suffer in some way every single day. If we want to model the humility of Jesus, we must allow ourselves to suffer—that is to say, we must deal with the great issues of life according to the Scriptures, even when we do not fully understand them.

One more way we are to model the humility of Jesus is through death. Paul tells us in verse 8, *"he (Jesus) humbled himself by becoming obedient to the point of death, even death on a cross."* This, of course, is the essence of Passion Week—the week just before Easter. This is the story of Good Friday. This is the death of Jesus, which we celebrate every time we gather around the table of the Sacrament of the Lord's Supper. Since Jesus died, we too will have to die. Oh yes, we will have to die a physical death someday, if the Lord does not come again before our day comes. But we die in many other ways before that. Because the death of Jesus—in our place, on our behalf, yet without guilt—does a saving work in the life of a Christian, it causes us to more and more appreciate its meaning and its power, and brings us to a point of deep repentance and dying to self and to sin.

During the period before Easter, many Christians, families, congregations, and denominations set aside some special time to rehearse these truths in their own lives. Some more liturgical denominations celebrate what is known as Lent, and make this extended period from Ash Wednesday to Good Friday a time of practical application of the process of dying to sin. That's why people give up things during Lent. They are dying to sin. Of course, the problem with so many people is that this has simply become a religious ritual without any internal spiritual meaning. Right after Easter you would think it was Fat Tuesday all over again (the day before Ash Wednesday when many people indulge to excess in what they are planning to give up the next day), because they go right back to their same attitudes and practices. No, true dying to sin and to self would have a more lasting effect, just as physical death has a very lasting effect.

Even if some people have turned a valid religious practice into a meaningless ritual, it does not mean we should not take time to reflect on our need to model Jesus' suffering, even to death. We should do this because each believer should seek the same attitudes of humility as Jesus did—allowing ourselves to be human, allowing ourselves to suffer, and allowing ourselves to die to sin.

All that makes for very good theory, doesn't it? If you and I were really perfect, or even pretty close to perfect, we could just wrap up this chapter right now. All I'd have to do is tell you what are you supposed to do and you'd go out and do it like good little Christian boys and girls who follow the model set for them by their fine Christian parents, right? But we know better, don't we? Life just doesn't work that way. And the reason is that this is not the way God made it to work. Each believer—each child of God—has to *work* at maintaining attitudes of humility. They just do not come naturally. This was true of Jesus himself as well.

That's the important thing in this Kenosis passage, that we are studying. As verses 6 and 7 put it, "*who, though he was in the form of God, did not count equality with God a thing to be grasped, ⁷but made himself nothing, taking the form of a servant, being born in the likeness of men.*" This word at the beginning of verse 7, which the ESV and most other translations render *"made himself nothing,"* comes from the Greek word *kenosis* (which is why this passage has taken on that special name over the centuries). The word means literally to "empty oneself." For you grammar buffs out there, it is a reflexive verb, which shows the need for a personal decision on the part of the individual taking the action. What this is telling us is that Jesus' humility was *not* due to his original, divine nature. He had to "make himself humble." He had to empty himself of his divine power (but never his divine nature), and that took effort. That took work. That took a conscious act of his will.

To go back to our modeling concept from the beginning of the chapter, this is what we must do as his followers. We have to "empty ourselves," which means we have to work at getting rid of the things in our life that keep us from "modeling" the humility of Jesus.

Back in verse 3, we are given an excellent commentary on what we need to get rid of. Paul writes, "*Do nothing from rivalry or conceit, but in humility count others more significant than yourselves.*" What we have to get rid of, you see, is our pride, our self-centeredness, our vain conceit. That doesn't come naturally. We have to put out some effort. In fact, we have to practice it.

When we were raising our daughters, there were a few truisms that I would try to teach them on a regular basis. One was the fact that anything in life that is worth doing takes work. I would, of course, apply that to doing homework; that's a pretty good standard.

I would more often apply that to swim practice when I heard all the moans and groans about long, arduous practice sessions. I think swimming is a good illustration because all great champion swimmers start out with just some basic physical ability. You'd be amazed at how many people have a high level of swimming ability—probably millions of them. But from that basic starting point, the champions have to work. They practice, practice, practice, hopefully practicing the right things they've learned from their coach. You do understand, don't you, that practice does not make perfect—practice simply makes permanent. So they had to be practicing the right things, the right strokes, the right techniques. And, in the end, some are able to achieve their goals.

Two of our girls learned during high school that the rewards of swimming were not worth all the work. Nothing wrong with that—if you can achieve the kind of goals to which you aspire (swimming well, but not at championship level), there isn't a lot of sense in doing all that work. One of them continued her swimming, and that hard work brought her first a scholarship to a Division II school (Ashland University in Ohio), and then, in her sophomore year, the phone call came with an offer of a scholarship to the University of Nebraska. Swimming also brought her another reward—she is married to a fine young man who is the head swim coach at Delta State University in Mississippi.

That's the way it has to be in our lives as we deal with sin. We have to practice putting aside pride, putting ourselves first all of the time. We must practice humility. We must learn from the coach, which means we must learn what to do from the Bible and our spiritual leaders and counselors. Then we must practice it, and practice it, and practice it. Practice doesn't make it easy, does it? But it wasn't easy for Jesus to give up his divine power, take on the form of a human being, and partake in human suffering. He didn't have to do it. He volunteered for the team out of nothing but love for the rest of those new recruits struggling to make the team.

So, as we seek the same attitude of humility that Jesus exhibited, as we model ourselves after him in this category, we know we will have to work—it doesn't come naturally. Let me again put in a plug here for *Watching Over the Heart,* another book published by Metokos Press, written by Michael Sharrett. It's in our Emerging Authors series. It's Mike's first book, but trust me, it won't be his last. He has the unique ability to reach down into the deep, hidden spiritual recesses of our lives and bring them up to the surface where we can work on them. His book can help us indeed practice the humility we need in order to model ourselves after Jesus.

There is one final point of warning for us here in Philippians 2. While we are going about practicing humility, we must be aware that Satan is going to do everything in his power to stop us. The more people try to follow Jesus as their model, the more effort the devil will put out to stop them. One of the most effective ways he uses to stop them is to tempt them to self-exaltation. Here is the key final point—each believer should avoid *any* self-exaltation, even if others exalt and praise us.

When you examine this Kenosis passage in Philippians 2, you see this is the basic result of Jesus' own humiliation. Look at verses 9–11 again. "*Therefore God has highly exalted him and bestowed on him the name that is above every name, [10]so that at the name of Jesus every knee should bow, in heaven and on earth and under the earth, [11]and every tongue confess that Jesus Christ is Lord, to the glory of God the Father.*" Immediately following the ultimate humiliation of death on the cross of Calvary, God exalted Jesus to the highest place. Notice that there is *not* a reflexive verb here. Jesus is passive at this point. It is God who does the exalting.

We must follow this pattern as well. There is great danger when we start taking to heart exaltation and praise from others. If you begin to live even a moderately "successful" Christian life, you are going to look so different from people around you that you might begin to receive this praise, this exaltation. So watch out. Don't let it go to your head.

This doesn't mean that you can't exhibit any degree of self-worth. What the Bible warns against is self-exaltation. Understand who you are (basically a sinner saved by grace), and what gifts God has given you (we can do nothing apart from God), and seek to use those gifts to bring honor and glory to Jesus. That's what it means to have self-worth. That's biblical. Non-biblical self-exaltation is the problem.

I think the classic Palm Sunday picture is the one you should always remember. Jesus never denied that he was in fact the King of the Jews. He was. However, what he did was to demonstrate that even the King could be humble. So he rode into the capital city of Jerusalem on the back of a jackass instead of in a golden carriage (which he certainly deserved).

Understand who you are. Know your gifts and your role in life and in the church. Then take those gifts and put that role into practice—with humility. You can be humble without being humiliated! But you sure have to work at removing any self-exaltation—any self-praise—any patting of yourself on the back. If you follow that pattern, if you do indeed seek to model the same attitudes of humility as Jesus through your humanness, through your suffering, through your dying—if you really work at these attitudes and if you avoid any self-exaltation—then something amazing is going to happen. You will become like the person Paul is talking about in verse 1. "*So if there is any encouragement in Christ, any comfort from love, any participation in the Spirit, any affection and sympathy.*"

I want you to see how that verse will describe you. You will be encouraged. You will be comforted. You will enjoy participation (which I think is better translated "fellowship" in this context) with the Spirit. You will have affection and sympathy. Take a minute right now to think about this. Ask yourself, "Is that the kind of person I want to be?" Encouraged? Comforted? In fellowship with the Spirit? Affectionate? Sympathetic?

If your answer is yes (and if you indeed are a Christian, then I'm positive that your answer will be yes), then ask yourself another question. Who am I modeling my life after? Who is my hero, my idol? Whose image do I portray? There is probably someone in your life, either right now or in your past, who had a great impact on you. My point is that whoever that person is— however godly or ungodly he or she might be—that person must be replaced with Jesus! Jesus must become the true model in your life.

As we work through these twenty most important things that everyone needs to learn about Jesus, learn this material not just so you can get smarter, not just so you can pass some kind of examination, but learn this so you can put what you learn into practice in your life. That way you will in fact take on the proper attitude of humility, which will have exactly the same result as Jesus' own humiliation. Then both you and Jesus can end up together giving all glory to God!

Y ou would agree, wouldn't you, that there are some people who just seem very, very special? This is especially so for well-known people such as sports stars, great entertainers, politicians, what have you. I would venture to say that just about all of us would be awestruck if the president of the United States, or the top golfer in the country, or the top Hollywood starlet were to walk in the room where we were sitting. But isn't it also likely true that once you got to know any of these people on a close, personal basis, you would quickly learn of their humanness and discover that, after all, other than being really rich, they were not all that much different than you or I?

All humans are alike, especially in regard to the one thing we have in common, original sin. All humans, that is, except for one. You already know that I'm talking about Jesus. Jesus was a human like no other. The awe I described earlier would never wear off as you got to know him better. The *one* difference between Jesus and the rest of us is that *we* are sinners, and *he* was sinless. That is the only real difference in Jesus' humanness.

As we continue in this chapter to examine some of the most important events in Jesus' life, we want to examine Jesus' relationship to the Holy Spirit. They are both part of the divine Godhead; they are the second and third persons of the Trinity. So Jesus as God was divine in nature, but Jesus as man was human in nature. And in his human nature, Jesus needed the work of the Holy Spirit just as we do! I'll run rather quickly through a number of areas where that is true, and I hope you'll begin to see the reality of this point.

To begin with, when thinking about the sinlessness of Jesus, many people assume that since he was both God and man, sinlessness was just part of his divine nature. That is not the case. If it were, then he would not have been fully man.

We are told in the Bible that Jesus was subjected to *real* temptation—what you and I face. We see that in Hebrews 4:15: *"For we do not have a high priest who is unable to sympathize with our weaknesses, but one who in every respect has been tempted as we are, yet without sin.*

In chapter 4 of his gospel, Luke makes a big point about the work of the Holy Spirit in Jesus' overcoming temptation. Jesus relied on the Holy Spirit when he was tempted by Satan after spending 40 days in the desert in fasting and prayer. Luke 4:1 tells us, *"And Jesus, full of the Holy Spirit, returned from the Jordan and was led by the Spirit in the wilderness . . . ."* Then Luke 4:14 says, *"And Jesus returned in the power of the Spirit to Galilee, and a report about him went out through all the surrounding country."* Luke wants to make it very clear that Jesus needed the power of the Holy Spirit to overcome the temptation of Satan.

Now, let me ask you. If Jesus needed the power of the Holy Spirit to overcome sin, how much more do you and I also need the Spirit's power? We are bombarded by temptation every day. Everywhere we go . . . home, school, work, driving down the street, going to a sporting event, what have you . . . we face the enticement to sin.

Let me make a little confession to you. My wife and I attend just about every home game of the Virginia Tech women's basketball team. During each game, I usually go to the restroom three times. Now, please understand, this confession is not about prostate or bladder problems. This confession is about the fact that I just find it easier not to be tempted when the Hi-Techs (the Virginia Tech dance team) take the floor. I just get up and walk out.

You and I need to do everything we can to avoid temptation. When it does confront us—and it certainly will because there's no way to avoid it in our culture—then we must be able to stand up to it. We can't get that kind of power on our own. We desperately need the work of the Holy Spirit to help us.

OK, back to another area of Jesus' life. Let's think about the simple fact that he had to grow up, he had to mature. The Bible tells us that even Jesus the Son of God, because he was a human being, had to grow up just like every other human being. Notice what Luke tells us in chapter 2, verse 40. *"And the child grew and became strong, filled with wisdom. And the favor of God was upon him."* From where do you think his wisdom came? Who was the source of his total spiritual and intellectual growth? Well, the answer to these questions was predicted by the prophet Isaiah in 11:1–2. *"There shall come forth a shoot from the stump of Jesse, and a branch from his roots shall bear fruit. [2]And the Spirit of the Lord shall rest upon him, the Spirit of wisdom and understanding, the Spirit of counsel and might, the*

Spirit of knowledge and the fear of the Lord." You see, Jesus needed the work of the Holy Spirit to enable him to grow up: to gain wisdom, knowledge, understanding, might, and even the fear of the Lord.

Again, I ask, What about us? Well, we must rely on the Holy Spirit in order to grow up too! Frankly, that's something we should be doing all our lives, right? The fact is, humans don't even reach the stage of being "grown up" (or substantially mature) until they're about 30 or so. Jesus didn't set out on his ministry until after he had turned 30. The elements or lessons of our growing up, of our maturing, need to come from the work of the Holy Spirit. True wisdom isn't trying to work out a human, political solution to a problem. True wisdom is looking at the Bible and doing what it requires in order to solve the problem. True might doesn't come from going to a gym and pumping iron. True might comes from being absolutely confident that the position you are defending is a biblical one, not just a man-pleasing one. None of this wisdom, might, understanding, what have you, can be obtained without the work of the Holy Spirit in our lives to bring it about. Just like Jesus!

Another area where we see the Holy Spirit in Jesus' life is the start of his vocation, symbolized by his baptism by John the Baptizer. Now—please understand—that the baptism by John the Baptizer was *not* the same thing as Christian baptism. Christian baptism is a sign and seal of a person becoming a disciple of Jesus. John was doing his thing before Jesus called even one disciple. Rather, the baptism by John was to prepare the way for Jesus, that is, to get the attention of the people of Israel that the Messiah, who would himself institute true baptism, was coming.

Luke 3:21–22 tells us the story of what happened when John baptized Jesus. *"Now when all the people were baptized, and when Jesus also had been baptized and was praying, the heavens were opened, ^{22}and the Holy Spirit descended on him in bodily form, like a dove; and a voice came from heaven, "You are my beloved Son; with you I am well pleased."* You see, Jesus didn't need this baptism so he could repent of his sins, as others did. Jesus had no sins that required repentance, but Jesus needed this baptism. He needed this work of the Holy Spirit to consecrate and empower him for his vocation, for his public ministry.

His very first act of ministry following his baptism was to read the Scriptures during a worship service at the synagogue in Nazareth. Just think about the verses Jesus picked out of the entire Old Testament to read. They come from Isaiah 61:1–2, and Luke records the details of the event in Luke 4:16–21:

And he came to Nazareth, where he had been brought up. And as was his custom, he went to the synagogue on the Sabbath day, and he stood up to read. ^{17}And the scroll of the prophet Isaiah was given to him. He unrolled the scroll and found the place where it was written, ^{18}"The Spirit of the Lord is upon me, because he has anointed me to proclaim good news to the poor. He has sent me to proclaim liberty to the captives and recovering of sight to the blind, to set at liberty those who are oppressed, ^{19}to proclaim the year of the Lord's favor." ^{20}And he rolled up the scroll and gave it back to the attendant and sat down. And the eyes of all in the synagogue were fixed on him. ^{21}And he began to say to them, "Today this Scripture has been fulfilled in your hearing."

Clearly, Jesus needed the work of the Holy Spirit to anoint and empower him to fulfill his vocation as the Messiah, not to make him the Messiah or to make him God as some liberal commentators would have you believe. It was to confirm who he was by the work of the Holy Spirit.

How in the world does this apply to you and me? We are far from being anything like the Messiah! Well, are we really? After all, what does "Messiah" mean (or to use the Greek word for the same term, what does "Christ" mean?)? The simple translation of both words is "an anointed one." What, you say? You and I aren't anointed. Well, perhaps that is why we don't sense much fulfillment from our vocations. We do not realize that if Jesus needed this anointing, we need it even more.

To put it in its simplest terms, we need the work of the Holy Spirit in our vocations. In order to do any vocation well, or even moderately well, we can't do it on our own. The anointing of the Holy Spirit is not just something that ministers or preachers need. No, indeed, it is needed by everyone—no matter what your calling from God might be. Every teacher, every mechanic, every student, every engineer, every nurse, every prison guard, every housewife, every contractor, every accountant, whatever you might do, every worker needs the work of the Holy Spirit to enable him or her to do his or her job in a way that glorifies God. You do not necessarily need a special worship service with laying on of hands (although that might be fun to do at a Labor Day service some time). But you do (through prayer, through understanding how the Bible applies to your vocation, through fellowship with other Christians going through the same experiences) need the filling of the Holy Spirit in order to succeed in whatever you may end up doing.

There is one final area of Jesus' life to examine how he needed the work of the Holy Spirit, his death. While chapter after chapter of the New Testament deals with this event, I want to focus on just one verse, Hebrews 9:14. *"How much more will the blood of Christ, who through the eternal Spirit offered himself without blemish to God, purify our conscience from dead works to serve the living God."* Jesus needed the work of the Holy Spirit to enable him to go to the cross to die for us, to provide the sacrifice for sins that you and I have committed.

This act of redemption is, of course, the very heart of the gospel. Every single person needs to acknowledge that he or she is indeed a sinner and is unable to save himself or herself from the penalty of sin, that is, eternal death and damnation. Most of us don't like to admit we ever made a mistake or are guilty of anything. In order to be in a right relationship with God, however, we have to get past this pride and humbly confess *all* of our sins. Then—and only then—will the shed blood of Jesus *"purify our conscience from dead works to serve the living God,"* as the author of Hebrews puts it.

Now let's take this one step further. Let's assume for a moment that everyone reading this is already a Christian. (By the way, that is almost never the case, but let's makes that assumption here anyway.) We Christians have been saved by the blood, right? We have been born again, agreed? We're all going to heaven, hallelujah! So what? We didn't do anything at all to achieve that status. Our redemption is nothing "of us"—it is all of God! Oh, sure, the Holy Spirit applied all of that work to our lives, but we didn't do a thing on our part to earn it or deserve it. So tell me please, how is it that we can draw an analogy to our lives today from the work of the Holy Spirit in

Jesus in presenting his sacrifice on the cross? We've done that with the other elements of his life. How does this one work?

Let's go back to the very end of Hebrews 9:14 one more time. What did Jesus do for us? He *"[purified] our conscience from dead works to serve the living God."* Jesus' work in our lives is not simply a fire insurance policy to save us from the heat of hell. Jesus' death on the cross didn't just pay for a one-way ticket to heaven when we die. Jesus has redeemed us so that in this life we live in the here and now, we can *"serve the living God."* This means that each and every Christian must be involved in serving the living God, and if you included yourself in our assumption, this means you.

How do we serve God? How do we provide service on behalf of the God who has both created us and saved us? Actually, there are a lot of ways we can do that. Back in Luke 4:8, Jesus said this in responding to one of Satan's temptations: *"It is written, 'You shall worship the Lord your God, and him only shall you serve.'"* Here Jesus is making a connection between service and worship. So if you want to serve God better in response to all he has done for you, one thing you really need to be doing is worshiping God regularly with all your heart, mind, soul, and strength. Worship is not simply something nice to do. It is vital to your very well-being. It is the heart of the service that you are to render to our God. If you are not worshiping God, you are not serving God.

What are some other ways we can serve God? If you were to run a word study of "serve," "service," and "servant," you would find dozens and dozens of occurrences in the New Testament alone. Let me highlight a few.

Matthew 6:24 says, *"No one can serve two masters, for either he will hate the one and love the other, or he will be devoted to the one and despise the other. You cannot serve God and money."* We serve God by not serving money. In other words, we must practice sound financial principles in our lives, in our families, in our businesses, and in our churches.

In chapters 24 and 25 of Matthew, there are parables teaching us our responsibility for taking care of God's household. In other words, we serve God through volunteering to do work in the church. If you are not involved in helping at church, your service to God is lacking.

John 12:26 tells us, *"If anyone serves me, he must follow me; and where I am, there will my servant be also. If anyone serves me, the Father will honor him."* We serve God by following Jesus, which is to say, being aware of and following both the model of his life and his teachings of both faith and practice.

Acts 6:2 contains another important way to serve: *"And the twelve summoned the full number of the disciples and said, 'It is not right that we should give up preaching the word of God to serve tables.'"* This verse, in context, speaks to the need for two categories of work in the church—the work of "preaching the Word of God" and the work of "serving tables." The twelve apostles didn't have time to concentrate on preaching and on mercy ministries (which is the proper understanding of "serving tables"). So they created the position of deacon in the church, an office that would take care of these mercy ministry needs of people both in the church and outside. Now, you don't have to be a deacon to do this—every Christian should be involved at one level or another.

Second Corinthians 9:12–13 instructs, *"For the ministry of this service is not only supplying the needs of the saints, but is also overflowing in many thanksgivings to God. [13]By their approval of this service, they will glorify God because of your submission flowing from your confession of the gospel of Christ, and the generosity of your contribution for them and for all others."* The cheerful giving of our tithes, plus offerings of love over and above our tithes to God's work, is, in fact, service to him.

Matthew 20:26 warns, *"It shall not be so among you. But whoever would be great among you must be your servant."* Here we see that those who are committed to the service of God end up becoming the people who are considered the greatest in the kingdom of God. It is kind of the reverse of our civil society. In spiritual terms, the more you serve, the higher your position.

Now, let's go back and make sure we understand the linkage here. Jesus sacrificed his life—not only that Christians might be saved—but also that they might be in a position to offer service to God. If Jesus needed the work of the Holy Spirit in his life to make his great sacrifice, how much more do we mere mortals need the work of the Spirit to enable us to give back to God our sacrifice of service.

So you see, there was nothing Jesus could do within his human nature without the work of the Holy Spirit in his life. And we are no different. We need to seek more and more to be filled with the Holy Spirit as we follow Jesus.

A s we begin this chapter, I've got to mention a few of those big, fancy theological terms, as much as that distresses me. The reason is, if and when you begin to study the systematic summaries of Christian doctrine (such as the Westminster Confession of Faith and the Catechisms), you find some words used in ways that made perfect sense back then (and still make sense today) but they just are not the words that we normally use, even when talking about Jesus.

One of those words is "mediator." When you read the Westminster documents, you find the word "mediator" all over the place. There is an entire chapter (Chapter 8) in the Confession of Faith on Jesus as our Mediator. There are seven questions (36–42) in the Larger Catechism about Jesus as our Mediator. All of the concepts covered in these sections of the confessional standards are good, and true, and important, but they are used there in ways that we don't generally use them when we speak about Jesus today.

For instance, Larger Catechism Question 36 asks, "Who is the Mediator of the Covenant of Grace?" Well, in the volume *God the Father,* we will discuss the Covenant of Grace in detail. But really, we have already learned the answer to the question in this book. Back in Chapter One, when we learned that Jesus was both God and man at the same time, we learned that, because of this, Jesus was able to mediate or go between God the Father and mankind, to make it possible for people to be saved from eternal punishment for their sin. The matter takes up four more catechism questions.

I bring this up to make you aware that in this book, we are not using the same theological terms in the same order as the systematic standards of the church. Rather we are learning the crucial truths that we must all understand about who God the Son is, who God the Father is (in the book *God the Father*), and who God the Holy Spirit is (in the book *God the Holy Spirit.*).

Having said all of this by way of excuse for not using the theological term "mediator" in this volume, I now want to introduce to you three theological terms that I *do* want to use. Most writers categorize the person and work of Jesus into three parts. You could consider them what the Westminster standards call his three "offices," or positions, that Jesus holds. The three are:

- Jesus as Prophet

- Jesus as Priest

- Jesus as King

We will cover his work as Prophet in this chapter. Then we will have an additional chapter for Jesus as Priest, but it will take two chapters to cover Jesus as King.

When we think of prophets, we usually think of the Old Testament. There were a bunch of them back in those days. We know the names of those who were "writing" prophets. The four major prophets and the twelve minor prophets pop into our minds immediately (even if we can't name them all).

The works of the four major prophets are Isaiah, Jeremiah and Lamentations (he wrote both books), Ezekiel, and Daniel. The works of the twelve minor prophets bear the names of each: Hosea, Joel, Amos, Obadiah, Jonah,

Micah, Nahum, Habakkuk, Zephaniah, Haggai, Zechariah, Malachi. (You might want to pick up another volume in this series titled *The New Geneva Introduction to the Old Testament*. It will give you brief reviews of each book's content.) The difference between a major and a minor prophet is not the quality of their work. It's not like the major and minor baseball leagues. Rather, the majors wrote longer books and the minors wrote shorter books.

Now, Isaiah and his friends were not the first prophets. There were some fellows known as the "former prophets," and they authored a lot of books of the Bible: Joshua, Judges, 1 and 2 Samuel, 1 and 2 Kings, 1 and 2 Chronicles, Ezra, Nehemiah. All were written by the former prophets, some of whom to this day remain nameless.

There was one more former prophet whose name we know quite well. He authored the first five books of the Bible. Moses was the first prophet and set the standard for prophets, so to speak. We learn from his books that Moses wrote what it is that prophets do. First, Numbers 12:6 tells us, *"And he said, 'Hear my words: If there is a prophet among you, I the Lord make myself known to him in a vision; I speak with him in a dream.'"* Second, Deuteronomy 18:18 goes a bit further. *"'I will raise up for them a prophet like you from among their brothers. And I will put my words in his mouth, and he shall speak to them all that I command him.'"*

What is it that God's people are to do about all this? In Deuteronomy 18:15 that *"'The Lord your God will raise up for you a prophet like me from among you, from your brothers—it is to him you shall listen.'"* So the prophets receive their words from God, they speak (and/or write) God's Word to the people, and the people are to listen, which includes understanding and applying the messages to their lives.

God gave his people a way to test whether a prophet was a true one. In Deuteronomy 18:22 we learn the third mark of a prophet, *"When a prophet speaks in the name of the Lord, if the word does not come to pass or come true, that is a word that the Lord has not spoken; the prophet has spoken it presumptuously. You need not be afraid of him."*

Now what does all this have to do with Jesus? Well, Jesus referred to himself as a prophet on a number of occasions. Take for example Mark 6:4 where he was referring to himself. *"And Jesus said to them, 'A prophet is not without honor, except in his hometown and among his relatives and in his own household.'"* Even more importantly, the people themselves recognized Jesus to be a prophet. Look at the following occurrences during Jesus' life.

After Jesus raises a widow's son from the dead in Luke 7:15–16 we find this: *"And the dead man sat up and began to speak, and Jesus gave him to his mother. [16]Fear seized them all, and they glorified God, saying, 'A great prophet has arisen among us!' and 'God has visited his people!'"*

Along the road to Emmaus, not long after Jesus' resurrection from the dead, he encountered two men and asked them what they were discussing. We find this in Luke 24:19. *"And he said to them, 'What things?' And they said to him, 'Concerning Jesus of Nazareth, a man who was a prophet mighty in deed and word before God and all the people . . . .'"*

So we know that God speaks to his people through his prophets. We know that Jesus was a prophet. We also know from Chapter Three that Jesus was the Messiah, the

Mediator. Therefore, the simple logic is that Jesus' work on earth (and still in heaven where he lives) has multiple parts, multiple motives. We'll see in the next chapter that Jesus was and is a priest. In Chapters Nine and Ten, we'll learn that Jesus was and is a king.

The "office" of prophet, however, gets the least press these days. It doesn't seem all that glamorous. But it should be the one that gets the most attention, or at least equal time, because Jesus' work as a prophet is important to you and me.

Peter gives us some insight to this in his great sermon on Pentecost. We find these words in Acts 3:22–24.

> Moses said, "The Lord God will raise up for you a prophet like me from your brothers. You shall listen to him in whatever he tells you. [23] And it shall be that every soul who does not listen to that prophet shall be destroyed from the people." [24] And all the prophets who have spoken, from Samuel and those who came after him, also proclaimed these days."

Do you see it? Jesus is a prophet, like Moses. In fact, Jesus is the greatest prophet, the one about whom all the prophets of the Old Testament talked. We won't take the time to repeat all of those predictions we covered primarily in Chapter Three. But the important thing for us to see is that it's just as Moses said it would be. God has indeed raised up the great Prophet, and that Prophet has spoken God's Word to us and we should listen to him. That prophet's name is Jesus, God the Son.

Again, Jesus actually identified himself as a prophet as he carried out those three crucial tasks of all prophets. First, what he spoke came from God the Father. In John 8:26–28 we read, "'*I have much to say about you and much to judge, but he who sent me is true, and I declare to the world what I have heard from him.' *^{27}*They did not understand that he had been speaking to them about the Father.* ^{28}*So Jesus said to them, 'When you have lifted up the Son of Man, then you will know that I am he, and that I do nothing on my own authority, but speak just as the Father taught me.'*"

The same thing is true for the second principle we learned to be a mark of a prophet. Jesus as Prophet proclaimed God's Word to the people. We find this beginning in Matthew 4:17: *"From that time Jesus began to preach, saying, 'Repent, for the kingdom of heaven is at hand.'"*

The third principle was also true of Jesus as Prophet. He would foretell the occurrence of events, not just events related to his second coming (we will have an entire chapter on that topic), but even historical events in the near future. His predictions always came true. About forty years before it occurred, he predicted that Jerusalem would be destroyed in A.D. 70. In Luke 19:41–44 we read these words:

> *And when he drew near and saw the city, he wept over it,* ^{42}*saying, "Would that you, even you, had known on this day the things that make for peace! But now they are hidden from your eyes* ^{43}*For the days will come upon you, when your enemies will set up a barricade around you and surround you and hem you in on every side* ^{44}*and tear you down to the ground, you and your children within you. And they will not leave one stone upon another in you, because you did not know the time of your visitation."*

It is simply amazing how accurate these verses are—foretelling Rome's armies arriving and surrounding the city, starting the long-term siege of the city under Vespian (beginning in A.D. 67), and then under the leadership of Vespian's son Titus breaking through the walls and destroying Jerusalem in A.D. 70.

So we can see that all three tasks of an Old Testament prophet were fulfilled by Jesus. Indeed, Jesus was the greatest and final prophet.

It's obvious, of course, that Jesus spoke all of these words while he was on earth. We even have "red letter Bibles" to help us focus on the words of Jesus. Wouldn't it be nice if we had lived when Jesus was on earth so we could have *heard* those words? But that was two thousand years ago. We don't have Jesus with us in the flesh now so we have to depend on some other way to hear what he has to say to us—some other way for Jesus to function as a prophet.

That brings us back to Jesus' role as the great Mediator. He uses a special way to mediate his work, if you will, to speak to us today. That is through the work of his Holy Spirit.

You see, while it is true that the prophets of the Old Testament told us about Jesus, they could not do that by their own ability. We see this in the classic text on this issue, 2 Peter 1:19–21. *"And we have something more sure, the prophetic word, to which you will do well to pay attention as to a lamp shining in a dark place, until the day dawns and the morning star rises in your hearts, [20]knowing this first of all, that no prophecy of Scripture comes from someone's own interpretation. [21]For no prophecy was ever produced by the will of man, but men spoke from God as they were carried along by the Holy Spirit."*

It was the primary work of the Holy Spirit to make sure the written word (that you and I know as the Bible) was inspired and without error. Today, Jesus works through the same Holy Spirit as you read the words. The Holy Spirit was there when the Scriptures were written and he is there when you read them. If you are looking for Jesus the Prophet to speak to you today, you simply have to open the Bible and see what it says.

James Benjamin Green, a famous Southern Presbyterian teacher who wrote the often-consulted *A Harmony of the Westminster Presbyterian Standards* (Richmond; John Knox, 1951), tells us how whatever our need may be, Jesus deals with that need through his work in one or more of his three offices (Prophet, Priest, and King):

As prophet, he meets the problem of man's ignorance, supplying him with knowledge. As priest, he meets the problem of man's guile, supplying him with righteousness. As king, he meets the problem of man's weakness and dependence, supplying him with power and protections.

A problem today is that knowing this does not seem to be enough to satisfy many people, even Bible-believing Christians. Some would say that it is not enough to know that Jesus is the great and final prophet; they want Jesus to keep speaking to them—to tell them what to do, to guide them if you will. Let me tell you a story to help you understand the problem with this concept.

I first read this story in Jay Adams' book titled *The Christian's Guide to Guidance* (Stanley, NC: Timeless Texts, 1998), and reprint it here by permission.

The following story appeared in a magazine called *The Concerned Presbyterian* in the summer of 1996. It concerns a dispute between one Mr. Jim Dunn and the First Congregational Church of Akron, Ohio. And I must tell you . . . it is true. It actually happened!

It seems that Mr. Dunn believed that God told him to go live outside First Congregational. So he took his dog and set up housekeeping in a tent in the front yard of the church. At the time the article appeared on the Associated Press wire service, Mr. Dunn, dog, and tent had been in place there for some thirteen months. Mr. Dunn could have used a homeless shelter two blocks from the church, but that was not where God had told him to go.

Apparently he also received some sort of revelation about taking showers—he abstained from such! He refused a new sleeping bag to replace the soiled one he had been using and rejected gifts of food unless the donor specified that it had come in response to God. "I'm not living my will," Mr. Dunn allowed, "I'm living God's will . . . ."

For all that (the article continues with editorial comment), we prefer Mr. Dunn's clarity of purpose to the muddleheaded (thinking) of the Reverend Bob Mollard, the administrative minister for the church, who is reported to have said, "If God called Jim to live in our front yard, who are we to say God didn't."

Well, the Reverend Mr. Mollard may not have thoroughly and clearly learned the biblical principles that explain how God guides us, but you and I need to have that knowledge. We learn from the Scriptures that God indeed does *not* guide people in the way that Mr. Dunn and Mr. Mollard think he must.

The issue before us is does Jesus still fulfill his role as Prophet through direct revelation, that is by speaking to us in a voice or vision? Obviously, those who hold to Pentecostal and Charismatic theology believe that they can and do receive direct revelation from God that is separate from the Bible. Historic Protestants do not believe that. They believe the canon of the Bible is closed; in other words, God no longer reveals himself directly to people, but speaks to us through the Holy Spirit as we read the written word, the Bible.

Even some non-Charismatic evangelical leaders seem at times to be saying they believe in continuing revelation. One evangelical, non-charismatic scholar, who is normally quite trustworthy in his teaching (and who will remain nameless for his own protection), wrote this in a recent book. "If any man's will is to do God's will, not only will he know that Jesus and His teaching are from God, but he will be told if he is out of the way." He then quotes Isaiah 30:21, which says, *"Your ears shall hear a word behind you, saying, 'This is the way, walk in it.'"*

That passage of Scripture, however, speaks physically of the prophets who had been silent since the people of Israel had dismissed them. They were beginning to prophesy again and Isaiah is giving them advice. This verse has nothing to do with personal guidance by direct revelation.

As much as you and I might wish that he would, Jesus does not speak to you and me directly to tell us what he wants us to do. If he did, then poor old Jim Dunn in Akron,

Ohio, might still be sleeping in that tent in front of First Congregational Church!

There is a very big difference between wearing a bracelet with the letters "WWJD" on it (What would Jesus do?) and wearing one with the letters "WWJS" (What would Jesus say?). We can indeed learn from the ethical and moral principles taught in the Scriptures those actions we should do, and can be sure that they are what Jesus would do because they are biblical. But we cannot listen to the words of Jesus, either directly from his mouth or through the speaking of the Holy Spirit in direct revelation (as many declare today). The only thing we have to go on is the Bible.

Please understand. The Bible is also the *best* thing we have to go on because it is one sure source of truth and of revelation from God that any of us can have. The only way to truly understand the Bible is to have the ongoing ministry of the Holy Spirit in your life. And, the only way to truly have the ongoing ministry of the Holy Spirit in your life is to have been born again. That means we must also have the work of Jesus as Priest applied to our lives. (We will discuss that more fully in Chapter Twelve.)

Chapter Eight
Priest – "Who is Your Priest?"

Over the years I have served as the interim pastor of a number of churches. I think six or seven at least. This story comes from one of those experiences.

The telephone rings. "Good morning, Presbyterian Church," I say.

"Is Pastor Dave there?"

"No," I respond, "he's at home packing, getting ready to leave for Gainesville on Wednesday. This is Mr. Clements. May I help you?"

"No thanks!" (Phone hangs up abruptly.)

A little while later, the phone rings again. "Good morning, Presbyterian Church."

"Is Pastor Dave there?"

"No. The packers are at the manse and he's making his final moving preparations. This is Mr. Clements. I'll be the interim pastor for a while. May I help you?"

"No! I *have* to talk to Dave. Good bye!"

At first, I didn't quite understand what was going on. But after a repeat of this kind of incident a number of times over several weeks, both in person and on the phone, it became clear that the people of this church had grown to depend totally on their pastor to tell them how to solve all the problems of their lives. They did not come merely for advice and spiritual uplifting. They came seeking and receiving a direct answer to specific questions. Now, some of you might feel that this is quite normal for people in a church. It takes a while for them to confide in their new pastor, especially one who would be with them only temporarily.

(Let me assure you that my analysis of this situation turned out to be correct.) The overwhelming judgment of the congregation about their previous pastor was that his sermons were unintelligible and without application. His organizational ability was non-existent. His stands on theological issues and church polity (government) during a time of crisis in the church were either unknown or could be called strictly fence-sitting. But he still was viewed as the greatest pastor in the history of the church, simply because he was a "good visitor."

I'm convinced this is what accounted for the lack of one dry eye among the ladies (and a few men too) in the congregation at his going-away reception. This church wasn't just losing its pastor; it was losing its priest.

Nor was the situation there a unique or isolated one. In discussing it with many other pastors over the years, as well as experiencing the same phenomenon myself a number of times, I have found agreement among most, that what people in churches today seem to want is a man of God to do their "God-work," their "God-thinking," for them.

The problem with people having that desire is that they are completely failing to recognize a great truth from the Word of God. That truth is central in Hebrews chapter 4: there is only *one* adequate source of solutions for the problems of a Christian—God.

As we seek to answer the basic question posed by the title of this chapter, let's examine the teaching of chapter 4 of Hebrews. Beginning with verse 16 we read, *"Let us then with confidence draw near to the throne of grace, that we may receive mercy and find grace to help in time of need."*

The principle here is very clear, isn't it? We know who is sitting on the throne of grace; it is God himself. So, if we belong to Jesus, and we have some kind of problem, we are to take it to God, not just to a pastor, not just to a counselor, but first to God. The one who sits on the throne of grace is sure to provide for us through his magnificent grace.

Another thing this verse teaches us, by induction at least, is that even though we are Christians, we are not free of problems. The verse assumes that problems exist, not for everyone all the time, but for different people at different times. Christians, like everyone else, regularly have problems. Most Christians, though, at least those who have memorized the Lord's Prayer and those who have sung hymns such as "Sweet Hour of Prayer," understand that we look to God when we have needs and problems.

We wish we could come up with a way that keeps us problem free, don't we? But we can't. Paul couldn't. James and Peter couldn't, and for sure David couldn't. They all knew their lives were not free of problems. Some were brought on by life experiences; many were brought on by their own actions. No, we have to face facts; we will all have problems.

Well, since we are unanimous that no one is without problems, it's clear that we've got to find a source of the solution for them. Certainly, the Scriptures make it clear that the solutions of the world—that is, any man-made solution—is doomed to failure. As Paul wrote to the church at Corinth

(1 Corinthians 3:19), *"For the wisdom of this world is folly with God."*

That truth is the reason that the vast majority of counseling systems being touted today are doomed to failure. They are more or less based on the *"wisdom of the world,"* and to a greater or lesser degree depend on man's principles. This is why the people in the church who were looking for Pastor Dave felt helpless when their priest left them. They were dependent on him for solutions, instead of allowing him to show them how to go to the proper source themselves.

What is the proper source? It almost should go without saying that only a sovereign God can solve our problems. If the wisdom of the world is doomed to failure, then the solution must come from outside the world. In fact, the solution must come from the creator of that world, from the *"giver of all good gifts,"* as James refers to God. When all is said and done—when all the methods have been ultimately judged—the answer must be that a Christian is to take all of his problems to God, and to God alone, for final solutions.

The writer of Hebrews does not just give us a platitude without telling us how it is possible. To a Christian, or should I say, most especially to a Christian, the awesomeness and greatness of God is almost overwhelming. To say that we've merely got to approach God with our problems is most certainly frightening, or at least it makes us think doing so is impossible.

I think the facts of our day support this judgment. It must be impossible to approach God, because there certainly are a lot of people—a lot of Christians—who are not getting their problems solved. Hebrews 4:16 tells us that we are even supposed to approach God *"confidently."* But most people aren't doing it at all. So there must be a reason why people are *not* taking their problems to God for solution.

Could it be that they don't know him? Could it be that they are afraid of him? Could it be that they don't know how to approach God, and therefore can only approach men? Well, they obviously either have forgotten or have never learned the proper way, the way that is taught in Hebrews 4:15. We must approach God through an effective, understanding mediator. *"For we do not have a high priest who is unable to sympathize with our weaknesses, but one who in every respect has been tempted as we are, yet without sin."*

You see, there is no reason to be afraid. We can be confident in our approach to God to bring him our problems for solution, because, contrary to much of popular opinion, we are able to identify with God. Isn't it true that the thing that draws us to a person, as either a friend or a counselor or a mentor, is that we are able to confide in them? That is because we are able to identify with them. It's sort of a feeling that he is pretty much like we are, so he's apt to understand us better.

This is why young people think they can best identify with someone who is not yet over 30. It's also why working in cross-cultural ministries is very difficult. The point here is that it is when someone is of the same basic nature that we are that we sense a true feeling of understanding. When that is missing, trust must be built.

Well, the Bible tells us the same thing. In generalities, Jesus refers to it in his conversation with Nicodemus in John 3:6 when he says, *"That which is born of the flesh is flesh, and that which is born of the Spirit is spirit."* And, of course, it was precisely this truth that made all other creatures God had created unsuitable for Adam as a helper. Only the *"bone of my bones and flesh of my flesh"* would do, he shouted in Genesis 2:23.

Now, do you notice that this is as far as the Scriptures will go? There is no further breakdown, specifically. Oh yes, Paul does speak of being a Jew to the Jews and a Greek to the Greeks, but this is in matters of culture, not in something inherent. So the basic requirement of understanding for a man is someone who is truly human, who has an inner being that can relate to others. We've got to have at least this aspect before we can sense a feeling of identity. That, you see, is a key element of a true priest.

Well, the beauty of our proposition is that we can approach God because we *do* have just this sort of true priest. Jesus is this sort of mediator through whom we can approach God with our problems. We know from the Bible that Jesus was completely human. Hebrews 4:15 has already told us that he was *"tempted,"* and that he can *"sympathize."* If there were time, we could go throughout the Bible and find reference after reference that clearly shows us how Jesus, the second person of the Trinity, was truly human.

But, you might ask, so what? If the key issue is that Jesus was human, why do I need him? Aren't there a bunch of other humans who can help me approach God? Mohammed comes to mind and all those Buddhist gurus!

Well, we've got the answer to your question, and it is the next key issue that must be true of our mediator, our priest. It's at the very end of verse 15: he must be *"without sin."* God cannot look upon sin, so in order for someone to be our go-between with God, he must be sinless. (If you have not yet read Chapter Four, and particularly the final section in which we discussed the primary reason for the necessity of the virgin birth, please go back and do that now.)

At this point, you must be sure you recognize that the Bible clearly teaches that Jesus was the only human ever to live who was *"without sin."* You see, Jesus died once in time and space for all his people. (We will look at this in great depth in Chapter Twelve. In a sense, that chapter will deal with the issue of the priest becoming the sacrifice. But for now, we need to see that Jesus' death was not just for our eternal life in heaven, but also for our life now, on earth.) Jesus died that we may live a life in which we are able to overcome our problems.

This is why a Christian's approach to God must be through the understanding, effective mediation of Jesus. It is the key, central, ongoing ministry of our Savior in heaven today—one of the two essential parts of the work of Jesus as Priest. (We'll deal with the other one in Chapter Twelve.)

So where are we? We've seen that a Christian must take all of his problems to God, and that his approach to God must be through the mediation of Jesus. But this is just looking *up* the path, isn't it? This is just seeing half of the law of dynamics, which teaches us that for every force there must be a counterforce. Now we've got to look to see the force coming the other way, from God to us.

This point is in Hebrews 4:16. Let's read it again. *"Let us then with confidence draw near to the throne of grace, that we may receive mercy and find grace to help in time of need."* Here it is clear that a Christian receives *both* mercy and grace from God. While the terms "mercy" and "grace" are closely related, they are distinct enough that we should treat them separately.

In the original language of the New Testament, the word "mercy" is a passive form, and therefore almost certainly refers to something in the past for its main emphasis. The word "grace," however, is an active form, and therefore applies to present and future aspects of our needs. So the best way for us to view these two great categories of gifts from God is through the big theological terms of "justification" and "sanctification."

We receive mercy from God through our justification. In his opening salutation at the beginning of 1 Peter, the apostle makes this comparison clear when he writes at verse 3, *"Blessed be the God and Father of our Lord Jesus Christ! According to his great mercy, he has caused us to be born again to a living hope through the resurrection of Jesus Christ from the dead . . . ."* I hope you saw it there. It was God's mercy that brought us our new birth, our justification. Paul pretty much says the same thing in Romans 9:23 when he refers to Christians as *"vessels of mercy."*

Even though the act of regeneration, of being born again, is a onetime act, and even though justification is a once-for-all-time pronouncement of our status before God, yet the writer of Hebrews commands us to be continuously coming boldly to God for this mercy. This kind of coming over and over again, this sort of "keep on keeping on" attitude of the Christian life, applies in the area of justification as we continuously confess our sins. Even though all of our past, present, and future sins were forgiven at Calvary, still the mercy of their forgiveness is always intertwined with our confession of those sins.

Think about the last time you were worried to death about something sinful you had done, especially as it related to another person. You were reluctant, or perhaps fearful, to tell the other person what you had done, and to ask for forgiveness. Finally, God gave you the strength and you confessed that sin. You confessed it to God and to the other person. Do you remember how you felt after that? How the relief just sort of came over you? In some cases, it might even have affected you emotionally and physically right then. Well, that's receiving mercy from God!

Now, what's important here is that we confess our sins to God, not to a priest or even a counselor. We confess them to God!

Turning to the second great gift we talked about, the gift of grace, one of the primary definitions of grace is this: "a state of being protected by God." Grace is something that we continue to receive from God, over and over again. God uses grace to bless us, and to enable us to live for him. So this gift applies to the theological term of "sanctification." You see, we need grace in our life all the time. We need a constant inflowing of grace, as sanctification is a constant process in our lives until we reach heaven.

Pulling all this stuff together, grace is what we need to solve our problems! Paul wrote in 2 Corinthians 12:8–9, *"Three times I pleaded with the Lord about this, that it should leave me. But he said to me, 'My grace is sufficient for you . . . .'"* Sometimes God grants a solution to our problem, and sometimes he gives us the ability to face the problem without it being solved. That is, grace is God's answer to the problems that we bring to him, coming through the mediation of Jesus. This is "where it's happening" in the Christian life!

While there is much more detail on all of this in the book *God the Holy Spirit*, let me give you the briefest of outlines on this topic here. The Bible teaches that there are three basic "means of grace" or three principal ways by which God gives us his grace. One is the Word of God, a second is prayer, and the third is the sacraments of the church.

First, let's look at the Word of God. Paul writes to Timothy in 2 Timothy 3:16, *"All Scripture is breathed out by God and profitable for teaching, for reproof, for correction, and for training in righteousness . . . ."* That's a lot of different uses of grace, isn't it?

Second is prayer. Psalm 145:18 tells us, *"The Lord is near to all who call on him, to all who call on him in truth."* Being "near" is another way of saying being with us. When God is with us, he is providing us grace. So, prayer is a must.

Third, we have a means of grace in the sacraments that is not always recognized nor well understood. There are two sacraments, baptism and the Lord's Supper. Well, I guess the individual act of baptism could be understood as a means of grace, but let's examine that. Baptism is a sign of God's covenantal protection over a person; it is God's promise to work in the life of the individual.

The same principle is at work in the Lord's Supper. The sacrament of the Lord's Supper involves the work of the Holy Spirit in the life of the individual. Every time we partake of the elements of communion, we receive grace directly. The elements don't somehow turn into the actual blood and body of Jesus. There is no magic there. But Jesus is really present in the sacrament through his sending us the Holy Spirit.

There are some, including me, who believe this principle is expanded even beyond the actual event of communion, that the giving of grace is involved in the total ministry of the particular church. Take a look at Acts 4:32–33. *"Now the full number of those who believed were of one heart and soul, and no one said that any of the things that belonged to him was his own, but they had everything in common. And with great power the apostles were giving their testimony to the resurrection of the Lord Jesus, and great grace was upon them all."* Here we find a description of the church functioning as it should. People with spiritual needs were having their problems solved. People with temporal needs were having their problems solved. All was as it should be. And what does Luke say of this wonderful situation? *"Great grace was upon them all"*!

"Wait a minute," you say. "You've lost me. This chapter hasn't been about reading your Bible. This chapter hasn't been a sermon about a strong prayer life. This chapter hasn't been about seeking and participating in a church with biblical fellowship. This chapter has been about a Christian properly solving his or her problems."

That's correct. This has been a chapter about a Christian correctly solving his problems—through the Word of God, through prayer, and through the communion of the saints found in the ministry of the church. That's how a Christian is *supposed* to solve his problems.

You see, the Word of God will not speak to you if it is always taught by someone else. You must allow grace to mediate in your life through the work of the Holy Spirit, which is to say, the work of Jesus. Our prayer life will be meaningless if we pray just because we're supposed to. Or worse yet, if we let the pastor do the praying for us instead of praying for ourselves in the confidence that our prayers are really effective, the prayers offered by the pastor will not be a means by which God gives us his grace. Our own prayers will really help us solve our problems, because we bring them to God through the mediation of Jesus.

Any church will fail if it is simply program-centered, preacher-centered or counseling-centered, instead of being Jesus-centered. Our basic question in this chapter has been, Who is your priest? Jesus stands ready to be your great High Priest—right now, today—you don't need anyone to be a go-between with him. Hebrews 4:14 says, *"Since then we have a great high priest who has passed through the heavens, Jesus, the Son of God, let us hold fast our confession."* Jesus is our *high* priest. Jesus is the only mediator between man and God. Of course pastors and counselors, and even Christian friends, can help us along in solving our problems. They can provide exhortation and even point us in the right direction. But you must be careful never to see them as a substitute for the real Priest in your life.

As Christians, we must each one of us learn how to take all of our problems to God alone through the mediation of Jesus, our great High Priest. Only Jesus is truly of our nature, human, yet able to talk face-to-face with God the Father and effectively carry to him our prayers. If we handle our problems in this way, then they will be solved through God's great mercy and grace.

Finally, let's again be reminded that Jesus fulfills his office of Priest in two ways. Here we have looked at his priestly role of being mediator between God and man. In Chapter Twelve, we'll see his very special, onetime function as priest on the cross of Calvary.

J esus serves in his office as King in two distinctly different ways. First, he serves as King in his church—which will be the topic for this chapter. But he also serves as King in the world. We will cover that topic separately in the next chapter.

Let's begin this chapter with a little high school civics lesson. We want to review the various ways in which countries—nations—have been and are being governed. Let's examine them through some caricatures.

First, there is the communist form of government. That is where everybody works and turns over all profits and earnings to the state, which then pays them a starvation wage and keeps all the rest of the money to spend on tanks and guns—or something like that.

Then there is socialism. That's where everybody has his own job, but the state takes 95% of each person's income in taxes, and turns around and gives money to everybody who asks for it for anything they need—or something like that.

Next, there is democracy. That's where people elect other people to run their government for them, pay them a salary, and expect them to perform miracles, but don't want to pay any taxes at all (but do anyway)—or something like that.

Finally, there is monarchy, with a king (or queen). That's where the king owns everything. He is in complete control. He sends other people around to all the cities and towns and villages and houses to be sure that the poor people are doing what they are supposed to do and paying the appropriate taxes, and the king just does whatever he wants to do, no matter whether the people like it or not—or something like that.

While I have just given caricatures of these various forms of government, I think we all pretty much understand how they are supposed to work. In the United States, we certainly detest communism, we don't much like socialism, and we would rather not live under a king. No, here in America we like good old apple pie, motherhood, and Fourth of July democracy. That's the American way!

Don't get me wrong. I'm not knocking democracy here. I'd just as soon live under it than any other system, as long as we do what is needed to make it work and as long as we can keep corruption out of it. I'm proud that America runs on constitutional principles as a republican form of democracy. But there is a problem. And that problem is in many of the churches in America.

The problem is that because Americans are so enamored with the democratic way, they honestly believe that it is the only way to run anything, and therefore they think that it is the proper way to run the church of Jesus Christ.

If you hold this opinion, I want to say quite frankly that this is not what the Bible teaches. Democracy is not the form of government that Jesus would have for his church, in America or in any other place in the world. The church of Jesus Christ is not to be governed simply the way we would like it, the way we think is best. The church of Jesus Christ must be governed the way the Bible tells us it is to be run.

The great Scottish expositor John Brown explained it this way: "A Christian Church is a very free society. But they mistake the notion who consider it a democracy. It is a monarchy, administered by inferior magistrates, chosen by their fellow subjects, who are to execute the king's law" (John Brown, *Epistle to the Romans* [London: Hamilton and Adams, 1857], 511). You see, what Mr. Brown is saying, and saying truthfully, is that the church is a monarchy. The church of Jesus Christ is governed by a King and his magistrates.

Jesus is King of everything in the world. He is therefore the King of his church. He is a complete and sovereign king. He's not like the king or queen of England. That monarch holds the position in name only, and really the people run the government no matter what the king or queen says. No, Jesus is not at all that kind of puppet king or the kind of democratic monarch they have in England. He is a sovereign king. He is the supreme head of everything.

We see this theme over and over again in the Scriptures. The prophet Zechariah gave us a famous prophesy of just this fact in Zechariah 9:9. *"Rejoice greatly, O daughter of Zion! Shout aloud, O daughter of Jerusalem! Behold, your king is coming to you; righteous and having salvation is he, humble and mounted on a donkey, on a colt, the foal of a donkey."* The fulfilling of that great prophecy of Jesus' kingship was clearly and inspirationally viewed by Matthew (in Matthew 21:4) as he told the story of Jesus' triumphal entry to Jerusalem on the first Palm Sunday.

Another famous prophetic passage of the Old Testament deals with this same theme. It is from Isaiah 9:6–7. *"For to us a child is born, to us a son is given; and the government shall be upon his shoulder, and his name shall be called Wonderful Counselor, Mighty God, Everlasting Father, Prince of Peace. Of the increase of his government and of peace there will be no end, on the throne of David and over his kingdom, to establish it and to uphold it with justice and with righteousness from this time forth and forevermore. The zeal of the Lord of hosts will do this."*

Of course, this famous passage and its underlying story are the inspiration of so many of our great Christmas hymns. Take for example, "Angels, from the realms of glory, wing your flight o'er all the earth; Ye who sang creation's story, now proclaim Messiah's birth: Come and worship, come and worship, worship Christ, the newborn King." Or, "O come, all ye faithful, joyful and triumphant, O come ye, O come ye to Bethlehem; Come and behold him born the King of angels . . . ." Or, "Joy to the world! the Lord is come: Let earth receive her King . . . ." Throughout its history, the church has always sung great hymns to this special biblical truth: Christ is King.

Going back to Zechariah 9, we see that the last half of verse 9 tells us three important things about the person of Christ the King. First, he is righteous. Second, he is endowed with salvation. And third, he is humble. Let's try to see what we can learn from these three things.

First of all, Jesus as King is righteous. That is to say, he's the kind of king who is virtuous, honest, and just; who calls things the way they are. If someone is innocent, he will surely pronounce him innocent, but if someone is guilty, the sentence must be pronounced. Being a righteous king demands that he punish those who deserve punishment. Since the Bible tells us in Romans 3:23 that *"all have sinned and fall short of the glory of God,"* then it is consistently true that as a righteous king, Jesus would punish sinners.

Dr. Bob Rayburn, who is now with the Lord but was president of Covenant Seminary when I attended in the early 70s, had been an Army chaplain during the Korean War. Bob would give this illustration of the King's justice. "A rough but sincere corporal once said to me, 'Chaplain, you don't believe in this hell stuff, do you?' I replied, 'Corporal, I have only one source of information and that is the Bible. And the Bible tells me there is an awful hell awaiting those who reject the love of God in Jesus. But,' I proceeded, 'it's this way, Corporal. You are going to exist through all eternity in God's universe somewhere. You cannot get outside of God's sovereign power and rule. If you receive God's love as demonstrated in his Son Jesus, you will be at home in God's universe as a member of God's household. But if you reject Jesus, who died for your sins on the cross, it is a logical necessity that you will be in hell wherever you are in God's entire universe.'" In other words, a righteous king must punish sin or he would no longer be righteous.

It is in the next attribute that we find our solution to our dilemma. For not only is Jesus as King righteous, he is also endowed with salvation. That is, he himself is the fountain of all salvation. In his death at Calvary, he makes the free offer of salvation to all who would believe in him.

Several other Bible versions translate this term *"endowed with salvation"* from Zechariah 9:9 as *"victorious."* In a sense, that is not far off if we view Jesus' victory as victory over sin and the grave. This is the only victory that really matters for you and for me. Without Jesus as our King having won that victory, we would be without hope. But he did win! And he is endowed with salvation, which is offered freely to all who would believe. So the call to each one is to trust him, to receive by faith that gracious offer of salvation that comes from the King.

Not only is Jesus as King a righteous person, not only is he endowed with salvation, Zechariah 9:9 tells us that he is gentle and lowly, that he is humble—so humble he rides on a donkey. Now, doesn't that seem to be incongruous? Here is the King of the world, the only truly just judge ever to walk on earth, and the Bible tells us he is meek and lowly. Actually, this verse is the one quoted by both Matthew and John in their gospels on the first Palm Sunday, as Jesus rode into Jerusalem on a donkey. Even in this humble, meek, and lowly way, the Gospel writers all agree that the triumphal entry on Palm Sunday was a manifestation of the kingship of Jesus.

Most of us would expect any king who had the kind of sovereign power of Jesus would exert it with great pomp and circumstance. But think about that for a minute. About the only glimpse a poor commoner like you or me ever gets of a king like that . . . is on television or in a movie, or we might read about it in a newspaper the way we do about Queen Elizabeth in England.

But Jesus is not that kind of King. He humbled himself, by becoming just like you and me. He took on the human identity in every way—except he did not sin. Even though he was the Son of God, he lived and walked and suffered and died just as you and I must live and walk and suffer and die. He did it so that by his perfect victory over sin, he could pay the penalty for our sin on Calvary; and in the grace in his resurrection, you and I can have the promise of victory also—if we trust in him.

Now, you might be asking, "How does Jesus execute his office of a King? As King, what does he do?" That is a good question. In fact, it is one of the questions answered in the Westminster Larger Catechism, one of the historic Presbyterian confessional documents. The answer to Question 45, which we will proceed to investigate in the light of the Bible, goes as follows:

Q. How does Christ execute his office as a King?

A. Christ executes the office of a king, in calling out of the world a people to Himself, and giving them officers, laws, and censures, by which he visibly governs them, in bestowing saving grace upon his elect, rewarding their obedience, and correcting them for their sins, preserving and supporting them under all their temptations and sufferings, restraining and overcoming all their enemies, and powerfully ordering all things for his own glory, and their good, and also in taking vengeance on the rest, who know not God, and obey not the gospel.

This is a lengthy answer, but we will only deal with the portion of it that directly affects officers in the church, although we will see in fact that what the officers do is carry out just about all of these functions in his church in the name of Jesus. The answer begins, "Christ executes the office of a king . . . in giving his people officers, laws, and censures, by which he visibly governs them . . . ." The key words here are "officers," "laws," and "censures." Let's examine these three items in reverse order.

First, Jesus gives us censures. That means he intended for the church to discipline its people when necessary. In Matthew 18:15, Jesus tells us, *"If your brother sins against you, go and tell him his fault, between you and him alone. If he listens to you, you have gained your brother. But if he does not listen, take one or two others along with you, that every charge may be established by the evidence of two or three witnesses. If he refuses to listen to them, tell it to the church. And if he refuses to listen even to the church, let him be to you as a Gentile and a tax collector. Truly, I say to you, whatever you bind on earth shall be bound in heaven, and whatever you loose on earth shall be loosed in heaven. Again I say to you, if two of you agree on earth about anything they ask, it will be done for them by my Father in heaven. For where two or three are gathered in my name, there am I among them."*

We need to study this entire paragraph from the Bible as a unit. Too often it is separated, and it really is one paragraph—one basic concept. We often hear the last verse, *"Where two or three are gathered together in my name, there am I among of them"* quoted at a prayer meeting—especially when only a handful of people show up. While it is true that the Lord is really with us when we enter into corporate prayer and worship, that's not what Matthew 18:20 is trying to teach us because this section is about church censures. It is about church discipline.

In the very next verse in Matthew 18:21, we find Peter asking Jesus, *"Lord, how often will my brother sin against me, and I forgive him? As many as seven times?"* Please notice, Peter wasn't talking about a prayer meeting. He was still talking about the power of the church to forgive sins—about church discipline. You see, it was to the disciples—it was to the leaders of the church, it was to the magistrates of the King—that this power of censure was given. Jesus executes his office of King in the area of censures through his magistrates. For a full discussion of church discipline, see my book *Biblical Church Government*.

Let's now look at the second item on that list from the answer to Larger Catechism Question 45: "officers, laws, and censures." Let's look at laws. How does Jesus execute the office of King by giving laws? Isaiah spelled it out pretty clearly for us in Isaiah 33:22. *"For the Lord is our judge; the Lord is our lawgiver; the Lord is our king; he will save us."* Jesus is the great lawgiver. Again, in Matthew's gospel, we find Jesus himself picking up this theme in the Sermon on the Mount. Matthew 5:17–20 instructs:

> *"Do not think that I have come to abolish the Law or the Prophets; I have not come to abolish them but to fulfill them. For truly, I say to you, until heaven and earth pass away, not an iota, not a dot, will pass from the Law until all is accomplished. Therefore whoever relaxes one of the least of these commandments and teaches others to do the same will be called least in the kingdom of heaven, but whoever does them and teaches them will be called great in the kingdom of heaven. For I tell you, unless your*

righteousness exceeds that of the scribes and Pharisees, you will never enter the kingdom of heaven."

What Jesus is teaching here is that the law applies to us. The law—the Word of God, the commandments—is for us. That is, these things are to govern our very lives, and those who do and teach the law are the ones who will be great in the kingdom of heaven. In other words, the officers, the magistrates, those who teach and enforce the law of God in the name of the King are the leaders of the church. Jesus fulfills his office of King by giving the law to his church.

Be careful that you don't read parts of the Bible that speak of certain laws that are no longer valid, and apply that assumption to the entire law. Some laws speak only of the special civil and ceremonial laws of the Old Testament, which foreshadowed Jesus. This "Jewish" law, as we could call it, has indeed passed away. But the law that we know today as the "moral law," the commandments of God, will never pass away. Not even one "iota" or "dot" of the moral law has been changed.

So far, we have seen the biblical basis for the last two items on our list from Larger Catechism Question 45: "How does Christ execute the office of a King? By the giving of officers, laws, and censures." We have looked at censures. We have looked at laws. Now we must begin our look at the subject of officers.

In chapter 4 of Paul's letter to the Ephesians, the apostle is writing about unity in the church. His main theme in the first half of the chapter is the church and how it is supposed to work together. Beginning at Ephesians 4:4 we read, *"There is one body and one Spirit—just as you were called to the one hope that belongs to your call—⁵one Lord, one faith, one baptism, ⁶one God and Father of all, who is over all and through all and in all."* We see clearly Paul's theme of oneness and unity.

How does this all come about? Paul continues in verse 7, *"But grace was given to each one of us according to the measure of Christ's gift."* The key word here *"apportioned"* (in the NIV), which was translated as a *"gift"* in the ESV), was speaking about something essential in the life of the church. This apportionment, these gifts, are described beginning in verse 11. *"And he gave the apostles, the prophets, the evangelists, the pastors and teachers, ¹²to equip the saints for the work of ministry, for building up the body of Christ, ¹³until we all attain to the unity of the faith and of the knowledge of the Son of God, to mature manhood, to the measure of the stature of the fullness of Christ."*

We need to follow Paul's train of thought here. His goal is unity. That is maturity in the church. How does it come about? It happens through very special, very necessary people in the church, whose role is to prepare God's people for works of service. These are the special sorts of *"gifts"* that Jesus gives to the church.

In verse 11, Paul lists four different types of officers. Remember, we need to be careful of the punctuation here. In the King James, it appears that there are five items in the list, but the best way to punctuate the original Greek is to do it so there are only four items on the list: prophets, apostles, evangelists and pastor-teachers.

Just what are these four classes of people? What are the prophets, apostles, evangelists and pastor-teachers? Why, they are the officers by whom Jesus executes his office of a King. They are the magistrates through whom he rules his church. The only one of these four remaining today is the office of "pastor-teacher," and it is also sometimes referred to by the terms "bishop" or "elder."

So remember your King Jesus. Remember that this King is indeed the head of the church. It is important that we seek to determine how our King would have us organize, function and work in the church today. He is sovereign over us. Jesus rules!

We can be comfortable with that because he is righteous. He is endowed with salvation. He is humble. He is not like any other king we might have ever heard about. Our King has decided, and he has declared, that he will rule his people, which is to say he will rule his church in the way he has decided— through his censures, through his laws, and through his officers.

Chapter Ten
King: Part II – "I'm the King of the World"

As we pointed out in the previous chapter, Jesus serves in his office as King in two distinctly different ways. In Chapter Nine, we saw how he serves as King in his church. But he also serves as King in the world. We will cover that topic in this chapter.

In a sense, I could have used the same title—"Who's In Charge Here?"—for this chapter as well. Just look at the stories you see on TV; people are always asking that question, but without using the words.

Take China for instance. In China, the national government is so determined to keep population growth under control that an abortion is required in many cases if a family that already has one child shows up with an expectant mother again. It is not just allowed, mind you—it is required!

The International Monetary Fund is constantly discussing how to deal with the almost certain default of a number of Third World nations on loans from the World Bank. National governments are refusing to pay their just debts because it is just too hard.

Political and economic freedom is still denied to many people in too many countries. Look how hard it is to bring that about in Afghanistan and Iraq. Those stories hardly make the front page any more. The stories that deal with governmental matters are just too common.

Now even in free countries—even in America—the authorities are requiring the submission of churches and individual Christians to more and more government control. You know the issues: the celebration of Christmas, prayer in public schools. Not long ago in Missouri, a 12-year-old student was disciplined by her principal for saying grace privately and silently before lunch in her own school cafeteria.

So politically, economically, morally, ethically—more and more each day it seems—the nations of this world are making new laws and enforcing new requirements on their people that run in direct contradiction to the political, moral, and ethical teaching of the Word of God.

If we had only newspapers to read, we would probably answer the question "Who's In Charge Here?" by saying that the leaders and rulers of the nations are in charge. They are not only in charge, but doing just about anything they darn-well please—thank you very much.

To these claims Jesus answers clearly in Psalm 2, "I'm the King of the world," which is to say, "I'm in charge here!" The very basic premise and first major point to learn from Psalm 2 is that the nations of the world must not do what they believe to be right. The nations of the world must serve and obey King Jesus.

Even though the psalm has this truth as its overall emphasis, it should come as no surprise to us to find rebellion on the part of the nations around us today. In fact, the psalm itself tells us that this will happen. Look at verses 1–3. *"Why do the nations rage and the peoples plot in vain? ²The kings of the earth set themselves, and the rulers take counsel together, against the Lord and against his anointed, saying, [3]'Let us burst their bonds apart and cast away their cords from us.'"*

Do you see what the rulers of the nations are doing? They are raging, rioting, plotting, scheming, taking stands, gathering together, breaking chains, throwing off their bonds. They are doing everything they can do to oppose the law of God. The bonds and cords in verse 3 describe the feelings that these nations have about God's law, and how badly they try to get out from under it.

While they may not realize it—while there may be no conscious, public decision as they pass their laws and hold their conferences and make decisions that affect the lives of billions of people—what they are in fact doing is acting in direct opposition to the one true and living God, to his Word (Jesus), and to his law. Their actions are rebellious because God requires that all men everywhere—even the leaders, kings and nations—must repent and believe in Jesus. And they must follow his ways and walk in his paths.

As a Presbyterian minister, I am oath-bound to a confession of faith, one of the great Reformation documents setting forth and continuing to instruct in a very objective way the teachings of the Bible. In the chapter in the Westminster Confession titled "The Law of God," we find these very important words:

> The moral law does forever bind all, as well justified persons as others, to the obedience thereof, and that, not only in regard of the matter contained in it, but also in respect of the authority of God the Creator, who

gave it. Neither does Christ, in the Gospel, any way dissolve, but much strengthens this obligation.

Later on, the confession explains clearly that this keeping of the law in no way saves anyone. Yet still, all men, everywhere—the "justified ones as others" (in other words, the Christians and non-Christians)—are obligated to serve and obey Jesus as King.

But as we look around us, we see more and more unjustified persons, nations, rulers and kings rebelling against Jesus and his law. So it makes it very difficult from a human perspective to answer the question, "Who is in charge here?"

Even though we see this blatant rebellion, we must also see the clear promise of the Scriptures that rebellion against the law of God will result in sure judgment. Look at verse 1 of Psalm 2. The raging, the plotting, is all in vain! It's not going to do them any good in the long run.

Now look at verse 4. *"He who sits in the heavens laughs; the Lord holds them in derision."* God simply scoffs at the nations. He openly laughs in their face.

The Bible tells us that it is a fearful thing to fall into the hands of an angry God. This great God—the God who gives his own obedient servant people a multitude of blessings and promises—also will give those who defy him an even greater multitude of curses and judgments. Psalm 2 is very helpful in our understanding of the differing ways in which God deals with the *"ones justified as others."*

In Psalm 23, we find the very familiar fact that God's rod and staff are the shepherd's instruments by which he guides his flock. They are his tools for comforting his own people. But in verse 9 of Psalm 2, we also see God still leading, still guiding the unjustified ones, this time with an iron rod. *"You shall break them with a rod of iron and dash them in pieces like a potter's vessel."* I don't think we need a whole lot of explanation to show that this iron rod is not going to be very comforting to those who rebel. In fact, the metaphor shifts in the last half of verse 9 where we see the nations and rulers being shattered like a potter's clay pot.

In light of this, we must be reminded that each and every one of us is simply clay in the hands of God the Potter. He made us from nothing. He has the final authority over us. He has the power, the ability, and yes the will to refine or destroy any or all of his creation that does not serve and obey him.

Let's think some more about that illustration of the potter and the clay. The potter has in front of him a number of vessels and every one of them is imperfect. There is nothing wrong with the potter, mind you—the problem is all with the clay. That's the result of original sin.

So, here is this potter with all of these imperfect vessels. What are his choices? He wants to keep only perfect vessels. He has really only two choices. Refine, rework, and remake them until they meet his perfect standards. That is how he deals with the justified ones, those of us who are Christians. Sometimes the refining process may not be very pleasant to us. If he has to use a "fire" to soften us, it might even hurt a bit, but at least we are in the process of being refined to ultimate perfection. We are going to make it!

What is his other choice? The other group—the not-justified—are headed for the ash heap. They will be shattered and destroyed. They will not make it.

Now, this is probably not too difficult to understand when we apply it to individual lives or when we personalize the teaching of Scripture one-on-one. What we sometimes tend to forget is that the Bible doesn't always individualize its teaching. Psalm 2 is one of those instances. The picture in view here is an international one. The picture includes nations, rulers, and kings. Here there is a corporate, political application of this same potter/clay illustration. The "them" in verse 9 who get ruled with the iron rod and dashed to pieces are the "them" from back in verse 8. *"Ask of me, and I will make the nations your heritage, and the ends of the earth your possession." "Them"* refers to the nations. It is the ends of the earth. This is an international psalm, not an individual psalm.

OK, so far we've learned what is required of the nations of the world. Let's turn our attention now to the question, "Why?" Why should the nations serve and obey King Jesus? The nations of the world must serve and obey Jesus because the nations of the world are all under the authority of King Jesus. That authority is expressed in Psalm 2 in two major ways, different yet supporting.

The first way the principle is expressed is through the clear fact that Jesus has the authority of a King. Look at verse 4 again. The picture is one of a King on his throne. *"He who sits in the heavens laughs; the Lord holds them in derision."* The picture here is heaven and the one sitting down is the one who is sitting on the throne ruling. This is the one who is really in charge here! Verse 6 helps us see that even better. *"As for me, I have set my King on Zion, my holy hill."* Not only is Jesus sitting on this throne, he has been installed by God the Father himself!

Now the purpose of any installation ceremony is to let the people know who belongs in a certain office. When ministers are installed in their churches, the purpose is to make it very clear that this minister is assuming the authority of office in the church. When a president of the United States is installed every fourth January (we happen to call it "inaugurated"), he is installed in a position of authority.

In verse 6, we see Jesus being installed as King in Zion on God's holy hill. Now, this is not just some localized event, taking place in Jerusalem.

Of course, Psalm 2 may have been originally written for the earthly event of David's installation over the twelve tribes of Israel. (Remember his first seven years he was only the king of Judah). This specific event is described in 2 Samuel 5:9.

If Psalm 2 were only typically a messianic psalm, this could be the case. Several of the messianic psalms (those that have direct reference to Jesus as the Messiah) had original application to some specific event in Israel. But others did not have such direct application. They were written as messianic psalms to begin with. They always had application only to the messianic reign of Jesus (Psalm 45 or Psalm 110).

For our purposes, it makes little difference whether Psalm 2 is directly or typically messianic. The term *"anointed"* in verse 2 is the Hebrew *"Meshiach,"* which comes from the root *"Mashach,"* to anoint. *"Meshiach"* is the Messiah, the Christ (to use the Greek term). Psalm 2 is a messianic psalm. It is about the Messiah, Jesus. There is no doubt whatsoever about the messianic nature of Psalm 2.

So Zion, God's holy hill in its messianic application, is not Jerusalem. It is heaven, the new Jerusalem. And it is from there, heaven, which we see in verse 4, that this King is laughing.

My friends, I am afraid that far too many evangelical Christians in America today tend to think of our Lord simply through his personal name, Jesus, which refers to his role as Savior. I don't want to downplay that in any way. Jesus is my personal savior. I trust that he is yours. Without that fact, there can be no entrance into heaven for any of us. But he has two names. Jesus is his personal name, and the name of his office is Christ (from the Greek). It is the one in common usage today. Better yet, "the Messiah" (from the Hebrew) tells us that he is King.

The kingship of Christ is a doctrine that we hear so little about in our churches today—let alone in the world. It is no wonder that the nations, rulers, and earthly kings are not aware of this great truth.

Yet, as if being called King of the world were not enough, Psalm 2 tells us that Jesus has authority and that the nations must serve and obey him because he is the eternal son of God.

If Jesus were simply another king, someone would probably try to take his throne away. In fact, the Antichrist's basic purpose is to dethrone God's anointed. The Antichrist does not want to "un-save" us, he wants to "un-king" us . . . but it will never happen because our King Jesus is indeed the eternal Son of God. (Read through Isaiah 6 and 7 thoroughly and you will see this pictured in the story of Ahaz.)

Psalm 2:7 is a crucial verse to understand. *"I will tell of the decree: The Lord said to me, 'You are my Son; today I have begotten you.'"* We have here one of the classic statements of the Bible about the sonship of Jesus. This verse is so important it is quoted three times in the New Testament.

Hebrews 1:5 tells us, quoting this verse, that Jesus is far better than any angel. *"For to which of the angels did God ever say, 'You are my Son, today I have begotten you'? Or again, 'I will be to him a father, and he shall be to me a son'?"* The reason I say he is far better than an angel is that he is the Son of God. This Son about whom the author of Hebrews is writing is called by the very name "God" in verse 1:8. *"But of the Son he says, 'Your throne, O God, is forever and ever, the scepter of uprightness is the scepter of your kingdom.'"*

In Acts 13:33, we see this same verse from Psalm 2 being quoted in the context of Paul's sermon in Pisidian Antioch. *". . . This he has fulfilled to us their children by raising Jesus, as also it is written in the second Psalm, 'You are my Son, today I have begotten you.'"* Paul uses Psalm 2:7 here to show the fulfillment of God's promises. The resurrection of Jesus was the ultimate proof that Jesus was in fact God's son. Without the resurrection, there could be no eternal sonship. Jesus did not become God's Son at the resurrection! He was God's Son before time began and his resurrection means he will be God's Son for all eternity forward. Acts 13:33 seems simply to refer to Jesus' resurrection as proof of this eternal relationship.

But *"this day"* referred to in Psalm 2:7 is not the day of the resurrection. The reference is not to Jesus' resurrection or even the day of Jesus' birth. My Old Testament professor in seminary, R. Laird Harris, makes an excellent point. The form of the verb "to beget" used in verse 7 is not the causative conjunctive that is used when speaking of a father begetting a child, but rather is the simple conjugation that refers to general relationships. (Sorry about the Hebrew grammar lesson here, but it is crucial!) There is no thought in Psalm 2:7 of any time of origination of the Son. *"This day"* refers to the eternal relationship of the love between the Father and the Son.

Then in Psalm 2:8, we see the importance of this sonship, because Jesus is the *only* heir and he inherits everything (all the creation, all the people, all the nations). You see, Jesus is not just the King and head of his church; he is "the King of the world." In spite of this, all nations have not yet bowed down to worship their King.

Verse 12 of the psalm calls these nations to *"kiss"* the son. *"Kiss the Son, lest he be angry, and you perish in the way, for his wrath is quickly kindled. Blessed are all who take refuge in him."* The nations need to pay due homage to this Son of God who is their King because his rule over them is eternal.

Submission to the Son is not something that will wait for the final judgment day. It will be too late for any changes then. This must be taking place right now. You and I as individuals cannot delay our turning to Jesus as Savior, and neither can the nations delay turning to Jesus as King.

Do not be put off by the future tense of the verbs in God's decree and promise to Jesus in verses 8 and 9. *"Ask of me, and I will make the nations your heritage, and the ends of the earth your possession. ⁹You shall break them with a rod of iron and dash them in pieces like a potter's vessel."* This making, this possessing, this breaking, will be totally and completely fulfilled at the day of judgment, when it will be too late for the nations to change their minds. But the requirements of serving and obeying Jesus are for right now—today. They are for this age or dispensation, and for every age or dispensation. Jesus is King now and forever, just as Jesus is Savior now and forever.

Now, we've seen what is required in Psalm 2: the nations of the world are to serve and obey Jesus. And we've seen why this is true: the nations of the world are under the authority of Jesus, as King and eternal Son. Our final task, however, must be to help us understand how all this is to come about. So we must also learn that the nations of the world must apply the law of God as the basis of their rule.

You see, the Old Testament did not have one set of regulations from God for Israel and something different for everyone else. No, the law of God applied to every nation: Israel and all her neighbors. This is clear in the early chapters of Amos where he applies the truth of God's law to Damascus in Amos 1:3–5, to Gaza in 1:6–8, to Tyre in 1:9–10, to Edom in 1:11–12, to Ammon in 1:13–15, and to Moab in 2:1–3. Only then does he turn to apply the law of God to Judah, the southern kingdom, in Amos 2:4–5, and finally on his intended hearers (Israel, the northern kingdom) in 2:6 and following. You see, it was all the same law—for *"the ones justified as others."*

Romans 13:1–2 brings this same truth to bear in the New Testament. All governing authorities exist because God has ordained them. *"Let every person be subject to the governing authorities. For there is no authority except from God, and those that exist have been instituted by God. ²Therefore whoever resists the authorities resists what God has appointed, and those who resist will incur judgment."*

If these governing authorities—these nations, rulers, and kings—are servants of the one true and living God, then it is God's rules, commands, and law that are to be the basis for rule by the governing authorities. Do you remember that section of the Westminster Confession we looked at earlier in this chapter? That law is for all—the *"justified ones as others"*! Well, Westminster uses Romans 13 as the Scriptural basis to make the New Testament application of that truth.

Now, if these rules, these governing authorities or nations, are to apply the law of God as the basis of their rule over people, *how* are they to do it? Psalm 2 tells us of at least three different ways. First of all, Psalm 2:10 says they are to apply it with wisdom. *"Now therefore, O kings, be wise; be warned, O rulers of the earth."*

Let me pause here to give you a little Bible quiz. Where does wisdom come from? If you know the Psalms, then you know the answer (Psalm 19). David, in writing Psalm 2 and so many other psalms, certainly knew the answer. Wisdom comes from the law of God, from the Scriptures!

So let's go back to our opening illustration. How about those nations of the world who are defaulting on their international debts? If they were to obey the law of God, what should they do? If God's Word were the basis for their rule, they would pay back their debts. Fairly simple, isn't it?

How about the situation in China where abortions are required in families that already have one child? This is another simple application of the law of God. Whatever your position is on abortion (whether you see it always as murder, or whether it is justified in certain instances such as threat to life of the mother), it is clearly sinful to do it just so the size of the family can be controlled by the state.

Take any international, political, economic, or moral question you want that affects the nations of the world. Apply the clear teaching of Psalm 2 to the law and teaching of God as found in his Word, and you will come to the right decision.

Notice also that the psalm tells the nations that they are to apply the law of God with fear and trembling. Verse 11 says, *"Serve the Lord with fear, and rejoice with trembling."* The serving, the obedience is to be done in fear. The rejoicing (or as I prefer the translation of this particular word, the "living") is to be done with trembling.

You see, the ultimate threat is that of God's judgment, wrath, and destruction. We saw that in verse 12. Jesus does not fear the nations of the world; verse 3 tells us he simply laughs at them. It is the nations of the world that must, in fear and trembling of their ultimate destiny if they fail to obey, apply the law of God as the basis of their rule.

Finally, in the last phrase of verse 12, we are told that the nations of the world are to apply the law of God with trust. *"Blessed are all who take refuge in him."* Does this mean that ultimately the nations of the world must be governed by those who follow Christ? The verse says blessed are all who trust in Jesus. Surely we must say that only one who is trusting in Jesus alone for salvation can be honestly and fully blessed. God calls on all men everywhere to repent and follow him, and to take refuge in the arms of Jesus.

That even applies to the rulers and kings of the world. So it logically follows that Christians should prepare and fit themselves to seek political and economic leadership in this world. It also logically follows that our mission strategy should be to reach those who will be leaders and rulers of the nations. For certainly, only those nations that base their political, economic, moral, and ethical laws and policies on the principles of truth in the Word of God will ultimately take leadership in the international community. And that will be because they will be blessed by God.

David wrote this psalm almost 3,000 years ago but its messianic application is eternal. It is as true today as it was then because Jesus is the same yesterday, today, and forever. He is the eternal Son of God. He is King Jesus. All the nations of the world are to serve and obey him, and apply the law of God with wisdom, with fear and trembling, and with trust.

Trust only in Jesus because it is Jesus who is "King of the world."

If you are reading this during a time of devotions, you may want to quietly (or loudly if you so choose) sing a few verses of "All Hail the Power of Jesus' Name!" But be sure to include the fifth verse, which begins, "Let ev'ry kindred, ev'ry tribe, on this terrestrial ball, to him all majesty ascribe."

No matter where you are reading this, I call on you to fulfill the Great Commission (which we'll discuss more fully in Chapter Nineteen) and take the good news of the gospel to all the nations of the world so they, too, may *"kiss the Son."*

L et's begin this chapter with a couple of stories—
one fictional, one true. First, the fictional story
(although I am confident that stories just like this
have actually happened thousands of times in the past
hundred years).

About a year after they got married, Joe's wife Mary went
to a revival meeting at the local Baptist church, and came home
and said, "I've been saved by the blood of Jesus. My sins are
forgiven. I'm going to heaven! Isn't that wonderful?"

Joe wasn't too sure about how wonderful it was because
now who was going out drinking with him every Saturday night?
And what was Mary going to start telling him about the porn he
liked to watch late at night. And . . . well, you know the rest.

Anyway, Mary kept bugging him and bugging him—and
(dare we call it this) kept nagging him—and finally he too went
to a revival down at the Baptist church. Sure enough, the
preacher talked about sin and guilt, and how everyone needed
his sins paid for by the shed blood of Jesus to enjoy eternal life
in heaven, and Joe walked the aisle that night. Mary was so
happy she cried all the way home.

However, just going to church, walking the aisle, and
making a profession of faith wasn't enough for Joe. He was an
accountant, and probably should have been a detective

because there was nothing he would rather do than research things and learn everything he possible could about them. So, he began reading his Bible.

He had been told not to worry too much with the Old Testament, so he really dug into the New Testament. As he read, he would write himself notes to look up things later. After a few months, Joe had a list of verses he had read that he just did not understand. Not only did he not understand them, they scared him. Here is the list:

Romans 3:21–22: *"But now the righteousness of God has been manifested apart from the law, although the Law and the Prophets bear witness to it—*[22]*the righteousness of God through faith in Jesus Christ for all who believe. For there is no distinction."*

Romans 5:18–19: *"Therefore, as one trespass led to condemnation for all men, so one act of righteousness leads to justification and life for all men.* [19]*For as by the one man's disobedience the many were made sinners, so by the one man's obedience the many will be made righteous."*

Ephesians 4:24: *"And to put on the new self, created after the likeness of God in true righteousness and holiness."*

Philippians 3:9: *"And be found in him, not having a righteousness of my own that comes from the law, but that which comes through faith in Christ, the righteousness from God that depends on faith."*

1 Timothyt 6:11: *"But as for you, O man of God, flee these things. Pursue righteousness, godliness, faith, love, steadfastness, gentleness."*

Hebrews 12:14: *"Strive for peace with everyone, and for the holiness without which no one will see the Lord."*

1 Peter 1:16: *"Since it is written, 'You shall be holy, for I am holy.'"*

1 John 3:10: *"By this it is evident who are the children of God, and who are the children of the devil: whoever does not practice righteousness is not of God, nor is the one who does not love his brother."*

Now all those verses from Paul about righteousness were confusing enough, but his preacher said not to worry about them because they all referred to the Jews of Paul's day. The only thing that applied to us today was that the blood of Jesus washed us clean and took away our sin. But some of those other verses were really troublesome.

He wanted to believe the Bible, but what was he supposed to do about things such as, *"Strive for peace with everyone, and for the holiness without which no one will see the Lord"?* That sure looked to Joe as though it was saying that without holiness, he wasn't going to heaven.

Now he had tried really hard to clean up his act. He had gotten rid of all the porn, he quit carousing on the weekends, he stopped swearing at work, he was working hard at being a better dad and husband, but . . . no holiness, no heaven? Just last week the preacher had said that he can't ever achieve holiness in this life.

What was all this about what Peter was saying: *". . . since it is written, 'You shall be holy, for I am holy.'"* That was a quote right from the mouth of God. He couldn't write that off as some man's opinion.

Then there was John, the one with all the "tests" for how you are doing in your Christian life. He wasn't too sure he cared much for John. What about the one from the third chapter? *"By this it is evident who are the children of God, and who are the children of the devil: whoever does not practice righteousness is not of God, nor is the one who does not love his brother."* Joe understood what evidence was, and this said that the evidence you belonged to God was that you *"practiced righteousness."* That put him back to all those verses from Romans that had started the whole problem. Poor Joe. No one had taught him about the active obedience of Jesus.

But let's turn to the second story; this one is a true story about a guy who had been taught about the active obedience of Jesus. In fact, he had taught others that concept many, many times.

In the late 1930s, a number of ministers and churches left the mainline Presbyterian church in the North and formed a new denomination. We know that group today as the Orthodox Presbyterian Church. Over the years a number of other groups have formed, from both Northern and Southern heritage Presbyterian churches. Some of these groups have been even more conservative, more concerned about the authority of the

Bible, and more concerned about the historical teaching of Presbyterianism.

The leader of the very first group was a man who had been a longtime professor at Princeton Seminary, and more recently had helped form the faculty at Westminster Seminary in Philadelphia. When the first of these new denominations was finally formed in 1936, Dr. J. Gresham Machen was elected as the first moderator.

In order to meet with groups throughout the country who wanted to learn more about this new denomination, "Mach" traveled extensively. In January of 1937, while he was traveling on a denomination organizational trip, Machen suddenly took ill and died. John Muether, the OPC historian, tells the story of his death in *"This Week in the OPC."* From the OPC denominational web site, we read:

> *During the Christmas recess at Westminster Theological Seminary, Machen agreed to travel to North Dakota to speak at some of the churches in the six-month-old denomination that he had helped to found. He took ill during the trip but insisted on fulfilling his obligations when he arrived in the twenty-degree-below-zero weather. After speaking in Leith and then in Bismarck, his condition worsened to the point where he was hospitalized for pneumonia.*

In *J. Gresham Machen: A Biographical Memoir*, Ned B. Stonehouse records Machen's death in this way:

On New Year's Eve Mr. [Samuel J.] Allen called briefly and offered prayer. And then Machen told him of a vision he had had of being in heaven: "Sam, it was glorious, it was glorious." And a little later, "Sam, isn't the Reformed Faith grand?" The following day he was largely unconscious, but there were intervals when his mind was thoroughly alert. In one of those periods he dictated a telegram to his colleague John Murray which was his final word: "I'm so thankful for the active obedience of Christ. No hope without it." And so he died at about 7:30 p.m. on January 1, 1937.

Now, here's a man who had an advance glimpse of heaven just before he died (which is quite common), and what he brought back from that glimpse and wanted his best friend and colleague John Murray to know concerned the active obedience of Jesus, because he understood that without it, one cannot see heaven. Somehow, in his pre-death experience, Machen was able to confirm what he had long been teaching in seminary—that without the active obedience of Jesus, one would not be found in heaven.

This was exactly what was scaring Joe the more he read his Bible. Happily, he lived down the street from a Presbyterian elder who knew a little bit about church history. This elder reminded Joe that Martin Luther's whole crisis was not about whether the blood of Jesus could pay for his sins, but whether Martin would ever be righteousness enough to qualify for heaven (let alone to qualify for the priesthood, which was Martin's immediate crisis).

This elder helped Joe work through the verses in Romans and showed him how Luther resolved the issue. Luther was afraid he needed perfect righteousness in order to go to heaven—and, in a sense, he was right. That is the standard by which God allows one into heaven.

But then the elder showed him that just as God had counted Abraham's faith to him as righteousness (Romans 4:3), each believer in the same way (through faith) could have the righteousness of Jesus (which is to say his active obedience) imputed or counted to the believer. Somehow, Machen saw how that worked out in heaven.

Who knows what he saw? I certainly don't. But I do know one Old Testament story that gives a vivid, wonderful picture about how it all works out. (You know, it's a shame that Joe's preacher said not to bother reading the Old Testament, or he might have seen this picture and figured it out for himself.) We briefly introduced this picture in Chapter Three when we talked about theophanies, because it involves a pre-incarnate appearance of Jesus as the Angel of the Lord. It's the picture in Zechariah 3:1–7 of Joshua before the Angel of the Lord. Let's revisit this vision, but this time look carefully at everything that is going on.

Then he showed me Joshua the high priest standing before the angel of the Lord, and Satan standing at his right hand to accuse him. ²And the Lord said to Satan, "The Lord rebuke you, O Satan! The Lord who has chosen Jerusalem rebuke you! Is not this a brand plucked from the fire?" ³Now Joshua was standing before the angel, clothed with filthy garments. ⁴And the angel said to those who were standing before him, "Remove the filthy garments from him." And to him he said, "Behold, I have taken your iniquity away from you, and I will clothe you with pure vestments." ⁵And I said, "Let them put a clean turban on his head." So they put a clean turban on his head and clothed him with garments. And the angel of the Lord was standing by. ⁶And the angel of the Lord solemnly assured Joshua, ⁷"Thus says the Lord of hosts: If you will walk in my ways and keep my charge, then you shall rule my house and have charge of my courts, and I will give you the right of access among those who are standing here."

Back in Chapter Three, we drew the picture the vision gave us. Zechariah the prophet saw in his vision three primary people: one was Joshua the high priest of Israel, the second was the Angel of the Lord, and the third was Satan. Recall also that in this vision there was great evidence of cherubim all about, serving the Angel of the Lord. Joshua the high priest was not alone, but rather, all the priests of Israel were also seen in the vision (the main point being that Joshua was their representative).

We also saw that the setting of the vision was very clearly the Day of Atonement. That was the one day in the year when the high priest of Israel would enter into the Holy of Holies in the tabernacle or temple. He would enter into the very presence of God, and at that time the sin of the people of Israel was forgiven—at least symbolically.

So the picture before us is the Angel of the Lord representing God, Joshua representing every single Christian (every single true child of God), and Satan the archenemy of God. And what was Satan doing? He was telling God that he should not allow Joshua to remain in the presence of God. What was the reason for this indictment? Joshua was not clothed properly. Joshua was covered from head to foot with human excrement. In other words, Joshua represents the true inner picture of every person's heart . . . total depravity in its ugliest, filthiest picture. Man is covered with iniquity and stands before God with a great need for cleansing.

What was the response of God to Satan's charges? Joshua could stay; Satan had to leave. Why? The true child of God, regardless of his initial state or condition, is called into the presence of God not because of his righteousness or because of his works, but rather because of the unconditional electing grace of God. It is God who chose Jerusalem, Joshua, and every single true Christian. So that is a picture of all of us. We are all standing in the presence of God, covered from head to foot with our sins and iniquity in great need of cleansing, but God allows us to remain in his presence because of his electing grace.

What do we do about the problem of sin? We must take care of this problem of being filthy from sin because God cannot look upon sin, and there we are in the very presence of God.

As we look at Zechariah 3:4, we find that Joshua does not take care of the problem of his filth. We as individuals do not have the ability to cleanse ourselves. In other words, you and I can do nothing. We are utterly helpless to take care of the problem of our sin and pollution that would separate us from God. God must do it for us. And so in verse 4, the Angel of the Lord says to the cherubim, "Take off these filthy clothes." You see, God does this cleansing himself.

Now, in verses 4 and 5 there are three definite steps to this cleansing process. First, there is the removal of the filthy garments, as we have just read in verse 4. Second, there is the re-clothing with festal garments at the end of verse 4: *"I will put rich garments on you."* Then in verse 5, there is the crowning with a priestly turban. The King James Version, *"set a fair mitre,"* is better translated *"put a clean turban on his head."*

Now let's look at these three steps from the vision in a little more detail to try to understand what they really mean to you and me. Remember, through all this, it is you and I—those called to be children of God—who are undergoing this cleansing, just as it was you and I who had the gall to stand in the presence of God covered with our filth. We are the ones undergoing this cleansing and we need to understand what it is all about.

First, think about the removal of the filthy garments. That is explicitly explained right in our text, verse 4. The removal of the garments symbolized God's taking away our iniquity, our sins. *"See, I have taken away your sin,"* says the Angel of the Lord. Again, it is God who takes our sins away. We can't do it. Paul writes, *"one who sins is a slave to sin"* (Romans 6:16). No matter how hard any one of us tries to do what is good or to keep even the moral law of God, it is impossible to do by ourselves. We are all sinners. We are all filthy. Only God can remove our filthy garments. It is only by God's sovereign grace that we may be cleansed.

How does this cleansing come about for you and for me? Do we not all know it so clearly? It is by the blood of Jesus Christ, spilled at Calvary, that we are cleansed. There is no other way. Jesus Christ, who was perfect—who had no filth whatsoever—had to die so that our sin, our pollution, our filth could be washed away in his blood. Oh, what a great promise, what a great act this was. Jesus Christ, the sinless, died for the sinner.

I think probably, and hope that, everyone reading this today knows that promise. Certainly, we know it intellectually. We have heard the story of the gospel before. I hope that we each know it personally, in our hearts. I hope that cleansing is a reality in our own lives. There is one way to tell and that is to be sure that the cleansing is as thorough as the Bible calls for. I'll tell you what that is in a minute.

So this means that the next two steps are also true of us. You see, the cleansing of God does not stop with stripping us of our filthy garments. He doesn't leave us to run around naked. Rather, he clothes us with other garments. He clothes us, in fact, with festal garments. This change of raiment mentioned in verse 4 quite clearly gives us the garments to be worn by the high priest upon entering the Holy of Holies on the Day of Atonement.

What does the white robe represent? It represents the righteousness of Jesus. If we are truly cleansed of our sin, then we must be re-clothed with the righteousness of Jesus. In many evangelical churches in the world today, this very, very important point either has been forgotten or is being purposely ignored. But we must not ignore it. This re-clothing in the righteousness of Christ is a must. It is essential to our salvation. It is essential to our justification. Without being re-clothed in the righteousness of Christ, we cannot call ourselves Christians. We are re-clothed in the active obedience of Jesus. Machen must have seen these garments!

Isaiah had prophesied, *"'Their righteousness is from me,' says the Lord."* Well, we see it right here in Zechariah. The re-clothing in righteousness comes from God, just as the taking away of the filthy garments of sin and iniquity also comes from God. So our righteousness is a gift from God. Our righteousness is not a result of our own efforts. Paul writes in Romans 5:19, *" . . . by the one man's [Jesus'] obedience the many will be made righteous."* In this context, the free gift in view is clearly righteousness.

Elsewhere, in Romans 8:4, Paul makes it crystal clear that this is necessary. It is not some extra alternative. He writes, *"The righteous requirements of the law might be fully met in us."* In 2 Corinthians, he puts it this way, *"God made him, who had no sin, to be sin for us. So that in him we might become the righteousness of God."* Can you see it? We have not only been justified by the blood of Christ, we have also been made righteous. We have not only had our dirty clothes stripped from us, but we have been re-clothed in the righteousness of Christ. Romans 4:25 says, *"He was delivered over to death for our sins, and was raised to life for our righteousness."* You see, the work of Jesus does not stop with paying the penalty for our sins. Jesus was raised again for our righteousness so that God the Father might look out at us and see us, not standing around with our sins cleansed and otherwise naked, but as he sees his very own Son. Our cleansing is thorough. It takes the filth off us and re-clothes us in clean garments—in the righteousness of Jesus.

There is one more step in this vision that affects our cleansing. It's described in Zechariah 3:5. Here we see Zechariah getting all excited. He's watching this picture before him. He sees the high priest being properly re-clothed to fit the picture of the Day of Atonement in the Holy of Holies. Zechariah knows his Bible. He knows the passage in Exodus 28 that describes this outfit and that in verses 36–39 there is something else that is needed. The priestly turban must be worn. So Zechariah gets involved in the vision. In verse 5, he speaks right up. *"Then I said, 'put a clean turban on his head.'"* Zechariah wants everything to go just right.

Now, why was that turban special? We don't have time to examine it in great detail, but we can get the basic picture. It was pure linen with a blue cord; a golden plate engraved with the words *"Holiness to the Lord"* was suspended on the turban. As the high priest entered the Holy of Holies on the Day of Atonement, God (who was enthroned among the cherubim) would see this consecrated plate first, indicating that this person had the right to be there. Without that turban and that plate, he could not be there.

You might remember the story of Uzziah, the great and good king of Israel. He dared to enter the Holy of Holies without being properly clothed and he got leprosy. Where? It was right in the middle of his forehead where that plate should have been hanging from the turban. God struck Uzziah with leprosy because he was not equipped with the proper mark of holiness.

We must understand that each of us is called to be a priest in the service of Jesus. We must be prepared to serve as we have been called. We too must have this mark of *"Holiness to the Lord"* emblazoned on our foreheads.

The Book of Revelation says that in the end times each person bears a mark. Some bear the mark of the beast (Satan) and are clearly identified as his people. But others bear the mark of the Lamb. They are clearly marked as belonging to Jesus. What is that mark? It is the mark of *"Holiness to the Lord."* That mark is the clothing in the white robe of righteousness of Jesus Christ. It is the real mark of a true Christian: holiness.

That mark is the definite consequence that must ultimately come from our cleansing. It comes only as a result of the active obedience of Jesus. If it is not there, then our cleansing is not really from God. Oh, we may pretend to have washed out our robes a little. We may try to clean up our lives enough to get by in the church. We may have even done enough to fool our families and friends into thinking we are Christians and have been cleansed by God. But you can't fool God. If he has cleansed you, then he has done a thorough job. If he has cleansed you, then the consequences of verse 7 must apply to you. *"This is what the Lord almighty says: If you will walk in my ways, and keep my requirements; then you will govern my house, and have charge of my courts, and I will give you a place among these standing here."*

I hope you can see it. God will give us great and wonderful privileges. We may serve as prophets, priests, and kings in his kingdom. We will be allowed to walk freely in his presence. We will be no longer limited to visit the inner sanctuary of the Holy of Holies one day a year. We may walk with him every day.

But we have these privileges *only*, he says, if we keep his requirements, or in other words, only if we are clothed in the righteousness of Christ. We have these privileges only if we bear the mark of a Christian. When we bear the mark of "Holiness to the Lord," only then do we have full access to this promise.

Now, be careful here. I am not saying that we must earn this right by our obedience. Joe's pastor was right when he said we can't earn our salvation. We cannot earn anything. Our forgiveness of sins is not only paid for by the blood of Jesus as a free gift from God, but God also gives us our holiness, our sanctification. That too is a free gift from God. The important point is that God gives them *both* to each and every Christian. Grace comes both from the active obedience of Jesus (he perfectly kept the law of God) and the passive obedience of Jesus (which he suffered on the cross—we'll get to that in just a few chapters).

If you want to say that you are justified, then you must say that you are being sanctified . . . and show it in your life. If you want to call Jesus your Savior, then you must call him your Lord . . . and show it in your life. The fact that we are growing in sanctification is evidence that we are wearing the white robes of righteousness of Jesus.

We cannot dare to walk in the presence of God calling ourselves by the name of his Son without that badge on our foreheads, *"Holiness to the Lord."* We must be aware that we are different. Perhaps it was all those badges that Machen saw and recognized as evidence of the active obedience of Jesus.

By active obedience, Jesus kept the law perfectly. His virgin birth, and living a life that perfectly fulfilled the moral law of God, resulted in his sinlessness so he could be a spotless sacrifice. His perfect fulfilling of the moral law of God made him righteous before God. This active obedience, when imputed to us by God's grace, allows us to wear those white robes representing his righteousness and the badge of *"Holiness to the Lord."* All of this was and is necessary for us to have eternal life.

Joe was right to seek to understand those verses, and he finally figured out that the evidence was crucial. That evidence came to him just as his justification came to him—by the saving grace of God in the work of Jesus.

Chapter Twelve
Passive Obedience – "When Jesus Surveys the Wondrous Cross"

The material in this chapter is adapted from a sermon preached by Dr. Sinclair Ferguson at the March 1998 Ligonier Conference in Orlando, Florida, and is used by permission.

In order to set the stage, the context for this chapter, let's look together at Mark 14:22–42 in its entirety. Then we'll go back and examine certain elements of this passage more closely.

> [22] And as they were eating, he took bread, and after blessing it broke it and gave it to them, and said, "Take; this is my body." [23] And he took a cup, and when he had given thanks he gave it to them, and they all drank of it. [24] And he said to them, "This is my blood of the covenant, which is poured out for many. [25] Truly, I say to you, I will not drink again of the fruit of the vine until that day when I drink it new in the kingdom of God."
>
> [26] And when they had sung a hymn, they went out to the Mount of Olives. [27] And Jesus said to them, "You will all fall away, for it is written, 'I will strike the shepherd, and the sheep will be scattered.' [28] But after I am raised up, I will go before you to Galilee." [29] Peter said to him, "Even though they all fall away, I will not." [30] And Jesus said to him, "Truly, I tell you,

this very night, before the rooster crows twice, you will deny me three times." ³¹But he said emphatically, "If I must die with you, I will not deny you." And they all said the same.

³²*And they went to a place called Gethsemane. And he said to his disciples, "Sit here while I pray." ³³And he took with him Peter and James and John, and began to be greatly distressed and troubled. ³⁴And he said to them, "My soul is very sorrowful, even to death. Remain here and watch." ³⁵And going a little farther, he fell on the ground and prayed that, if it were possible, the hour might pass from him. ³⁶And he said, "Abba, Father, all things are possible for you. Remove this cup from me. Yet not what I will, but what you will." ³⁷And he came and found them sleeping, and he said to Peter, "Simon, are you asleep? Could you not watch one hour? ³⁸Watch and pray that you may not enter into temptation. The spirit indeed is willing, but the flesh is weak." ³⁹And again he went away and prayed, saying the same words. ⁴⁰And again he came and found them sleeping, for their eyes were very heavy, and they did not know what to answer him. ⁴¹And he came the third time and said to them, "Are you still sleeping and taking your rest? It is enough; the hour has come. The Son of Man is betrayed into the hands of sinners. ⁴²Rise, let us be going; see, my betrayer is at hand."*

"When I Survey the Wondrous Cross" is without a doubt one of the most popular hymns in Christian music. In just about everyone's "Top 25" list (at least until a few years ago) you would always find this hymn.

The hymn concerns how you and I, as human beings living after the time of Jesus' crucifixion, knowing that the first Easter has come and gone and that Jesus has risen from the grave to overcome death, sing these words of how the cross looks to us. What does it really mean in our lives?

I would suggest there are other ways to survey the wondrous cross. Other eyes can look at that same incident nearly two thousand years ago, and the voices connected to those eyes might sing different hymns. Over the years, I have preached sermons based on the perspective of people who were at the scene that day at Calvary. I've tried to see how others such as Thomas, Peter, John, the Roman centurion, the thief, and others have looked at the cross.

Two other important sets of eyes also surveyed the wondrous cross. The first of these were the eyes of God the Father. The prophet Isaiah helps us to understand what the cross looked like to God the Father, sitting on his throne in heaven, looking down at Calvary that day.

In writing about the Suffering Servant whose name and time were still unknown, Isaiah is able to see that the one of whom he writes in chapters 50 through 53 was born for the very reason of dying. He was sent to earth for the expressed purpose, wish, and determination of his heavenly Father. It is God the Father who sent his son Jesus to die at Calvary.

Those of us who are parents know what it is like to see a son or a daughter involved in some important or special event. You know the feeling you get when you watch your child participate in a program at church or in an athletic contest, or receive an honor at a graduation ceremony. When your child stands in front of a congregation of your family and friends taking vows of church membership or perhaps marriage, you stand back and say (at least to yourself, if not out loud), "That's my boy!" or "That's my girl!"

The relationship of God the Father and God the Son is very much like that. Jesus calls his heavenly Father "Daddy" (*Abba* in the Greek) in Mark 14:36. As "Daddy" looks down from heaven a few short hours later, he sees his son hanging on the cross, suffering the eternal pains of hell. And the heavenly Father points the myriads of hosts of angels surrounding him to the cross. Jesus could have instantly called to earth those myriads of angels to remove him from his threat of imminent death. Then the Father says, as it were, to his angels, "Do you see him? That's my boy! That's my boy!" That's just a glimpse of how God the Father must have surveyed the wondrous cross.

As we examine Mark 14:22–42, we find details of the night before Jesus died. You see, we have here one of those rare passages of the Bible where we sense that we are standing on holy ground. I say that for this reason. The source of this passage has to be Jesus himself. We aren't reading simply the words of Mark, nor the words of Peter or others as they relayed incidents and stories to Mark. Starting in verse 35, the only human observer to this event is Jesus himself! He has left the disciples behind. In fact, when he comes back a little later, he finds that they are sleeping, so he returns once again alone into the garden to pray and to communicate with his heavenly Father.

I think we can properly surmise that some time in those 40 days after the resurrection and before Jesus' ascension to heaven, the three disciples (verse 31 tells us they were Peter, James, and John) who went the deepest into the garden that night must have asked Jesus what happened after they had fallen asleep. Jesus must have shared with them this most sacred moment in his experience, and told them how on this occasion he found himself in agony. He said that he had fallen on the ground as he wrestled with the destiny that God had given to him. In other words, verses 35 and 36 give us a clear picture of how Jesus surveyed the wondrous cross!

Clearly, Jesus wanted you and me to know of this incident. Through the inspiration of the Holy Spirit, it is included in all three of the synoptic Gospels (Matthew, Mark, and Luke). In all three cases, it is the key incident that connects the institution of the sacrament of the Lord's Supper with the Lord's crucifixion, and why I say that we could also properly call it the sacrament of the Lord's crucifixion.

What is happening here is that Jesus has gone out in the garden, and has found himself at a "table that has been prepared for him in the presence of his enemies." As he surveyed this picture, his whole being shuddered. The cup he must drink runs over, and it is overwhelming to him. (We will talk more about this cup later in the chapter.)

As Jesus consciously began to survey what he was about to do on the cross of Calvary, he revealed to us a series of steps or stages that take us to the very heart of the gospel. He discloses the very center of what it means for us to find salvation in Jesus, the great and gracious, dear Savior whom we have come to trust, know, and love.

What are these steps or stages? The first of them is this. Our Lord, as he was surveying the wondrous cross, was brought into personal isolation. We see this as we examine how the scene was physically set. Jesus took his disciples away from the world of activity and out into this isolated garden, called Gethsemane. Next, he further isolated three of them from the others in order that they might stand with him in his hour of trial and darkness. Then, in Mark 14:35, we see that Jesus himself drew apart from the three, and quite physically made it plain that what he was about to experience isolated him from the whole of humanity. This isolation was not just outward and physical. It was inward and spiritual isolation as well.

Jesus referred to this in the next scene, when the armed crowd, tipped off by the traitor Judas, came to the garden to arrest him. Speaking to the chief priests, the officers of the temple guards, and the elders who were standing there in opposition to him, Jesus said, according to Luke, " . . . *this is your hour, and the power of darkness.*"

What did he mean? How was this an hour of darkness? Think back to earlier in Jesus' ministry, just after his baptism by John. God revealed to the world that this Jesus of Nazareth was indeed his own dear, unique son. Remember what happened next? Satan took Jesus into the wilderness, and four times tempted him to give up his work and accept Satan's kingdom and rule. Four times Jesus rebuked him. So what did Satan do? He left him and looked forward to a more suitable time to take him. Satan hadn't given up. He had just stalled awhile to try to gain tactical advantage, we are told in Luke 4:13.

Jesus recognized this when he was in the Upper Room. There was a feeling of uneasiness in the room, especially when Jesus revealed that Judas was to be his betrayer and that Satan had come to dwell in him for this purpose. Satan's time had come again and Jesus recognized that he had entered into a new stage of his cosmic conflict against the powers of darkness.

In the midst of this great conflict, what did Jesus' closest friends (the three disciples who were always with him at the major events of his ministry) do? They fell asleep! He came back and woke them up, but they fell asleep again! Clearly, Jesus was left to fight this spiritual battle by himself. He was totally isolated in facing and withstanding all the hellish powers.

God the Father did send an angel to minister to Jesus as he faced this great spiritual battle. Luke tells us about the angel in his account. But do you remember when it was that the angel came? It was not at the beginning of the struggle. The angel came at the end of the battle, after the anguish, after the suffering. Jesus faced all of that alone—isolated. Just as he had spent the 40 days and nights of temptation in the wilderness isolated, he now faced the greatest physical and spiritual battle of all.

How bad was this struggle? The isolation was so overpowering that Jesus actually asks his heavenly Father to change his mind! He prayed to God (in Mark 14:36) for the cup to be removed from him. Jesus knew that this cup was going to involve—for the very first time in all of eternal history—the Son being isolated from his Father. Relatively speaking, that means little to you and me. You and I will never— never—fully understand what it means to live 33 sinless years in unbroken, unclouded fellowship with God, then experience total separation from him.

As one who, in his divinity, had lived for all eternity in passionate fellowship with God the Father, he had never been isolated from him, even as a man. Now, for the first time in human history and eternal history, Jesus the God-man was entering into uncharted territory. Jesus had told us (in John's Gospel) that everything he did was what he had seen his Father do. Everything he did was what the Father had instructed him to do. But now as he surveyed the wondrous cross of Calvary, he had become overwhelmingly conscious that he must face it in isolation. He was all alone, unable to see what his Father was doing or to hear what his Father was saying.

In a real sense, Jesus saw that he was about to fulfill the prophetic utterance of Psalm 69. Jesus knew he was facing the waters of isolation from God because he knew the words of Psalm 69:1–3. *"Save me, O God! For the waters have come up to my neck. ²I sink in deep mire, where there is no foothold; I have come into deep waters, and the flood sweeps over me. [3]I am weary with my crying out; my throat is parched. My eyes grow dim with waiting for my God."*

The first stage that Jesus surveyed on his way to the wondrous cross was isolation. The second stage was spiritual desolation, also expressed outwardly and physically.

We understand, don't we, that what Jesus suffered spiritually was essential to our salvation. But we must never downplay his physical, human suffering. When we look at all three accounts of this scene (Matthew, Mark, and Luke) and put them together, we see his physical suffering.

Jesus went into the garden. He isolated himself from the disciples and then, contrary to the Jewish custom of standing to pray with his eyes lifted up to heaven, he fell down and prayed. Sensing the burden of what he was about to experience, he could not physically stand. Mark 14:35 says he literally *"fell on the ground and prayed."*

There is some sense that this was not just a single act but that after he fell, he tried to raise himself up again to pray in the normal way but the burdens pressed him to the ground once again, and again, and again. The pressure of the burden of this cup produced drops of sweat. His sweat was not just water but drops of blood oozing out from his skin as he prayed to God, *"Father, all things are possible for you. Remove this cup from me."*

I don't know about you, but it is just absolutely amazing to me that Jesus would share this deep insight into his emotional life with us. He didn't have to, you know. No one saw this scene. No human heard him utter those words of desperation. But Jesus wanted you and me to know what he went through as he surveyed the wondrous cross.

Even before he went off by himself in the garden, he had turned to the three disciples and told them, *"My soul is very sorrowful, even to death"* (Mark 14:34). In relating this story to his readers, Mark says in verse 33 that Jesus, at the very outset of leaving the Upper Room, *"began to be greatly distressed and troubled."* Why was that?

There in the garden, isolated, by himself, Jesus was able to see fully, clearly, and totally what it was going to cost him in the next few hours. Surveying the wondrous cross cost him not only physical and emotional stress, but distress within his very soul.

I remember a great Christian of another age referring to this passage in Mark as expressing the confused, restless, half-distracted state produced by physical derangement or mental illness. You see, Jesus was entering not only into the territory that Psalm 69 described, but also into the territory in which Psalm 23 can no longer be experienced. It would not be possible for him to say, *"Even though I walk through the valley of the shadow of death* (the valley of deepest darkness, like Gethsemane), *I will fear no evil."* Oh, but he did have something to fear. He was filled with fear. "No man ever feared death like this man," said Martin Luther so clearly of this passage.

Why? It was because there was no man or woman who ever lived to whom death was so unnatural, so undeserved, so unrighteous. In his humanity, Jesus was simply overwhelmed by a sense of spiritual desolation because his imminent death was so seemingly irrational.

Just a few days earlier, John 12:27–28 reports, Jesus was discussing his coming death with his disciples, and he said to them, " *'Now is my soul troubled. And what shall I say? "Father, save me from this hour:"? But for this purpose I have come to this hour. ²⁸Father, glorify your name.' Then a voice came from heaven: 'I have glorified it, and I will glorify it again.'"*

For the next four days, he marched steadfastly toward the cross. But now in the Garden of Gethsemane there was something new. "What shall I say now? I shall say, 'O my father. O, my father, if it is possible, let this cup pass from me." Jesus enters into an experience of human isolation, and into a deep experience of spiritual desolation.

As he does so, we move to the next stage, which is the very center of the meaning of the cross. Jesus becomes our "propitiation." Some of you may not be familiar with that word. It is crucial to our understanding of what Jesus saw as he surveyed the wondrous cross, so let me first describe it for you, and then briefly define it..

We have heard Jesus ask his heavenly Father to, if possible, take *"this cup from me."* What was this cup he was talking about? Earlier in the Gospels, Jesus had spoken of the cross as his cup, and what Jesus saw now so clearly is that to which "this cup" refers. When he speaks about the cup, he refers to those passages in the Old Testament that tell us about the cup coming from the Lord's right hand. Many of the prophets speak about this cup.

Isaiah writes of it in the midst of the passages about the Suffering Servant, in Isaiah 51:22. *"Thus says your Lord, the Lord, your God who pleads the cause of his people: 'Behold, I have taken from your hand the cup of staggering; the bowl of my wrath you shall drink no more.'"*

The same thing is found in the prophecy of Jeremiah 25:15–16. *"Take from my hand this cup of the wine of wrath . . . . [16]They shall drink and stagger and be crazed because of the sword that I am sending among them."*

Likewise in Ezekiel 23:32–33 we read of the *" . . .cup that is deep and large."* Now we pay special attention to this next section. *"You shall be laughed at and held in derision, for it contains much; [33]you will be filled with drunkenness and sorrow. A cup of horror and desolation."*

Finally, Habakkuk 2:26 says, *"You will have your fill of shame instead of glory. . . . The cup in the Lord's right hand will come around to you, and utter shame will come upon your glory!"*

So this is the cup that Jesus was anticipating—the cup of God's wrath for sin would be poured out on him.

Just a few hours earlier, while they were at the Last Supper, Jesus had offered the Cup of Blessing to his disciples. In the Passover meal, the Cup of Blessing is intended to honor the Messiah. Mark 14:25 tells us that Jesus said, *"Truly, I say to you, I will not drink again of the fruit of the vine until that day when I drink it new in the kingdom of God."* He is refusing the cup that was rightfully his!

Then he went out into the Garden of Gethsemane and the Father brought to him another cup, saying, "This cup is filled with my wrath, with my scoffing, my derision and suffering. It is the cup of my outpoured judgment upon sin. And it is coming round to you!" You see, this cup is the fulfillment of the prophecy that Jesus had just proclaimed. *"I will strike the shepherd, and the sheep will be scattered"* (Mark 14:27).

In the Old Testament, on the great Day of Atonement, there was a ritual in which something of this scene was expressed. In Leviticus 16:7–10, God gives instructions to Moses to take two goats for a sacrifice. Two goats were needed, one to express the outer significance of what propitiation for man's sin would require, and the other to express the inner significance of the propitiation. One of the goats had men's sins confessed over it, then it was slaughtered and its blood was used in the ordinary way to represent atonement for the sins of the people. But the other goat (whose title has come into use in our language), the scapegoat, was held by someone who was counted worthy for that task. The sins of the people were confessed over that goat as well and then it was led out and made to wander in the isolated wilderness until it died. So this was a picture of the sins of the people entering not simply into death as in the case of the first goat, but into a no-man's land where one wandered in the wilderness in the presence of a wild demon, with sin being borne upon one's being. That's why as Jesus entered into the reality of Psalm 69, where the promises of Psalm 23 no longer apply, he now also entered into the reality of Psalm 22:1: *"My God, my God, why have you forsaken me?"* Why? And God's answer is, "My son, you are becoming the propitiation, the atoning sacrifice, for the sins of my people." Jesus' death on the cross served the purpose of both goats, death and spiritual isolation.

This brings us to the whole point of the chapter, and for that matter, the whole point of Jesus having to face that awful cup of death on the cross. You see, Jesus enters into isolation and spiritual desolation, because he comes forward to offer himself as a propitiation – a substation payment by one persone for another - for our sins. In doing so, he enters into the realm of personal substitution.

I hope you see that the most awful thing about the horrible death that Jesus suffered is that he didn't deserve it! He was sinless. As Isaiah put it in the Suffering Servant passages (Isaiah 53:4–6, emphasis added):

> *Surely he has borne **our** griefs and carried **our** sorrows; yet we esteemed him stricken, smitten by God, and afflicted. [5]But he was wounded for **our** transgressions; he was crushed for **our** iniquities; upon him was the chastisement that brought **us** peace, and with his stripes **we** are healed. [6]All we like sheep have gone astray . . . and the Lord has laid on him the iniquity of us **all**.*

In Mark 14, Jesus made that clear to his disciples, just as he seeks to make it clear to you and to me today. In Mark 14:22–24, he institutes the sacrament of the Lord's Supper, taking from the table what the Jews called the Cup of Blessing that ultimately belonged to the divine Messiah, and he thrust it into the hands of his disciples, saying, "All of you drink it. This cup is for you."

You see, Jesus gave to us the Cup of Blessing, which we call the Cup of the Sacrament of the Lord's Supper. He didn't drink it. Instead, he went out into the Garden of Gethsemane and there (thank God) drank instead the cup of isolation, the cup of spiritual desolation, and the cup of the overwhelming wrath of God—the cup of propitiation and substitution. While we drink the Messiah's Cup of Blessing that should have been drunk by Jesus, he drank the cup of God's wrath that was the penalty for sins. The one we should drink is the one Jesus drank for us. He drank the Cup of the Sacrament of Crucifixion and he drank it to the last, bitter dregs.

There is no greater love than the love of God. *"In this is love—not that we have loved God but that he loved us and sent his Son to be the propitiation for our sins"* (1 John 4:10).

The second stanza of "Man of Sorrows" reads, "Bearing shame and scoffing rude, in my place condemned he stood. Sealed my pardon with his blood. Hallelujah! What a Savior!"

Hallelujah! Hallelujah! What a Savior!

Chapter Thirteen
Resurrection – "The World's Best Easter Sermon"

S ometime in the early 1930s, a communist activist addressed a huge assembly in Kiev, Ukraine, then part of the Soviet Union. He assailed Christianity for a solid hour, heaping on argument after argument, ridiculing the faith. Finally, he finished and looked down on what seemed to be the smoldering ashes of shattered faith. "Are there any questions?" he demanded! There was silence.

Then, after a long period, a man rose and asked permission to speak. He got up on the platform. There was silence as he looked around, first to the right, then to the left. At last he shouted—loud and clear—the ancient Christian greeting: *"Christ is risen!"* The vast audience arose as one man, and the response resounded like an avalanche—*"He is risen indeed!"*

I think we can honestly say that nothing is as ingrained in the Christian psyche and culture as is the truth of the bodily resurrection of Jesus over two thousand years ago. And the resurrection is our topic for this chapter.

Let me begin our examination with a question. Who do you think has preached the world's greatest Easter sermon? Was it one from a great preacher from church history such as John Knox or Charles Spurgeon? Do you think it was Billy Graham? If you have a Presbyterian background, do you think it might have been D. James Kennedy or R. C. Sproul? Perhaps you think it was Jerry Falwell or Jack Hayford, or another televangelist.

Well, I'm going to say that all of those guesses are wrong because the greatest Easter sermon ever preached comes right from the Bible. It's in Acts 13. Actually, it is the very first sermon recorded in the Bible that was preached by the Apostle Paul. I am sure he had preached many times before, but God's Holy Spirit inspired the recording of this one first.

Here is the world's greatest Easter sermon, which comes to you as God's holy, inspired, inerrant Word, beginning at verse 16:

So Paul stood up, and motioning with his hand said: "Men of Israel and you who fear God, listen. [17]The God of this people Israel chose our fathers and made the people great during their stay in the land of Egypt, and with uplifted arm he led them out of it. [18]And for about forty years he put up with them in the wilderness. [19]And after destroying seven nations in the land of Canaan, he gave them their land as an inheritance. [20]All this took about 450 years. And after that he gave them judges until Samuel the prophet. [21]Then they asked for a king, and God gave them Saul the son of Kish, a man of the tribe of Benjamin, for forty years. [22]And when he had removed him, he raised up David to be their king, of whom he testified and said, 'I have found in David the son of Jesse a man after my heart, who will do all my will.'

[23"]Of this man's offspring God has brought to Israel a Savior, Jesus, as he promised. [24]Before his coming, John had proclaimed a baptism of repentance to all the people of Israel. [25]And as John was finishing his

course, he said, 'What do you suppose that I am? I am not he. No, but behold, after me one is coming, the sandals of whose feet I am not worthy to untie.'

[26]"Brothers, sons of the family of Abraham, and those among you who fear God, to us has been sent the message of this salvation. [27]For those who live in Jerusalem and their rulers, because they did not recognize him nor understand the utterances of the prophets, which are read every Sabbath, fulfilled them by condemning him. [28]And though they found in him no guilt worthy of death, they asked Pilate to have him executed.

[29]"And when they had carried out all that was written of him, they took him down from the tree and laid him in a tomb. [30]But God raised him from the dead, [31]and for many days he appeared to those who had come up with him from Galilee to Jerusalem, who are now his witnesses to the people. [32]And we bring you the good news that what God promised to the fathers, [33]this he has fulfilled to us their children by raising Jesus, as also it is written in the second Psalm, 'You are my Son, today I have begotten you.'

[34]"And as for the fact that he raised him from the dead, no more to return to corruption, he has spoken in this way, 'I will give you the holy and sure blessings of David.' [35]Therefore he says also in another psalm, 'You will not let your Holy One see corruption.'

36"For David, after he had served the purpose of God in his own generation, fell asleep and was laid with his fathers and saw corruption, 37but he whom God raised up did not see corruption.

38"Let it be known to you therefore, brothers, that through this man forgiveness of sins is proclaimed to you, and by him everyone who believes is freed from everything 39from which you could not be freed by the law of Moses. 40Beware, therefore, lest what is said in the Prophets should come about: 41'Look, you scoffers, be astounded and perish; for I am doing a work in your days, a work that you will not believe, even if one tells it to you.'"

Within this truly great sermon, the one thing that stands out to me—the point I want to stress—is the reason that people gather every year on the special holy day known as Easter. Central to this message from Paul (as it is central to all true preaching) is the fact contained in verse 30, *"But God raised him from the dead."* Without the fact of the resurrection of Jesus Christ, there would be no gospel to preach. We might as well just go to a football game or invite some friends to a backyard barbeque because there certainly would be no reason to go to church. Not just on Easter—there would be no reason to go on any Sunday.

This world's greatest Easter sermon is not very complicated, but it *is* profound. The gospel of Jesus Christ is neither complicated nor erudite. But this world's greatest Easter sermon is a very beautiful message. That is the very nature of the gospel.

In thinking about the resurrection, there are three basic facts to remember. Three ideas are central to the gospel. The first is every human being in the world must die. The second fact is Jesus did *not* have to die. The third and last fact is that because Jesus rose from the dead on that first Easter morning, we can have eternal life through faith in Him.

I hope everyone reading this has already heard all of three facts. There is nothing unique, certainly nothing new, about these ideas, but perhaps you've never heard them put quite so bluntly or directly before. If that is the case, your initial reaction to the first fact that we all must die might make you think that this is not such a beautiful message after all. That's only because you are judging the first fact on its own without seeing the whole picture.

You see, the gospel is a package. It is a package that Paul preached so eloquently that Sabbath day many centuries ago. After giving the Jewish citizens of Antioch a short course in Old Testament history, Paul moved directly to this main theme of Jesus' resurrection. In doing so, he drew from the Old Testament an illustration that brings home our first fact.

As the Jews looked back over their long and illustrious history, one of the names that stood out as the greatest among them was the name of David. David had been their beloved king. It was through David's descendants that God had promised to the people of Israel a great Messiah, who would lead them in the world. Certainly, David was one of the greatest of all men who ever lived. In Acts 13:36, however, Paul very bluntly tells his hearers that after David had "served his purpose," he died.

That's a truth that applies to everyone. No matter who we are, no matter how great or how small our impact on the world may be, no matter what we do for ourselves—come what may in this world—*we will all die!*

You've probably been to a good number of funerals in your time, right? Please forgive me. I don't want to bring you any additional sorrow by talking about funerals. But I want everyone to see very, very clearly that death can be the most sorrowful thing that can happen to a person. When we are young and still living vigorous lives, we try hard not to think about death. We just eliminate the thoughts from our minds and go about our business as if death weren't true or that we could somehow escape it. But you can't escape! Everyone has to die.

Why must this be so? Well, if you've studied the first few chapters of the Bible (Genesis 1–3), then you know the answer, don't you? You know that ever since that original sin committed by our first parents, Adam and Eve, death is now an inevitable part of the creation. Like Adam and Eve, we too are sinners and we must die.

"But wait!" you say. "Your second fact was that Jesus didn't have to die, but you just said that everyone must die." That's a contradiction. How can both be true? Well, the historical truth that Paul preaches in Acts 13:28 is that even though Jesus' enemies *"found in him no guilt worthy of death, they asked Pilate to have him executed."*

When you read the story of the life of Jesus, you very quickly see that Jesus was different. Oh, sure, he is the Son of God, he's the Second Person of the Trinity, but I'm talking about Jesus in his humanity. When you read about the life of Jesus, what you see is that the man Jesus never committed a sin! He was sinless. He was without guilt. Since it is sin that is the cause of death, and Jesus was sinless, then he did not have to die.

This is where the Christmas story intersects with the Easter story. The Christmas story tells us that Jesus was miraculously born of a virgin. As a result, he was born without sin. So here we are with Jesus—sinless and guiltless—who did not have to die. And what happens?

We know that the Roman army in Palestine crucified him two thousand years ago. He was nailed to pieces of a tree that had been assembled in the form of a cross, and as he hung there, he suffered a very inglorious and horrible death. When the last breath of human life had passed from him, he was taken down from the tree and buried in a cave, which had been prepared to be the tomb of a rich man. That cave was sealed off with a giant rock that closed it completely.

Because of all the controversy surrounding Jesus' life, the Roman army guarded that cave day and night so that no one would tamper with the body. On the third day, however, the stone was rolled away by an earthquake and the tomb was opened. When the guards looked in that tomb that Sunday morning, the body had miraculously disappeared.

Remember that these are not just stories; this is not a myth. These are historical facts to which there were many witnesses. And the most important historical fact of all is the one we celebrate each Easter. It's the fact that Paul emphasizes in his sermon in Acts 13:30–31. *"But God raised him from the dead,* *³¹and for many days he appeared to those who had come up with him from Galilee to Jerusalem, who are now his witnesses to the people."*

Again, the fact that he was alive had many witnesses. A historian once said that the resurrection of Jesus from the grave is the best-attested fact in the entire history of the world. One cynical nonbeliever not too many years ago (a British journalist) started from the premise that the resurrection had to be a myth—it couldn't possibly be true—and did all the historical research he could possibly do in the modern world of the then-twentieth century. He finally came to the conclusion that the resurrection was real. It was clearly a historical fact! That man was Frank Morrison, author of one of the best-selling books of all time, *Who Moved the Stone?* He became a Bible-believing, evangelical Christian, as a result of his research and experience.

It is no wonder that this happened to Morrison. It had to happen! The resurrection is the pivotal fact of all human history and the Christian faith. Through our belief that Jesus died on the cross and was resurrected from death—through our faith, a gift from the Holy Spirit—we are able to understand the third central fact. You and I, every single one of us who believe, can know and live an eternal life.

Do you remember having awful thoughts when we talked about death at the beginning of this chapter? Well, just turn them around completely and think now about life forever—eternally. This kind of life is not the kind here on earth with all its problems and pains. It is an eternal life in our Father's house in heaven, in the many mansions of his kingdom. Another fairy tale, you say? Well, I'll be the first to admit we can't have the same kind of firsthand witnesses to heaven that we had to the resurrection of Jesus. But even if we don't have documented facts, we certainly have the promise of Jesus himself given to us in the Bible. The promise of eternal life in heaven is for all who believe in him.

It would be fun to sit around and speculate about what heaven is going to be like, wouldn't it? Now, there's an idea for a small group party some time. We all have our own ideas, don't we? I would think that would be a very pleasant way to spend an afternoon or evening with friends. Get your Bibles and commentaries out and read all you can find about heaven. The prophets Isaiah, Micah, and Zechariah describe it for us in the Old Testament. The Gospel of Matthew probably contains the best definition and parables about the mystery of the kingdom of heaven. And, of course, the book of Revelation contains a wealth of pictorial information about heaven.

No matter what you and I might come up with as different pictures of what heaven is like, the fact remains that heaven exists. And since it is there, I for one aspire to go there, don't you? I'm sure just about everyone would answer that question, "Yes." The Bible says that the only other option after death is hell, and based on the description given—lake of fire, eternal flames, pain and agony and suffering—we would not want to go there. Anyone in his right mind would want to be saved from spending eternal life there!

The next question then is what you need in order to be sure that heaven is your destiny. You say you understand our first central fact that each individual, including you and me, will die and deserves to die because of our sin. You say that you understand the second central fact that Jesus was without sin, and did not have to die; but he chose to die to pay the penalty that God demands for our sin. That penalty is death but Jesus paid the price on our behalf and took our place on that cross. And you say you even understand the third central fact that because of that finished work of Jesus on our behalf, we can go to heaven.

Well, you know all the facts! No problems there. And you agree, "Yes, it is all true!" But you may immediately ask, "Please tell me once again *how!*" If you are reading this book straight through in chapter order, you have already been exposed to the answer to the question of how to go to heaven.

Whether this is your first time to understand what I'm going to say, or your hundredth, please pay careful attention. Here are the wrong ideas about how someone goes to heaven.

We don't go to heaven just because we believe in the facts that we just rehearsed—that Jesus lived, died, and was raised again to life. James tells us that even the demons believe that. So, surely, it's not enough just to believe some facts.

We don't go to heaven because we believe some facts about Jesus *and* because we believe those facts, we try to live a good, Christian life. No one is good enough to live a perfect Christian life. Since God set the standard at perfection, and that is not obtainable, if that were the way to go to heaven, there would be no one there except Jesus, God the Father, and the Holy Spirit.

We don't go to heaven because we believe some facts about Jesus *and* then we make a decision that we will become a Christian. I know there are many people out there who teach something like this: that all you have to do is make a decision, and as a result of your decision, you are a Christian. But when you stop to think about it logically, if that sort of decision is something that we do on our own, through our own wisdom, thinking, efforts, and abilities, then it is doing "work." Ephesians 2:8–9 makes it very clear that our salvation from hell and a future in heaven *" . . . is not [our] own doing; it is the gift of God, not a result of works, so that no one may boast."*

So, we don't get to heaven because we believe certain facts; we don't get to heaven by being good enough; and we don't get to heaven by being wise enough to make a decision to become a Christian. Well then, how *do* we get to heaven?

The first half of Ephesians 2:8 that I left out just a moment ago says, *"For by grace you have been saved, through faith."* The way you are saved from hell to spend eternal life in heaven instead is through faith in Jesus. Faith *in* Jesus is not a decision *about* Jesus.

That subject was an essential part of the world's greatest Easter sermon. In Acts 13:38 Paul said, *"Let it be known to you therefore, brothers, that through this man forgiveness of sins is proclaimed to you, and by him everyone who believes* [in other words, everyone who has faith] *is freed from everything."*

Where does that faith, that ability to believe, come from? Do we conjure it up inside us? Do we wait until we grow strong enough spiritually to have it? Do we have to study a certain amount of the Bible to learn it? No, that's not it at all.

Ephesians 2 tells us that faith is the gift of God. The dictionary says faith is belief, devotion, trust especially *without* logical proof. If you think through the facts we've been talking about and come to a logical decision that they must be true, you are doing a "work." But Ephesians 2:8 says you have faith through grace, through a gift from God. Faith is something you are given, not something you decide.

You receive faith just like you receive any true gift. You just open your hands (or in this case, your heart) and receive it and say thank you. Now if you were to receive a freely given gift of $10,000,000—no strings attached—you'd probably want to say more than just a simple thank you, wouldn't you? Or if you were to receive a freely given gift of a replacement human heart just as you were to about to die, you'd probably want to say more than just a simple thank you, wouldn't you?

Well, that's the way it is with Christians. When we receive from God the gift of faith in Jesus, a gift that comes to us purely, simply through God's grace having done nothing at all on our part, and when it's the kind of gift that lasts for eternity and saves us from the most unthinkable eternal alternative, then we are overwhelmed and cannot say no.

Further, we would be saying more than a simple thank you. We would spend the rest of our lives, living in full commitment to Jesus, the Jesus who died in our place to pay the needed penalty for our sins. We would respond with love, not just to God, but to all those around us who so desperately need to receive that same gift we have received. Then we would be more like Jesus and it would be appropriate to call us by his name, Christian.

I'd like to end the lesson right here; this is indeed its high note. But Paul makes one more point in his sermon. Beginning in Acts 13:40, he says, *"Beware, therefore, lest what is said in the Prophets should come about . . . ."* In verse 41, Paul quoted from the prophet Habakkuk: *"'Look, you scoffers, be astounded and perish; for I am doing a work in your days, a work that you will not believe, even if one tells it to you.'"* The Old Testament prophecy about the Messiah, about the coming of God's own Son whom we call Jesus, is true. Jesus fulfilled all the Old Testament prophecy, and since the day of His resurrection there have been those in the world who hear the gospel message—this truly good, even great news—and who do not believe it. They are not given the gift of faith. They are the scoffers of the world, and unfortunately, they will surely perish.

If there is anyone reading this who continues to be a scoffer—who has not received the gift of faith and does not believe in Jesus—then, don't listen to Don Clements, listen to the very Word of God as spoken by the inspired apostle who preached the world's greatest Easter sermon. Keep reading and listening to it, and ask God over and over again to give you the gift of faith to believe it. Tell God your wonders and your doubts! Ask him to give you trust in Jesus alone for your salvation this very day. When he does, you will know the joy of that salvation, the joy of holding the keys to the mansions of heaven, the joy of eternal life (which begins *before* you die—immediately when you believe). Through faith in Jesus, whom God has indeed raised from the dead, you will be sure that you will go to heaven and live with Jesus, God the Father, and the Holy Spirit forever.

Chapter Fourteen
Ascension – "Glory on Thursday"

T he vast majority of Christians throughout the world gather on Sunday for worship services. We sometimes call Sunday "The Lord's Day" because it is the day that Jesus rose from the dead in his glorious resurrection.

Most Christians "celebrate glory" on Sunday, that is, they remember Jesus' resurrection into the glory of heaven. There are a few, such as the Seventh-Day Adventists, Seventh-Day Baptists, and the like, who worship on Saturday. They do so seeking to follow the Old Testament teaching that the Sabbath should be on the seventh day of the week, Saturday. They celebrate glory on Saturday.

Ordinarily, weekdays such as Monday, Tuesday, Wednesday, and Thursday don't cause too much excitement. They're just regular workdays. However, to some people, Friday is special. I'm not referring to those who are Jewish who worship on Friday. I'm referring to the fact that it's the last day of the workweek for many folks. Some people almost get religious about this fact, saying, "Thank God it's Friday!" I would venture to guess that many of them are not *really* thanking God but making an ungodly use of the term as a sign of emphasis.

I want to suggest that we give a little more attention to Thursday. This is not to say that we ought to transfer our regular worship service to Thursday, but we would do well to remember what happened to Jesus on a particular Thursday about two thousand years ago.

Sadly, many churches these days do not seem very impressed with that special event long ago. Some have never heard anything about a special Christian worship service held on Thursdays. Once upon a time, one of those was the well-known conference speaker and writer, R. C. Sproul.

R. C. tells a funny story about his introduction to a "liturgical year" celebration. R. C. had just returned from Amsterdam, where he worked on his doctor of theology degree. He had returned to the Pittsburgh area and was doing some secular work while he was trying to finish writing his dissertation. Well, one morning R. C. was driving with his new boss to play golf. It was 5:45 in the morning (they tell me golfers get up as early as preachers do), and R. C. was riding with his boss on their way to the links when they drove by a large Roman Catholic church. There, at that early hour on a Thursday, R. C. noticed that the parking lot was jammed with cars. He asked his boss, who he knew to be a nominal Roman Catholic, what could possibly be going on at the church so early on a Thursday morning? His boss thought for a moment, and then suddenly turned the car in at the church parking lot!

"R. C.," he said, "I can't play golf this morning. Today is the feast of the Ascension. I've got to go to church!" So for the first time in his ministry (R. C. had been ordained as a Presbyterian minister for almost ten years at this point), R. C. learned about a church celebration called the Feast of the Ascension.

It could well be argued that what happened to Jesus on Ascension Thursday was the *most* important event of his entire earthly life. It was extremely significant not only for him, but also for all who believe in him today. If that event had not happened, you could just as well forget about Jesus' birth, his teachings and miracles, his crucifixion, and even his resurrection. Though all those events would still be interesting, possibly even inspirational and educational, there would be no use making them into some kind of religion.

The concept of the ascension is far more than just going from one place to another. Ascension is the sign of assuming a throne. At the time of my writing, it has been fifty years since we've seen the queen crowned in England. When the next coronation comes along (whether is it Charles or his son William), you will see him walk up the steps and *assume* the throne. That's "ascension."

That special Thursday, forty days after Jesus' resurrection, made everything else about Jesus' life supremely important. The physician Luke, who was one of Paul's closest associates and longtime travel companion—the same Luke who wrote the gospel that bears his name—also wrote a book about the history of the early church. We know that book as the Acts of the Apostles (or more simply as Acts).

It is very significant to notice that Luke begins his history of the early church with this special Thursday event. Acts 1:1–11 says:

In the first book, O Theophilus, I have dealt with all that Jesus began to do and teach, [2]until the day when he was taken up, after he had given commands through the Holy Spirit to the apostles whom he had chosen. [3]To them he presented himself alive after his suffering by many proofs, appearing to them during forty days and speaking about the kingdom of God.

[4]And while staying with them he ordered them not to depart from Jerusalem, but to wait for the promise of the Father, which, he said, "you heard from me; [5]for John baptized with water, but you will be baptized with the Holy Spirit not many days from now."

[6]So when they had come together, they asked him, "Lord, will you at this time restore the kingdom to Israel?" [7]He said to them, "It is not for you to know times or seasons that the Father has fixed by his own authority. [8]But you will receive power when the Holy Spirit has come upon you, and you will be my witnesses in Jerusalem and in all Judea and Samaria, and to the end of the earth." [9]And when he had said these things, as they were looking on, he was lifted up, and a cloud took him out of their sight.

[10]And while they were gazing into heaven as he went, behold, two men stood by them in white robes, [11]and said, "Men of Galilee, why do you stand looking into heaven? This Jesus, who was taken up from you into heaven, will come in the same way as you saw him go into heaven."

That's the biblical record. On a Thursday, forty days after rising from the grave, Jesus ascended into heaven. He went up into the sky. That's a fact. "Glory on Thursday" was for Jesus, and also for you and me if we are joined to him by faith.

Let's think a little about Jesus' ascension, as the event has been called throughout Christian history. When we remember that unusual Thursday on which Jesus ascended into heaven, what should we think about? Well, first of all, we need to see Jesus' ascension as the reverse of his birth, sort of the *opposite* of Christmas.

When Jesus was born, God's eternal Son, the second person of the Trinity, actually became a human being. The fact that God became a "divine human" person in Jesus of Nazareth, whose natural mother was Mary and adoptive father was Joseph, still baffles and delights us, and invites our worship. He was both fully divine and fully human. When God became a man in Jesus, he humbled himself. He did that simply by becoming a member of our human race, voluntarily taking on himself the limitations of humanity.

What's more, God chose to take on himself the sin of humans. In the person of Jesus, God humbled himself by suffering the disgraceful death of the cross. In reading the Bible, we see the process of God's humiliation, which began at Jesus' birth, continued throughout his life, and ended with his death on the cross. That process of humiliation was initially reversed when Jesus rose from death to life, and was completed when he ascended back to glory with his Father in heaven.

So the overall picture of Jesus' life on earth looks like this. From birth to crucifixion is all humiliation. From resurrection to ascension is all glory. The first part of the picture is dark and dreary, and grim. The other part is dazzling and splendid. When Jesus was born, God became a human being. When Jesus ascended, the God-man Jesus entered into the fullness of the glory that he had with his Father in heaven even before the world began. Jesus' glorious exaltation is what Ephesians 1:20–21 is talking about when it says that God raised Jesus from the dead " . . . *and seated him at his right hand in the heavenly places, [21]far above all rule and authority and power and dominion, and above every name that is named, not only in this age but also in the one to come."*

If you want to grow as a Christian, you need to sit back at times and just think about Jesus. Think about what we have been considering here. Visualize Jesus' journey, as revealed in the Bible. He went from heaven's glory to this world—to the cross—to   hell—to   resurrection —and back to heaven's glory again. Jesus suffered and was glorified; and those who fix their eyes on Jesus in faith will also suffer in this life, yet be glorified in the life to come.

The second thing we need to consider in connection with Jesus' ascension is that Jesus is now the supreme ruler of all things. It might be easy for us to be impressed with the fact that the story of Jesus' life had a happy ending. After being crucified and buried, he rose to life again and ascended into heaven. Now, isn't that a nice story line? But if we react to Jesus' ascension only that way, we are missing the point of what happened.

When Jesus' disciples saw him being taken up into heaven, they were dumbstruck. (Can't you just picture them in Acts 1:10, standing there, gaping mouths wide open?) They witnessed Jesus' exaltation not only to a position of glory, but also to the position of supreme rulership. As Ephesians 1:20 says, God seated Jesus *"at his right hand in the heavenly places."* That term, *"his right hand,"* refers to Jesus' sovereign rule over the universe, over planet earth, over the nations, over the church, and over our lives.

Philippians 2:9–11 expands on this same theme. *"Therefore God has highly exalted him and bestowed on him the name that is above every name, [10]so that at the name of Jesus every knee should bow, in heaven and on earth and under the earth, [11]and every tongue confess that Jesus Christ is Lord, to the glory of God the Father."*

Our dismissal chorus at church each week says it all: "He is Lord!" Jesus ascended into heaven and now sits at the right hand of God the Father. By doing so, he announced his Lordship. Believers in the early Christian church were identified by their clear and simple confession, "Jesus is Lord." Only people who said that and meant it were considered to be Christians.

According to Romans 10:9, *" . . . if you confess with your mouth that Jesus is Lord and believe in your heart that God raised him from the dead, you will be saved."* When God saves you, you will truly believe that Jesus is Lord. According to 1 Corinthians 12:3, *"no one can say 'Jesus is Lord' except in the Holy Spirit."* So, a clear sign of the Spirit that you are saved and will go to heaven is that you do believe and declare that Jesus is Lord.

Remember, Jesus of Nazareth was crucified as a condemned criminal. No one has ever been humiliated as he was because no one ever deserved the humiliation less than he did. But God raised Jesus from the dead and gave him the name that is above every name. Jesus' ascension into heaven on that glorious Thursday proves that he is indeed the victorious Son of God. Jesus is Lord!

OK, so far we have understood two important lessons from the ascension. We learned first that the ascension was the opposite of Jesus' birth, reversing the cycle of humiliation and placing Jesus back once again to glorification in heaven. Second, we learned that Jesus' ascension was not just a private awards ceremony or a happy story ending, but the exaltation of him to the throne of sovereign authority and Lordship.

There is a third lesson we need to learn about the ascension—the "so what?" lesson. It's never enough just to learn more about historical Christianity or the stories about Jesus, as wonderful as those stories might be. The real question is, "What difference does it make in my life?"

Well, here's the difference. Every day I have to submit to the authority of Jesus in my life. I have to let him rule me with his love and power. As he put it himself while he was here among us (recorded in Luke 9:23), *"If anyone would come after me, let him deny himself and take up his cross daily and follow me."* I have to learn to live and love as Jesus did. I have to submit, deny myself, take up my cross, follow Jesus, and love others because Jesus is Lord, my Lord!

If you profess Jesus as your Savior, you also have to submit to Jesus. It's not enough to say that Jesus must have been a pretty good person, because no one says much bad about him. It's not enough to become excited about Jesus as some people do, going on and on about him and seeming to love him very much. Instead, what each of us needs to do is submit to the Lord Jesus Christ!

We have to confess that we are sinners and that our sins can be paid for only through the death of Jesus on the cross. Each of us must say, "I believe that Jesus died for me" and then we receive the gift of faith in him as our Savior. But we must also accept Jesus as our Lord and our Master. We must live our lives making all our life decisions based on what Jesus teaches us in his Word about what he wants us to do and how he wants us to do it.

The principles of guidance we learned in this book are absolutely worthless unless we acknowledge that Jesus is the Lord of our lives. We must follow his principles. Like everything else we do as Christians, we understand that we have no ability on our own to do a thing. Even following biblical principles of guidance can happen only as the Holy Spirit brings us God's power and grace to work in us and through us.

Jesus is Lord! I know that he is. Jesus' ascension to the place of exalted Lordship is a fact that is recorded in the Bible. Still, none of us were there to see what happened that day. Some people say that the account of Jesus' ascension is imaginary; it's like some kind of fairy tale. But it was a publicly witnessed event. Admittedly, one person cannot possibly make another person believe an event such as the ascension really happened. The Holy Spirit, however, *can* create faith in human hearts. Therefore, I have told you very directly what the Bible says and have called on you to believe it. I can and will also pray that the Holy Spirit will illuminate your heart so that you too will believe.

Today, right now, Jesus is Lord. Most people, including many members of Christian churches, don't want to hear anything about his Lordship. They want to live their own lives and achieve their own pleasure. "Forget about Jesus!" But the church is one place where the Lordship of Jesus must be continually acknowledged and experienced. The day is coming (we saw that in those verses we just read in Philippians 2) when every knee will bow before Jesus Christ. That is going to happen. Even those who reject Jesus now will someday be forced to bow before him and acknowledge that he truly is Lord.

In the church—now, today, every day—Jesus is confessed as Lord. Sundays are special because the Lord's glory is celebrated, but Thursdays are special too. (And so are Mondays and Tuesdays and Wednesdays and Fridays and Saturdays.) Maybe we should remember Jesus' ascension every Thursday (and every other day too), not just once a year on the special Thursday that is Ascension Day. The Lordship of Christ cannot be limited to just one day whether that day is Sunday, or Thursday, or any other day of the week you might select. Jesus is Lord *every* day. The effects of his ascension apply to our lives every single, solitary day that we live and breathe.

My prayer for you and for myself is that God's Spirit may more and more open our hearts and our wills and give us the grace we need to bow down to the Lordship of Jesus every day. And that as we humbly submit to our great Master and King, he will bless us and guide us, and (just as he promised in Acts 1:8) we will receive the same power he promised to each and every one of his disciples.

Chapter Fifteen
Second Coming – "The Sky is Falling,
the Sky is Falling"

When is Jesus going to return to earth? As Matthew 24:3 records it, his own disciples asked him that very question shortly before he died. So far, nobody has come up with the correct date, but it's not for a lack of trying.

Back in the 1980s, Edgar Wisenant, a contemporary of Hal Lindsay, the godfather of all the recent evangelical Bible prophecy fanaticism - wrote a book titled *88 Reasons Why the Rapture Will Be in 1988*. The book was selling so fast that stores had a hard time keeping it on the shelves.

Jesus must not have found those 88 reasons very convincing. The year 1988 came and went, and nothing happened. As you might expect, the book isn't selling very well anymore.

Another person who made precise predictions about the end was Charles Taze Russell, the founder of the Jehovah's Witnesses. Russell was absolutely certain that the world would end in 1914, but he himself died in 1916 without seeing it happen.

Russell's successor as head of the Witnesses' Watchtower Society was Joseph Rutherford. (Did you catch that name— *Watch*tower?) He coined the slogan, "Millions now living will never die," and revised the date, predicting 1925 would be the year the world would end. However, Rutherford saw 1925 pass by uneventfully and he died in 1943.

If we look farther back in history, we find people who thought Jesus would come again at the end of the first thousand years of the church's existence. As the year 1000 approached, some people stopped working, sold everything they had, and bought a little plot of ground near a church or monastery to wait on holy ground for Jesus to appear . . . sort of a "Y1K" phenomenon. Instead, the world moved into another millennium, and yet a third, without interruption, and those people had to find a way to make a living again.

Of course, there are dozens and dozens of other authors writing in similar ways today. If you run a search for "Bible prophecy" in Amazon's website, you'll get more than 400 hits. Certainly tens, if not hundreds of thousands of American Christians are extremely interested in biblical prophecy. The very popular "Left Behind" fiction series was based on this same premise.

Like any Christian who believes in the total truth of the Word of God, I too know that Jesus will come to earth a second time and establish in fullness and glory the kingdom of God and the new heaven and new earth. And like many Christians, I too long for that day because I know that all suffering will end for me then.

But unlike some Christians, I do *not* feel that we should expend an inordinate amount of the time God has given us to go around seeking and calling attention to such possible present signs. People who put so much of their effort and study into this matter of end-times prophecy that they have no time left for anything else remind me of Chicken Little.

You remember the Oakey Oaks crowd, right? Chicken Little and all her Misfits friends went running around yelling, "The sky is falling, the sky is falling." This continued until they were finally confronted by the wise old owl who revealed the truth to them. It had only been an acorn falling from a tree. So let's you and I look at our wise old owl, which of course is the Bible, and see what we can learn about the second coming of Jesus.

While there are a number of places in the New Testament we can learn about the second coming of Jesus, I believe the best place to start is with Jesus' own words in Luke 17:20–37:

> Being asked by the Pharisees when the kingdom of God would come, he answered them, "The kingdom of God is not coming with signs to be observed, [21]nor will they say, 'Look, here it is!' or 'There!' for behold, the kingdom of God is in the midst of you."
>
> [22]And he said to the disciples, "The days are coming when you will desire to see one of the days of the Son of Man, and you will not see it. [23]And they will say to you, 'Look, there!' or 'Look, here!' Do not go out or follow them. [24]For as the lightning flashes and lights up the sky from one side to the other, so will the Son of Man be in his day. [25]But first he must suffer many things and be rejected by this generation.

26"Just as it was in the days of Noah, so will it be in the days of the Son of Man. 27They were eating and drinking and marrying and being given in marriage, until the day when Noah entered the ark, and the flood came and destroyed them all. 28Likewise, just as it was in the days of Lot—they were eating and drinking, buying and selling, planting and building, 29but on the day when Lot went out from Sodom, fire and sulfur rained from heaven and destroyed them all—30so will it be on the day when the Son of Man is revealed.

31"On that day, let the one who is on the housetop, with his goods in the house, not come down to take them away, and likewise let the one who is in the field not turn back. 32Remember Lot's wife. 33Whoever seeks to preserve his life will lose it, but whoever loses his life will keep it. 34I tell you, in that night there will be two in one bed. One will be taken and the other left. 35There will be two women grinding together. One will be taken and the other left."

36And they said to him, "Where, Lord?" 37He said to them, "Where the corpse is, there the vultures will gather."

Our goal in examining this passage is to learn some important things about the second coming. We will not try to cover all the details, mind you. That would take far too long and require lots of speculation. Actually, I want to avoid speculation. I want to examine what our priorities as Christians in the early twenty-first century should be, in light of the fact of the second coming of Jesus to establish the kingdom of God on earth.

To begin with, we ought to be sure we all understand what is meant by the biblical term "kingdom of God" when it is used in such a context. Jesus uses this term many times in his teaching. Along with the synonymous term "kingdom of heaven," which is mostly used by Matthew, the term appears more than a hundred times in the Gospels, at least thirty-five of them here in the Gospel of Luke. With that many references to something, we can get a pretty clear picture of what Jesus is talking about.

In the very widest of outlines, we can divide teachings on the kingdom of God into two categories. First, to a great extent the kingdom of God is already on earth in the reign of Jesus through his church. You will remember we discussed that back in Chapter Nine. We know that from the impact of the final phrase in Luke 17:21 when Jesus said, *"[the] kingdom of God is in the midst of you."* Some translations say *"within you"* but that gives the wrong impression of what Jesus meant. It is not *in* each Christian; it is in the midst of all Christians, that is, in the church.

But Jesus is saying this as merely an aside. His real concern is to teach about the other major category of the kingdom of God—the coming of the kingdom in its fullness and glory at the second coming. Notice that to the Pharisees, Jesus spoke of the present reign of the kingdom, which was evident in him. To his disciples, however (Luke 17:22), he turned his attention to the other aspect, which of course is the second coming of Jesus to this earth.

So, the focus of this chapter is the second coming. We want to look for the issues you and I must know concerning the second coming and put aside all the crazy stuff and controversial differences of opinions concerning some elements. We want to focus on the things on which there is agreement among most Christians, or at least those who continue to follow the teachings of the Reformation.

Basically, we will look at three things. One will be what the second coming will be like in a general sense. The second will be what the results of the second coming will be for various people (since there are some real differences). Third will be to decide what is the most important thing that each of us needs to know about the second coming.

What is the second coming going to be like? One thing we know for sure from Luke 17 is that, when it happens, the second coming will be quite visible to everyone. It won't be a big secret! We get this from verse 20 in the ESV, which says, *"The kingdom of God is not coming with signs to be observed."* The King James Version renders the key word here *"with observations."* That is fine, but the NIV is very much off track when it translates this as *"does not come visibly."* You see the strong influence here of those who held strongly to a pre-tribulation, pre-millennium view of the Second Coming, involved in that translation team.

The Greek word used here is also used elsewhere in reference to watching the stars. Here it means that the anxious watching and searching of every phenomenon that might be an indication of the coming of the kingdom is just not necessary. Jesus' saying the kingdom does *not* come with such close observations must be taken to mean that such will not be necessary in order to notice the coming of the kingdom.

This interpretation is entirely in agreement with Luke 17:21. *"Nor will they say, 'Look, here it is!' or 'There!'"* Now this applies not only to the answer given to the Pharisees, it also applies to the second coming. These words are repeated in verse 23, and there as elsewhere they are concerned with the premature and false alarms that the Son of Man is about to come in the immediate future.

When Jesus says, *"The kingdom of God is not coming with signs to be observed"* he does not mean that we shouldn't heed the signs of the times. Rather, he rejects the idea that the ultimate coming of the kingdom is something that can only be detected by the well-trained eyes of the so-called prophecy experts. The kingdom's appearance will be so overpowering that nobody will be in need of any classes or correspondence courses in order to know what's going on. There will be no doubt about it to anyone.

In fact, in Luke 17:24, we see the illustration of lightning used. This picture is not necessarily meant to indicate the suddenness of the coming of the kingdom, but, in the context, is intended to illustrate how clearly it will be seen. We all realize that when lightning comes in whatever area we might be, we don't have any doubt about whether or not it has arrived. It can be clearly seen by everyone. This is the one way we can be sure of the nature of the second coming.

In spite of this, there are countless numbers of Christians who believe in a "secret" rapture. You've probably seen their bumper stickers, such as, "Caution: This car will be driverless in case of the Rapture." There is only one passage in the Bible that speaks of a "rapture" of any kind and that is 1

Thessalonians 4:16–17. It says, *"For the Lord himself will descend from heaven with a cry of command, with the voice of an archangel, and with the sound of the trumpet of God. And the dead in Christ will rise first. ¹⁷Then we who are alive, who are left, will be caught up together with them in the clouds to meet the Lord in the air, and so we will always be with the Lord."*

Our English versions speak of being "caught up." The Old Latin translation uses the word *"raptus."* Now, if this rapture, this being caught up to meet the Lord in the air, is preceded by a loud command, the archangel's thunderous voice, and the trumpet call of God, how can it be a secret? No, when Jesus comes, it will be public, visible, and noisy, and the whole world will know that the King has arrived and that history has reached its conclusion.

Even though the truth is that the second coming of Jesus will be able to be seen clearly, still there are going to be some people around who will ignore it. They won't ignore it because they aren't going to be able to see it. They just won't *want* to see it. Luke 17:25–30 teaches that the concept of the rejection of Jesus by *"this generation"* is not referring only to Jesus' particular age (although it was quite true back then). Rather we see a common usage of this term elsewhere in the Bible, and from that we find this truth applies to any and every generation.

So, the important idea in verse 25 does not involve any particular generation either before or after Jesus lived. It involves *rejection*. There will be people who have rejected Jesus as their Lord and therefore they will not want to see his return to earth. Jesus gives us two very well-known examples of just this sort of attitude from the pages of the Old Testament.

The first of these concerns the people at the time of the great flood. (Read Genesis 6–9 if you are not familiar with this story.) Just as all the people of the world except for Noah and his family had rejected the authority of God and had done their own thing and ignored God, so will there be people at the time of the second coming of Jesus who will ignore him. We certainly can't help but think that the people of Noah's time knew it was raining, as it never had before in history. They could clearly see that but still they rejected God. At some point when the floodwaters rose high enough, they realized too late the authority of God.

The same thing was true of the people involved in the second example, the people of Sodom and Gomorrah. (Read Genesis 18–19 if you are not familiar with this story.) Here, too, people had rejected God and his promises for them. When Lot told his sons-in-law the place would be destroyed, they thought he was joking. When it began to rain down sulfur, they learned too late that it was no joke.

I think we can see the same sort of thing in our own human natures, can't we? How many times have we been in a situation in our own lives where there was something true that could be clearly seen or known, and somehow we refused to react to it? We even have the modern cliché, "You can't see the forest for the trees."

In spite of the fact that the second coming of Jesus will be able to be seen clearly by all, there is a group of people who either will not understand this or will not believe this. They will misread some signs and make some false pronouncements about the coming of the kingdom. We find this taught in Luke 17:22–23. These are the "Chicken Littles" of the world.

It's true that we would all like to see the final establishment of the kingdom of God during our lifetimes. But we must be careful not to let this desire allow us to be led astray by people who keep pointing to signs they think are indicative of the immediate return of Jesus. Our day and age is full of such people.

I'm afraid there are many Christians who can easily be led away from the first priorities in their lives and spend all their time and efforts on becoming "observers." In truth, there is no need for such close observations. The whole impact of what we have been talking about is that, when the kingdom of God really comes in its fullness at the second coming of Jesus, all who have not rejected Jesus will clearly see it no matter how little or how much they know about Bible prophecy.

Since this is true, it is the logical conclusion then that what is important for us to know about the kingdom of God is not so much *when* it will come or what particular signs may or may not occur, but rather what the *results* will be. Since this is so essential, let's take a close look at these results.

Luke 17:34–35 shows us clearly that the first immediate result of the return of Jesus will be a complete and absolute division of all people into two categories. From their beds, from their work, from wherever they might be, people will be divided into two distinct groups. In explaining one of his parables

(Matthew 25), Jesus describes this division as that of sheep and goats. I think we could properly use some simple biblical language and just call these two groups the saved and the lost.

Let's look first at the lost and see what they are like. Luke 17:31–32 says one thing is true of the lost, that they are all hung up on their worldly possessions. The startling illustration used goes right back to the story of Sodom and its destruction. In Genesis 19, when God was leading Lot and his family away from the destruction, he told them very clearly not to look back. In other words, they were not to be concerned with anything connected with the worldly life they left behind. They were to trust completely in God. Yet Lot's wife could not hold that trust. She just had to look back on the home she had left behind. She turned into a pillar of salt. That truly is an example of what the lost person is like.

We can see that same picture today even among people in churches. People allow their own possessions, their own jobs, their own material wealth to be foremost in their minds and concerns. Within Christian circles, you often see it expressed by people who are more concerned with church buildings and finances than they are with the true teachings about Jesus— who he is and what he has done—and with the ministry that springs from that truth. Remember, these worldly things are not the sign of a Christian, but rather of one who is lost.

Another illustration of the lost person at the time of the second coming is found in Luke 17:37. In response to the question from the disciples of where the lost man would be left, Jesus uses the illustration of where *"the vultures will gather."* By the way, the King James Version is just plain wrong in this verse by using "eagles" for the translation. Clearly carrion-feeding birds such as vultures are in view here.

The point being made by Jesus is that the place where the lost will be left is a place of decay, where it would be common to find vultures. This then is the thing that is true of the lost person. He or she will be decayed, as we know full well that those who reject God are guilty of great moral decay. So, we must be sure there is not that kind of moral decay in our own lives.

There is a third illustration of what the lost person will be like, and this illustration comes in the most important verse in Luke 17, verse 33. The most striking thing about lost persons is that they will be seeking to save themselves. We certainly can see that they will not be successful.

Are you trying to save yourself? Are you trying to be good enough to be a Christian? I once heard a woman in a Presbyterian church where I was serving talking about a lady she wanted the Women in the Church to invite to speak at one of their events. The lady in the church was quite impressed with this woman's gifts. She said, "Oh, Mrs. So-And-So is such a good woman. I'd never be good enough to be a Mormon like she is—I'm just barely good enough to be a Presbyterian!"

I guess it's funny the first time you hear this story, but the more you think about it, the more you see how many people in the church still think they can somehow be good enough to make it to heaven. Or they think they can be good enough to be a church member. Or worst of all, they think they can be good enough to save themselves. But it will never happen! Only Jesus was good enough. Without Jesus, anyone who tries to be good, or to save himself, will surely be herded in with the goats. He will surely be lost on the last day.

What is Jesus telling us as he is talking to his disciples? What does he mean about people who will be more concerned with worldly possessions than with the things of God? What does he mean about people who will be guilty of moral decay? What does he mean about people who will try to save themselves? Maybe we better look at the other side of the picture, which is certainly a much brighter side.

The other side of the picture is in the other half of Luke 17:33. There is one simple reference made to the other type of person, to those whom we are referring to as saved. All we are told about the person who will be saved at the second coming is that he shall lose his life.

Seems a little contradictory on the surface, doesn't it? Those who will be saved are those who shall lose their lives. In order to understand this verse, we must understand the main teaching of the Bible. We must understand God's plan of salvation—his way of saving people. The great message of the Bible (from Genesis to John 3:16 to Revelation), throughout all the pages of the Gospels, is that the only way one can enter heaven or the kingdom of God is through knowing Jesus as Lord and Savior. There is no other true religion. There is only one way to be saved. (We will look at this in more detail in the next chapter as well.)

To really understand Luke 17:32, you have to understand the necessity of trusting in Jesus as both Savior and Lord. We trust in Jesus as Savior when we trust the fact that his death at

Calvary was atonement for all our sins. On the cross, he made a complete payment, once and for all, for the guilt and sins of anyone who trusts in Jesus.

A person cannot trust in Jesus as Savior and then not trust in him, at the same time, as Lord. That's what is meant in verse 33 by losing one's life. It means that you lose control of your life; you turn that control over to Jesus and let him be Lord and Master of it all. It means that you do things his way, not your way. It means that you follow the teachings of the Word of God in the Bible. It means that you become in reality a servant, a slave to Jesus, as Paul so often refers to the relationship. That is the way you lose your life.

When you think about it, what are you really losing that you need or want anyway? Is there anything that you need that God cannot provide for you? Of course not! God is a providential and all-powerful God, and he will clearly do anything that is necessary for you. So there is nothing you need that you lose by turning your life over to Jesus.

Now, if we understand clearly the difference between being saved and lost, we are in a position to understand the most important thing about the coming of the kingdom of God. It is not important for us to know precisely what it will be like when Jesus comes again because we already know we will be able to see it clearly when it happens.

So the thing that is important for us to be sure we know is what will be the results of the second coming, or to see the difference between being lost and being saved. By the time of the second coming, it will be too late to make any change from one to the other. The change must be made now, precisely because we can't know when he will come again.

The really important thing is to be sure that we will be found among the saved, among the sheep, when Jesus comes again. This means we have to be sure that we have "lost our lives," that we indeed trust Jesus to be the Lord of our lives. We don't hold back anything—not our leisure time, not our employment, not our finances—nothing. Only then can we be certain in our hearts and minds that Jesus is our Lord and that we will be found among the sheep. As I explained earlier, I am not talking about making a decision to trust Jesus, but I am urging us to be assured in our own hearts and minds that Jesus has saved us.

It's not difficult to tell the difference between a goat and a sheep, now is it? Suppose you were to see a goat walking around with a sign around his neck saying, "I am a sheep." You'd know full well that it was still a goat, right? Well, let me tell you. It is just the same way with you and me. A person cannot hang a sign around his or her neck saying, "I am a Christian," and fool God for one minute. The only way not to be a goat— the only way to truly be a sheep of the Great Shepherd—is for Jesus to put in you a trust in him as Lord and Savior.

We must not be swept along by all the "Chicken Littles" who scurry to and fro crying, "The sky is falling, the sky is falling!" We must keep our eye always pointed on the crucial issues of the gospel, about Jesus being Savior and Lord. Only those that are truly saved, those who are truly sheep, will live and reign with Jesus forever in the kingdom of God. We must be zealous to share the good news of the gospel so that any who are goats today might hear, might seek, and might know God.

Chapter Sixteen
Exclusiveness – "No Other Name"

B ack in the days when I was able to walk longer distances, I used to enjoy sightseeing. Particularly, I would enjoy learning about the early history of the town or region we were visiting.

Sometimes I would have read a lot of history before visiting a place such as Hawaii or Washington, D.C. Then the sightseeing would give reality to my mental pictures. But sometimes I would know absolutely nothing about the place before I arrived. In those cases, I was usually very fascinated to learn little-known historical facts.

One such place was Key West, Florida. Before our three daughters began going off to college, we would try to take a family vacation each year. Sometimes we would try to get away from the cold of winter in the Virginia mountains, and head south. One year we flew to Key West.

One of the first things we did when we arrived was to ride a trolley around Key West, getting several hours' worth of history as we toured. I had not realized that the original settlers of Key West were primarily people from the Bahamas whose main occupation was salvaging the many ships that wrecked on the great coral reef just offshore from the Keys.

Anyway, our tour guide went into great detail to tell us how these salvage experts would wait for some signal that a ship had wrecked, and they would all race from the port to see who would get there first. For many years, there were no rules in this business. Finally, however, the government passed a law that said the first captain to arrive on scene had salvage rights. He could then sign on only those others he wanted to help him take off all the gold and other valuables from these wrecked ships.

In hearing those stories, it dawned on me that "salvage" might not be the best word to describe what they were doing. Actually, "plundering" might be a more fitting description.

Usually when we think of words such as "salvage" or "save" or even "salvation," we think in terms of people being rescued from a tough predicament. For example, you might think of something like the incident that a fellow named Robert Bell writes about in his book, *In Peril on the Sea* (naming it by using a phrase from the famous hymn, "Eternal Father, Strong To Save.")

Bell tells about being saved after floating on a raft in the Caribbean for twenty days. It happened during World War II. Bell was only eleven years old when the freighter he was on was torpedoed. He was one of nineteen people who survived on an eight-by-ten-foot raft. By the time a British destroyer picked them up, two people had died, and the rest were nearly starved, covered with sores, and totally exhausted.

Bell tells in his book how he and his sister and mother could hardly fall asleep the first time they lay down on a real mattress after being saved from the sea. They were practically delirious with joy. Now, that's a story about being saved from real danger, isn't it?

In this chapter, I want to consider a very well-known statement in the New Testament about being saved. It comes from Acts 4:12: *"And there is salvation in no one else, for there is no other name under heaven given among men by which we must be saved."* The Apostle Peter made that statement soon after the Holy Spirit was poured out on Pentecost. Let's go back and pick up the context for this verse by looking at what was happening when Peter made that extraordinary statement of the exclusiveness of the Christian religion. Acts 4:1–12 says:

> *[1]And as they were speaking to the people, the priests and the captain of the temple and the Sadducees came upon them, [2]greatly annoyed because they were teaching the people and proclaiming in Jesus the resurrection from the dead. [3]And they arrested them and put them in custody until the next day, for it was already evening. [4]But many of those who had heard the word believed, and the number of the men came to about five thousand.*
>
> *[5]On the next day their rulers and elders and scribes gathered together in Jerusalem, [6]with Annas the high priest and Caiaphas and John and Alexander, and all who were of the high-priestly family. [7]And when they had set them in the midst, they inquired, "By what power or by what name did you do this?" [8]Then Peter, filled with the Holy Spirit, said to them, "Rulers of the people and elders, [9]if we are being examined today concerning a good deed done to a crippled man, by what means this man has been healed, [10]let it be known to all of you and to all the people of Israel that*

by the name of Jesus Christ of Nazareth, whom you crucified, whom God raised from the dead—by him this man is standing before you well.

[11]"This Jesus is the stone that was rejected by you, the builders, which has become the cornerstone. [12]And there is salvation in no one else, for there is no other name under heaven given among men by which we must be saved."

Notice the excitement, the drama, the conflict in that scene. Or maybe this story doesn't interest you at all. Things are going great for you. You feel fit as a fiddle. Your work is going reasonably well. School is humming right along. Everything's just fine, thank you very much. Being saved is the last thing on your mind.

If that is the case, I understand. But I also know that circumstances can change overnight. It doesn't take very much to throw us into a panic. An accident can paralyze a strong grown man. Or you may suddenly feel a sharp pain shooting down your arm as your chest tightens—you're afraid you may be having a heart attack. Think about September 11, 2001. I know, all of that seems long ago now. But there were literally thousands of families who suddenly had the rug pulled out from under them that day. Sooner or later, every one of us will find ourselves in a situation where we realize that we need help!

In a sense, the people living in Jerusalem on the day the events in Acts 4 took place had all just been confronted with something so stirring that it caused them to think about needing help. Just preceding this in Acts 3, a grown man they had known for many years had been miraculously healed from lameness since birth. He had been saved from a life of utter poverty and dependence.

That miracle had blown the city of Jerusalem apart. Everyone was talking about it, so much so that the religious leaders, feeling threatened, called the disciples of Jesus in to put a stop to this kind of thing. It was in this situation that Peter and John proclaimed the saving power of the name of Jesus.

The saving power of which Peter and John spoke, however, was not from drowning at sea or some great personal or health crisis; it was not even from some life-long handicap. Rather, the salvation that the disciples talked about is what the Apostle John described in its fullness as *"eternal life."* He wrote in John 3:15 *"that whoever believes in him* [Jesus] *shall have eternal life."* You see, ultimately Jesus is the only one who can save you. Jesus is the only one who can bring you eternal life. That's the heart of the message of the disciples that day in response to the threats from the religious leaders.

Take a close look at what Peter said in Acts 4:12. Look at it as if your life depends on it—because it does. *"There is salvation in no one else, for there is no other name under heaven given among men by which we must be saved."* Perhaps you are puzzled by that statement. How can we be saved only by the *name* of Jesus? After all, being saved by a name is certainly not a common idea.

Well, consider for a moment how names function in our lives. A personal name represents both a person and his work—what he or she does, who the person really is. Take

Dale Earnhardt for instance. The minute you hear his name (if you are any kind of NASCAR race fan at all), you get a picture of him in your mind. You think of his achievements, his being probably the greatest driver of all times, or even the picture of the crash that took his life. You see, the name Dale Earnhardt tells you a lot.

Think about some people who are so famous that they only need one-word names, or simply initials: Madonna . . . Tiger . . . Annika. You hear that name and immediately a great amount of information comes into your mind about the person and his or her work.

Even beyond the case of popular personalities today is the fact that in the Bible, the name of Jesus is more special. Back in those days, if someone proclaimed something in "the name of Caesar," it would have meant that the power of the emperor and his entire kingdom could be brought to bear on that particular situation. In modern history, the phrase "in the name of the king" or perhaps "in the name of the emperor" implies the authority and imperial power of that monarch.

Yet there is something even deeper than that at work in the biblical usage of a name. In the original language of the Old Testament, the word "name" was used as a sacred synonym for the name of God. In order not to break the Third Commandment (taking God's name in vain), the Hebrews would not even pronounce in their own language the word for God.

We believe it would have been pronounced as "Yahweh" (Yah-way), but they never said that word. They never even wrote that word down. They would always use a synonym.

Sometimes the synonym was "Lord" (*Adoni* in the Hebrew). That became the practice among Greek-speaking Jews of Jesus' day and age. But among the older Jewish people, the most common synonym used was simply the word "name." So when someone said "in the name" it was generally understood to be a reference to God.

So it is clear that when Peter and John say that the only way to find salvation is through the name of Jesus, they were just emphasizing the same thing Peter had emphasized in his sermon in Acts 3, that through the power of the name of Jesus, God had healed the man lame since birth. No doubt about it: this Jesus was indeed God, not just some new prophet.

When the Bible says that we can be saved through the name of Jesus, it means that the person and work of Jesus, the Son of God, makes salvation possible. The speaking of the *name* does not have a saving power in itself. You don't say "Jeeesus" in some special way and then some magic happens. But it is who Jesus is and what he has done that make salvation possible for everyone who believes in him.

I want to emphasize that the Bible in Acts 4 is speaking about salvation in the ultimate, eternal sense of the word. The Bible is not just talking about one crippled man's healing from his physical problem. Notice back in Acts 3 that the cripple's healing brought about a total transformation of the man. He had never walked before, but when he was healed, he jumped around and praised God as he accompanied the apostles into the temple. This unusually dramatic healing is a symbol of the total salvation referred to in the Bible. If we believe in Jesus, God will save us from eternal death in hell. That is *total* salvation.

"And there is salvation in no one else, for there is no other name under heaven given among men by which we must be saved." When you read Acts 4:12, you can see at least three elements in that sentence that emphasize Jesus as our only Savior—that emphasize the exclusiveness of Christ.

Peter, speaking on behalf of all the apostles, said three key things:

- *"no one else"*

- *"no other name under heaven"*

- *"must"*

In other words, to be saved, you *must* use this name. This name is necessary for salvation. It's like when someone urgently asks you for directions from your house to the hospital. You live here on High School Hill and so you tell them, "At the traffic light on Route 460, you *must* turn left. If you turn right you can't get there in time."

Now, does it offend or bother you (or others) to hear that you can be saved *only* through the name of Jesus? *No* other name. NO other way. Maybe you think you have another way. Maybe you respect Jesus of Nazareth, but you feel very uncomfortable with the idea that he is the *only* Savior. Jews,

Muslims, Buddhists, Hindus, Scientologists, New-Agers—none of them are saved. None of them will go to heaven. Isn't that some sort of exaggeration?

I used to think that way. The day I sat down with the pastor of the church my wife and I were attending in New Jersey to talk about spiritual things, he showed me the plan of salvation and said unashamedly that there was no other way, no other name. I argued. That didn't seem fair!

I'm afraid there are far too many people who consider themselves to be evangelical Christians, but have a difficult time with this point. They say they believe the Bible is the Word of God. They have personally put their own trust in Jesus for salvation, but they somehow believe (or at least, they act as if they believe) that there is some other way of salvation.

That's the way it looks to me at least. Why else would people be so reluctant to be involved in evangelism? If they *really* believed that Jesus was the only way to salvation—if they believed it with all their hearts, and thus knew that *anyone else* was destined for eternity in hell—they would demand that the church offer them training in how to tell people about Jesus.

If it bothers you to think that Jesus' name is the *only* way of salvation, let me tell you that it *really* bothered those Jewish religious leaders even more when they first heard it. Peter and John were not exaggerating for dramatic effect either. They knew very well that their statement about Jesus was more controversial and dangerous than anything else they could possibly say.

In Acts 4:12, the men who sat in that room judging the apostles represented an extremely elaborate system of salvation. Many of them were members of a strict religious party that had developed a way of achieving righteousness through keeping the law. For them, Jesus was the name of a crucified criminal. In their judgment, Jesus deserved to die, for he was guilty of blasphemy. He had called himself the Son of God.

When the apostles proclaimed that Jesus alone was the Savior, they were contradicting, insulting, and challenging these leaders. By rights, these religious leaders should have leapt from their seats and stoned these two blasphemers. But, according to verses 21 and 22 of this chapter, at the end of their discussions, *"when they had further threatened them, they let them go, finding no way to punish them, because of the people, for all were praising God for what had happened. [22]For the man on whom this sign of healing was performed was more than forty years old."*

What had happened was that the crucified Jesus had risen from the dead and had mightily performed a miracle through the apostles in the sight of everyone. The miracle was so spectacular that the Jewish leaders could not deny that something extraordinary had happened. They were angry when the apostles told them that the Jesus whom they had crucified was the only Savior. Even though the religious leaders wanted to keep this idea from spreading, they could not think of a single way to do so. Frustrated, they finally let the disciples go free.

Now then, the apostles' statement about the exclusive saving power of Jesus raises some serious questions for us today. For instance, what about people who have never heard about Jesus and therefore haven't had a chance to believe in him? What about the followers of other religions? Aren't many of them good people? Is the Bible really this *exclusive* about salvation?

I have raised these questions because they are real. I have not raised them because I have a perfect answer to all of them. I do not. For example, what about all those people who lived before Jesus was born? Did they perish because they never knew Jesus? It strikes me as extremely sad if that was the case.

The only way we can answer questions such as these is on the basis of the Bible. When we do that, we cannot keep from concluding that Jesus alone provides salvation for people of *all* times and places. Even Old Testament believers, living before Jesus, were saved through Jesus. Their religion pointed forward to a savior, a messiah, whose name turned out to be Jesus. Their entire religion was pointed forward to Jesus and was fulfilled in him. But there were others, the so-called "noble pagans" outside the influence of biblical religion, who by our definition perished because they would not have known Jesus. I cannot give a final answer on them. All I can say is that the Bible declares that salvation is exclusive; it is *only* in the one name of Jesus.

Please listen carefully. Even if you have problems with the concept of the exclusivity of Christianity (that there is only one way of going to heaven, through faith in Jesus), *do not let that keep you from believing in Jesus yourself.*

Admit that you don't understand why there is only one way of salvation. If you wish, admit that if it had been up to you, you would have come up with several ways of salvation. Admit, too, that as a human being you will never be able to understand the mysterious ways of God. Then remember that God has come into *your* life and has told you about Jesus, the only way of salvation. God has revealed to you that way of salvation in this message you have heard (most likely not for the first time) about Jesus.

Jesus paid for human sin by dying on the cross. He then rose from the dead and ascended into heaven. There Jesus continually prays for his children who are still in this world, surrounding us with his love and filling us with his Holy Spirit.

There comes a time when you and I have to put aside all our questions and arguments and take a good look at our own relationship with God through his Son, Jesus. Each of us must ask, "What about me? Do I really believe in Jesus as my Savior? Have I made him the center, the Lord of my life? Do I love him? Do I want to serve him? Am I willing to share his name with others?" Those are the most important questions we can ever ask. You need salvation more than anything else. Maybe you have a big "want list" for God to consider. What you *need most* is the assurance that you're saved from sin and hell. You need salvation.

I hope you understand what I am telling you in this chapter. It's really pretty simple. Peter sums it up in verse 12. *"There is salvation in no one else, for there is no other name under heaven given among men by which we must be saved."*

If you want to be saved, if you want to go to heaven, you must believe in Jesus. If you have close relatives or friends or neighbors, who you want to receive salvation, they must believe in Jesus. Share this message with them. There is no other name. There is no other way.

S hema Yisrael! Yahweh Elohim, Yahweh Achad! Va-ha-vat' et Yahweh Elohim bacal le-va'vet, vucal naf'sha-ca, vucal mo-day'ach!

These are two of the most famous verses from the Hebrew Bible. They are so famous they have a special name. They are called the *Shema (ssh-MAH)*, after the first word in the verses. They are so famous, in fact, that every pious Jew—even yet today—repeats them twice each and every day. They are the words from our text, Deuteronomy 6:4–5, spoken in the Hebrew language that Moses himself spoke and in which most of the Old Testament is written. Consider them again.

Shema Yisrael! Yahweh Elohim, Yahweh Achad! Va-ha-vat' et Yahweh Elohim bacal le-va'vet, vucal naf'sha-ca, vucal mo-day'ach!

Do you see that first word, *Shema*? It is an imperative. Moses is calling on the people of God (whose Old Testament name was of course Israel) to hear, to listen to something very important. It was so important that it bore repetition over and over again. What is that important? First, he says in verse 4, *Yahweh Elohim, Yahweh Achad! "The Lord our God, the Lord is one."*

Remember the context here. Deuteronomy is written as Israel is completing her forty years of wandering in the wilderness. The nation is poised to enter the Promised Land,

and before they go across the Jordan River, Moses is summarizing all that God has done for them up to this point.

The purpose of this summary is to remind Israel how God has shown his love and mercy to them. In Deuteronomy 5, Moses has just repeated the Ten Commandments. Now in Chapter 6, he is reminding them that their God, who Moses most frequently refers to by the name *Yahweh Elohim* (The Lord our God), is the one and only true God. There is no other God.

Many of you know how the story goes, don't you? In just a few short years, the people of Israel forgot this important truth that Moses had urged them to hear. They entered the Promised Land and quickly bogged down in the culture of the day. They worshiped all the idols, all the heathen gods of the people who lived in that land, instead of worshiping the one true and living God.

Now you say, just what does all this have to do with love? The title of our chapter said we were going to learn something about love. Even more importantly, what difference does it make anyway if those Jewish people three thousand years ago worshiped some idols? Let me answer those questions for you carefully because if you don't understand the answers, you not only won't understand this chapter's lesson, you probably won't understand what the Bible teaches about love.

The first question is, What does the call to Israel to hear that their God is the only true God have to do with love? The answer is in the very next words out of the mouth of Moses: *Va-ha-vat' et Yahweh Elohim bacal le-va'vet, vucal nafsha-ca, vucal mo-day'ach!* If you're reading the Bible in an English translation, it goes something like this: *"You shall love the Lord your God with all your heart and with all your soul and with all your might."*

Here is the great call to Israel to love God completely. How important is this one little verse, really? So what! So what if Moses said those words. So what if pious Jews today repeat these words twice every day. I'm not Jewish. I'm a Christian. Well, if you're a follower of Jesus Christ, let me tell you how important Jesus thought this verse was.

One day, one of those troublesome Pharisees had just heard Jesus rebuke the other Jewish leadership group known as the Sadducees. This Pharisee decides he will try to outdo his rivals and trip Jesus up. In Matthew 22:34, the conversation goes like this: *"But when the Pharisees heard that he had silenced the Sadducees, they gathered together. [35]And one of them, a lawyer, asked him a question to test him. [36]'Teacher, which is the great commandment in the Law?'"*

Tough question, right? The Old Testament law, which is a reference to the five books of Moses, contains an awful lot of important teaching. How could anyone, even this popular rabbi they called Jesus, pick out just one verse and say it was the greatest? Well, you know the rest of the story, don't you? Continuing at verse 37, we read, *"And he said to him, 'You shall love the Lord your God with all your heart and with all your soul and with all your mind.'"* Jesus is quoting from the *Shema,* directly from Deuteronomy 6:5. Jesus himself says this is the most important verse Moses ever said or wrote.

So you see, the fact that Israel had only one God was in and of itself the reason the people were called to love him. No other god, idol, symbol, or *anything* could or should detract from their love for the one true God.

The *Shema* is in the middle of Deuteronomy (which is filled with command after command after command given to the Israelites). Look at the words in the verses following Deuteronomy 6:4–5: observe, keep, obey, impress the children, talk about religious matters, use memory devices so you don't forget. We find the call to love God in the context of this great call to obedience. Right away, that ought to get our attention. You should be immediately asking yourself, "What does obedience have to do with love?" The answer is, when it comes to loving God, obedience has everything to do with it.

Loving God is nothing like loving your boyfriend or your new cocker spaniel puppy or your baby or your Grandma. Loving God is totally, completely different from any other love.

You've seen TV shows about archaeologists, haven't you? These strange little men with short pants and funny hats dig around in the desert sands of the Mideast and have dug up some pretty interesting stuff. One of the things we have learned from archaeology is, to the Semitic people of old (including Israel), the word "love" meant "faithful adherence to the king." It had nothing to do with affection or warm, fuzzy feelings. It had everything to do with obedience. That's why Jesus over and over again made the same point he did in John 14:21: *"Whoever has my commandments and keeps them, he it is who loves me."*

Loving God, again and again and *again* in the Bible, is related to obeying God. If you say you love God and you don't obey his Word, then you are as phony as a three-dollar bill. The technical word for it is "hypocrite."

It's kind of like a man who repeatedly says to his wife, "I love you," but then one day she discovers that he has been committing adultery with another woman. The words of love are totally without meaning to his wife, and the feeling behind the words, if there is any, is worthless.

Love—true, biblical, *agape* love—demands total, absolute dedication and obedience. Love for God has *got* to be *"with all your heart and with all your soul and with all your might."* God wants us to demonstrate our love for him *all* the time.

Do you know what's really sad? The vast majority of people who call themselves Christians today don't understand that point. The vast majority of Christians (and I'm sure that includes some of you reading this today) lack that kind of love for God. Let me illustrate this for you. Over the years I've become quite an expert in watching the way people drive. I find it really interesting. You basically see three kinds of drivers.

The first type I would call the "Worrywart Driver." Especially back in the Appalachian mountains of Virginia where I live, you see drivers who are fearful and never relaxed. They lack assurance. They sit at a stop sign even after it is their turn to proceed and wait until everybody for six blocks around gets out of the way. Then they slowly creep through the intersection. I'm not just talking about senior citizens; I see this kind of driving by people of all ages, both male and female.

Lots of Christians are like that, you know. They've heard about the promises of God and the great love that he has poured out on his people through the sending of his son, Jesus, to die in their place. They know they need that salvation. They need that forgiveness for their sins. They need to have that love of God demonstrated in their lives. But when they try to love God back, they are fearful, anxious, and worried. They just can't quite get across that intersection to the other side of the street where the street name turns to "obedience." Some of you are that kind of worrywart Christian.

The second kind of driver I like to call "Mr. Cruise Control." He gets out on the interstate and revs it right up to the speed limit (and perhaps five or so miles over the speed limit), then turns on the cruise and just moseys on down the road. Lots of Christians are like that, too. After their conversion, they start out in the Christian life all revved up. They start reading their Bibles. They go to church regularly. They even start giving a little more money to the Lord's work. Perhaps they volunteer to teach Sunday School or be a deacon, or what have you. Once they think they are up to speed, it's cruise control time for them. What they are doing is bringing their level of obedience up to a certain point, a level they have identified as the speed limit of the Christian life. Or rather, they think they have reached a level they have identified as the speed at which they can get along in church and still look good. But that's not the level that God calls for in the Bible, mind you. It's just the level that most other Christian cruise controllers like them are driving. Their obedience is set so as not to rock the boat of the culture in which they live or to get in trouble with the elders of the church for inactivity. And cruise they do, all the way (they hope) to heaven. There are probably some cruise controllers reading this as well.

There is a third kind of driver who illustrates yet another kind of Christian. Obviously it is not the drunken, drug-impaired, reckless driver on the road. Those are illustrations of non-Christians. No, this one is the one I call "the Dale Earnhardt Model."

I know, I know. I'm not back in Southwest Virginia now where everyone knows that racecar spelled backward is racecar. I've got a hunch though that there are enough race fans reading this that this illustration will work. It better! I got it from Jerry Bridges at a Ligonier Conference.

Now if you were not a fan of Earnhardt you have my permission to replace the name of this model with any NASCAR driver you like: Jeff Gordon, Dale Earnhardt Jr., one of the new kids, whomever—as long as the person you choose plays by the rules. When you used to see that black Chevy with the number 3 on it going around the track, you knew without looking that Dale Earnhardt was pushing his driving skills and abilities to the limits. He was always, always out to win the race. He would do anything in his power (legally, morally, and ethically . . . remember those qualifiers) to win the race!

The NASCAR driving model is what Moses meant when he said there in Deuteronomy 6:5, *"Love the Lord your God with all your heart and with all your soul and with all your might."* That's what we can learn about love from Dale Earnhardt. Dale drove with all his heart, soul, and might.

God is not looking for a bunch of timid, worrywart Christians who are afraid to cross the street. God is not impressed with a bunch of cruise controllers who operate the same during the week no matter what they might say or do on Sunday morning.

God wants us to love him and him alone because he is the one and only true God. He is the God and Father of our Lord Jesus Christ. He is the God who sent his only Son to die in our place to make us right with God. He is the God who loves us with even greater love than the Dale Earnhardt Model!

I need to take you briefly back to the beginning of the chapter now. So far, I've only answered one of our original two questions. Do you even remember the questions? Let me repeat them for you. They were, "What does all this talk about God being the one true God have to do with love?" I hope we've answered that. But there was a second question. It went something like this: "What difference does it make if those people three thousand years ago worshiped some idols anyway?"

Do you remember what the people of Israel did almost immediately after hearing the great *Shema* from the lips of the greatest prophet of all time (Moses)? They forgot! Some of them just put it into cruise control. Some of them were too fearful or too anxious to get even that much involved. And of course, some of them just drove recklessly through life trying to ignore God. Ultimately, nearly all of them ended up worshiping idols.

Folks, I hate to tell you, but you and I do the *very same thing* today. We fail to love God the way we should. We fail to connect the ideas of loving God with obeying his Word. We end up not loving him as we should. And nothing—I say, *nothing*—is worse than not loving God as we should.

Think about Dale Earnhardt one more time with me. Do you remember Daytona in 2001? Do you remember the *real* reason Earnhardt died that day? It wasn't any seat belt problem. It wasn't some other driver's fault. Dale died because he stopped driving number 3 with all his heart, and with all his soul, and with all his might. Instead of driving to win, he slowed down and tried to block so someone else could win. Oh, I know, I know. The two cars in front were ones driven by his firstborn son and another one he owned, but his reasons for blocking don't matter either. He died because he failed to drive the way he always had and the way he knew he should have been driving, with *all* his heart, soul, and might.

Do you think I'm making too radical an application to this piece of Scripture? Well, if you want radical, I'll give you radical. The true radical, Martin Luther, was a great sixteenth-century reformer. Let's let him help us understand the importance of this piece of the Bible. I'll give it to you straight out of R. C. Sproul's writing so you can measure the weight of its importance.

According to Sproul, it has been said many times that there is a fine line between genius and insanity, and that some people move back and forth across it. Some people believe Martin Luther was like that. In reality, Luther was not crazy. He was simply a genius. Before he became a priest, he studied the law. He had a superior understanding of the law, being heralded as one of the brightest young minds in Europe in the field of jurisprudence. Once he applied his astute legal mind to the law of God, he saw things that most mortals miss.

Luther examined the passage of Scripture we are studying today. He too saw how Jesus had sanctioned this passage as the great commandment. If he had been present here today, he would have been echoing "Amen" to most of the points I have made so far. But then he would have interjected a question, one that he in fact asked himself. He would have asked, "If this is the great commandment, what then is the great transgression?" Most people would answer his question by saying that the great sin is murder, adultery, or blasphemy, or just plain unbelief.

Luther disagreed. He concluded that if the great commandment was to love God with all the heart, then the great transgression was to *fail* to love God with all the heart. Luther saw a balance between great obligations and great sins.

Friends, you and I have got to see this balance in our own lives. We have got to see how badly we measure up to this standard of loving God with all our heart, soul, and might. We need to see it every time we do the opposite of loving God or every time we commit the great transgression of disobedience.

Let me close this chapter with one more allusion to good, ole Moses. Moses died before the children of Israel crossed over to the Promised Land. So picture him up in heaven watching them after he had preached this great sermon, which makes up just about all of the book of Deuteronomy. Early on in the sermon, he gives them these great words that Jesus himself would sanction as the first and greatest commandment.

Shema Yisrael! Yahweh Elohim, Yahweh Achad! Va-ha-vat' et Yahweh Elohim bacal le-va'vet, vucal naf'sha-ca, vucal mo-day'ach! "Hear, O Israel: The Lord our God, the Lord is one. You shall love the Lord your God with all your heart and with all your soul and with all your might."

Not very many years later after preaching this great sermon, he saw Israel fall away from this great God. They were worshiping idols, doing in their personal lives anything they felt like doing, loving themselves more than they loved God. They were having sex before they got married, cheating on their income taxes, smoking a little grass, holding back on their tithes so they would have enough for a nice vacation on the Sea of Galilee. Whatever. They were cruise controllers all the way. Oh, yes, they would travel to the temple when the holy days came—no doubt about that! But would they drive like Dale Earnhardt? Never!

How do you think Moses felt when he saw that? Well, I think I know how he felt because one day another great prophet was feeling kind of the same way. He had been preaching God's Word to the descendents of the people to whom Moses had preached. It was now ten or twelve generations later. Listen to what God told Ezekiel that day in Ezekiel 33:31–32. Remember, this is God himself speaking.

"And they come to you as people come, and they sit before you as my people, and they hear what you say but they will not do it; for with lustful talk in their mouths they act; their heart is set on their gain. ³²And behold, you are to them like one who sings lustful songs with a

beautiful voice and plays well on an instrument, for they hear what you say, but they will not do it."

That is exactly how Moses felt looking down from heaven. *"They hear what you say, but they will not do it." And do you* know what, folks? That's exactly the way your pastor feels if all you do is come to church month after month, year after year, and you hear the Word of God preached from this pulpit, but you do not put that Word to practice in your lives!

In the minds of far too many Christians today, preachers of the Word of God are treated as nothing more than *"one who sings lustful songs with a beautiful voice."* They are just another type of entertainer. Stepping on your toes in a sermon has about the same effect as watching a good movie. You walk out to your car and say, "Boy, I really enjoyed that!" but nothing ever happens. Nothing changes.

This is the curse of modern evangelical Christianity. People listen to sermon after sermon. They know it is the truth of the Word of God but it makes no difference in their lives. They just drive around on cruise control, that is, if they even have enough love for God to get out of the garage on Sunday morning!

But people, that is *not* what God wants. That is not pleasing in the eyes of God. Moses said it first. Jesus made it the gospel. God wants us to learn about love from Dale Earnhardt!

Shema Yisrael! Yahweh Elohim, Yahweh Achad! Va-ha-vat' et Yahweh Elohim bacal le-va'vet, vucal naf'sha-ca, vucal mo-day'ach!

"Hear, O Israel: The Lord our God, the Lord is one. You shall love the Lord your God with all your heart and with all your soul and with all your might."

Chapter Eighteen
Great Cultural Mandate – "You are the Salt
of the Earth"

O ur question for this chapter is, "Should a Christian be different from a non-Christian?" Certainly when we go to church, we are different. We worship God the Son as well as God the Father. We participate in special practices that only Christians can, such as baptism and the Lord's Supper.

But what about the rest of Sunday? Say while we're watching the Super Bowl or the Daytona 500? Should a Christian be different from a non-Christian during those hours? And what about Monday through Saturday? Should a Christian be different from a non-Christian every day of the week?

These are important questions, at least to my mind. You know, there was a time in the United States when everyone in the country knew the difference between someone who was a Christian and someone was a non-Christian. Christians stood out in society. But today the differences are greatly blurred. In most of the U. S. today, people assume that everyone is a Christian unless they specifically say they are something else— a Jew, or a Muslim, or an atheist, or a follower of one of the many Eastern religions.

However, this is a false assumption. Confronting this wrong assumption is precisely why Jesus begins the portion of the Sermon on the Mount immediately after what we know as the Beatitudes. I like to call this portion "Beyond the Beatitudes."

Jesus is talking about salt and light. In Jesus' day and age, there was a common saying in Roman society and culture that went like this: "There is nothing more useful than sun and salt." Everyone who listened to Jesus preaching that day at the foot of the mountain would have immediately recognized that he was using that very common saying as the basis for this teaching. Non-Christian Romans knew the value of light and the warmth that came from the sun (but explaining that is a different message). They also knew the value of salt. In fact, Roman soldiers were often paid in salt because it was so valuable in that society. That fact is the basis for our English word "salary," which comes from the root word for salt.

Jesus' key teaching on the subject of salt comes from Matthew 5:13. *"You are the salt of the earth, but if salt has lost its taste, how shall its saltiness be restored? It is no longer good for anything except to be thrown out and trampled under people's feet."* In this complex sentence filled with lots of important stuff, let's first be sure we understand the basic ingredients. Jesus speaks of "earth," "salt," and "you."

What does Jesus intend to teach when he uses the word "earth" here? One thing is for sure, he's not talking about the planet on which we all live. He's not talking about dirt. Rather, he's talking about people. He's talking particularly about interpersonal relationships.

I say that because of what he had just said in verses 11 and 12 at the end of the Beatitudes: *"Blessed are you when others revile you and persecute you and utter all kinds of evil against you falsely on my account. ¹²Rejoice and be glad, for your reward is great in heaven, for so they persecuted the prophets who were before you."* Here Jesus had been speaking of reverse interpersonal relationships and how common it was for non-Christians to persecute Christians. So when Jesus speaks of Christians being the salt of the earth, he means that they are the salt among people who are not Christians, or among the rest of the people on earth. So "earth" here refers to all non-Christians.

What about "salt"? Well, clearly Jesus was speaking about sodium chloride ($NaCl$)—that white stuff that exists in nature, and is mined, refined, and sold in boxes and shakers today. Salt was plentiful and cheap as I was growing up in Detroit. Many people living there didn't even realize it, but much of that large city is built over one of the largest salt mines in the world. Salt was plentiful in Israel as well. They had good quality salt. It was not mixed with too many impurities. So Jesus had in mind pure, unadulterated sodium chloride—good, old salt.

Now we get to the crucial part. Who is the "you" to whom Jesus addressed this teaching? When he says, *"You are the salt of the earth,"* to whom is he speaking? Well, he was speaking to the people who had become his followers. Principal among them were his chosen disciples, the Twelve. To put it into terms for our understanding today, he was speaking to Christians, and he is speaking to Christians as individuals, not as a group such as a church.

So pay careful attention to the material in this chapter . . . Jesus is speaking to you. He is telling you that you are the salt of the earth. Not that you will become the salt of the earth, but that you already are fulfilling that role. Now if we are, as Jesus says, the salt of the earth, we better be sure we understand the purpose of salt. That way we can understand our purpose as Christians, right?

Ask anyone what the purpose of salt is today, and almost all unanimously people will say it is to enhance the flavor of food. It is something you use while cooking or eating to make the food taste better (that is, if you enjoy that taste). Some Bible commentators today try to make that the application of what Jesus is teaching here. They teach that in order to be the salt of the earth, Christians are supposed to make life "zestier," to add flavor to the culture and to the society in general.

It is clear to me, however, that this is not what Jesus had in mind that day. In saying that, I realize I am going against the grain of some translations of the Bible, especially the King James Version and even the one I prefer, the English Standard Version. Those versions use the words "savor" or "taste." I think that is wrong. I think the NIV has it exactly right. *"You are the salt of the earth. But if the salt loses its saltiness, how can it be made salty again? It is no longer good for anything, except to be thrown out and trampled by men."*

Do you see the difference? The issue is substance, not taste. The old English word "savor" used by the KJV used to have the English meaning of "character" or "reputation," and that's why the KJV translators used that word.

In the New Testament, the Greek word Matthew used to translate what Jesus said that day was *moratayo*. This word is used elsewhere in the Bible to mean "fraud" or "nonsense" or "foolish." If Jesus had wanted to talk about salt adding flavor or taste to life, he would have used a different word. And so, I am sad to say, the ESV has it wrong. The NIV has it correct when it speaks of salt *"losing its saltiness."*

What Jesus had in his mind when he said that you are the salt of the earth is the primary use of salt in his day and age. Back then, salt was used as a preservative. Even today, salt is used as a preservative, and also as an antiseptic. Twice every day I clean out my sinuses with saline solution—salt water. In Jesus' day, the primary use and value of salt was to prevent and slow down decay. It was used to affect things that would naturally go bad if left unsalted, such as meat and bread.

Salt works invisibly and silently. It works inside things. In fact, you have to rub it carefully into meat or mix it thoroughly with bread dough if it is going to do its job. Jesus had this concept in mind when he said that you and I are the salt of the earth. In other words, Jesus is telling us (everyone who is his disciple, a Christian) that our purpose is to bring a redemptive quality to our society. This is the great cultural mandate. Our function in the world is to help keep society from going bad—to help restrain evil and moral decay, not just in ourselves but in all the earth (even among non-Christians).

Notice the implication that Jesus is making here. People of the earth, left to themselves, without the influence of Christians, would just keep getting worse and worse. The earth would decay. It cannot get any better on its own. And, of course, if we understand the teaching of the Bible elsewhere, we know why. This decay or moral evil is the result of sin in the world. Human society needs the influence of the people of God to keep it from decay from the effects of sin. It needed it in Jesus' day and age. It needed it throughout history, and it needs it still today.

Think about several illustrations of this basic truth. First, think about the positive influence of the godly patriarch Joseph in Egyptian society. Think about David and the other godly kings in Israel who affected nations around them. Think about Esther and Mordecai in Persia. Think about Daniel in Babylon. Think about the way the young churches of the New Testament shook up the world around them.

We can also find illustrations in history. Christian missionaries have frequently had a redeeming effect on primitive societies. You may recall the story (recently brought to the Hollywood screen) of the American missionary Jim Elliot, who with some friends more than fifty years ago were murdered by a tribe of Auca Indians in Equador. In spite of this terrible act, Jim's wife Elisabeth and the other missionary team members remained in Ecuador, bringing the gospel to this tribe of murderers and cannibals. Today, essentially all members of the tribe are wonderful Christians.

In England early in the nineteenth century, the great Christian statesman William Wilberforce stirred up his fellow Christians to bring about the abolition of slavery. In our own nation, the Great Awakening, led by the preaching of George Whitefield and Jonathan Edwards, changed our society in such a dramatic way that sociologists are still studying the phenomenon.

Still today, you and I are called on to be a positive influence in our society. We are to function as salt stemming the tide of evil and moral decay. The question is, then, how are we supposed to do that? The answer is basic. Jesus will expound the answer as he continues his Sermon on the Mount. But in a nutshell, it means that you and I as the salt of the earth are simply to apply basic biblical ethics and teaching to every sphere of our lives. We are to function as Christians in our families, in our schools, in our workplaces, in our neighborhoods. And we are to function in such a way that we have the effect of keeping the society (or that portion of it with which we have direct involvement) from going bad. We are to have the effect of restraining evil and moral decay.

Let me give you a quick aside on the concept of "sphere." This term is used technically in some theological circles when referring to "sphere sovereignty." By it, these people are suggesting (and I fully agree and support this view) that Jesus is sovereign over every "sphere" of life (government, economics, education, business, family, etc.). If Jesus is sovereign (which is to say, if Jesus is indeed the "King of the World" as we studied in Chapter Ten), then it follows that his principles and ethics should be followed. So it is up to Christians to teach and show the way on how to practice biblical truths.

So, how are we doing in this regard? Do you honestly think that Christians at the beginning of the twenty-first century are having the effect of being the salt of the earth to the extent that our culture and society are getting better? If it is true that, in society, things will keep getting worse without the influence of Christians, can you honestly say that Christians are functioning today the way Jesus intended for us to function? Or is our society getting worse? If you think things are getting worse instead of getting better, then guess what? You and I are part of the problem! If a society goes bad, part of the blame must be laid at the feet of Christians in that society.

Think about basic illustrations of this point in some of the familiar Bible stories. In fact, let's think about a very "salty" story—the story of Sodom and Gomorrah. Lot and his family chose to live in that particular community because it was rich with resources for living the good life. Abraham gave Lot first dibs on where he wanted to live, and Lot went for the best.

What happened in Sodom and Gomorrah? You can read all about it in Genesis chapters 18 and 19, but let me summarize the story for you here. Obviously, Lot and his family failed to have any significant godly influence on their society. Oh, I'm sure they were quite comfortable, probably even wealthy. That wasn't enough, however, when the band of homosexual terrorists showed up at Lot's door one night. Lot and his family had to run for their lives. Notice the irony in what happened to Lot's wife. As she lusted for the good life she was leaving behind and turned to look one last time (even though she had been clearly warned not to do that), she was turned into a pillar of salt—exactly because she had not been functioning as the salt of Sodom and Gomorrah while she lived there.

When you read the Old Testament prophets, you see time and time again the result in Judah and Israel of the people of God failing to function as the salt of the earth. Jesus was constantly blaming the Jewish religious leaders of his day for the same kind of failure.

Throughout history you find lots of examples of this principle. The Romans persecuted Christians, thus keeping them from being the salt of that society, and that society quickly self-imploded with evil and moral decay. In medieval Europe, the culture decayed from within the church itself as Christians (even the clergy) lost sight of their purpose to fulfill the great cultural mandate. They even purposely withdrew from society in the monastic movement, making things worse.

So let's cut to the chase here. Jesus says all Christians are the salt of the earth. Then immediately he adds the warning at the end of the verse: *"You are the salt of the earth, but if salt has lost its taste, how shall its saltiness be restored? It is no longer good for anything except to be thrown out and trampled under people's feet."* If you and I say we are Christians, but we are not having a Christian influence in our society (in other words, if we have lost our "saltiness"), what does Jesus say about that? He says we're not good for anything (which in today's vernacular means we're "good for nothing") except maybe to pave some roads. In other words, the world is just going to walk all over us! Jesus says that if someone claims to be his disciple and does not act like a Christian, he or she is a hypocrite; that person is worthless!

Recall my question at the beginning of this chapter about how Christians are supposed to look and act. How are they supposed to be applying basic biblical ethics and teachings to all of life? Well, let's apply Jesus' words to our families, our schools, our workplaces, and our neighborhoods.

If your spouse and children do not see you act like a Christian, then Jesus says you are not good for anything. Kids, if your parents, brothers, sisters, schoolmates, and teachers do not see you acting like a Christian (even though that may not be "cool" these days), then Jesus says you are not good for anything. If your neighbors and friends do not see you acting like a Christian, and would not know your religion if someone asked, Jesus says you are not good for anything. If your work associates do not see you acting like a Christian, Jesus says you are not good for anything. If your extended family members do not see you acting like a Christian, Jesus says you're not good for anything.

Each of us may have only a small sphere of influence here on earth. But in that sphere, people must see Jesus in the way we act, talk, and conduct our lives. If you are not functioning as salt within your little sphere of society, then you just plainly are not a disciple of Jesus. Jesus says his disciples *are* salt—not *should be* salt—they really *are* salt.

If you are not part of the solution to stem the growing tide of evil and moral decay in our society, then you are part of the problem. It's time to quit just talking the talk, and start walking the walk, or should we say salting the salt! Because if we don't, Jesus himself is warning us we are no longer good for anything except to be thrown out and trampled under people's feet. The world will walk all over us.

O n a dangerous seacoast where shipwrecks often occur, there was once a crude little lifesaving station. The building was just a hut and there was only one boat, but the few devoted members kept a constant watch over the sea. With no thought for themselves, they went out tirelessly searching for the lost, day and night.

Many lives were saved by this wonderful little station, and it became famous. Some of those who were saved and various others in the community wanted to become associated with the station and give some of their time and money and effort for the support of its work. New boats were bought and new crews trained. The little lifesaving station grew.

Some of the members of the lifesaving station were unhappy that the building was so crude and poorly equipped. They felt that a more comfortable place should be provided as the first refuge for those saved from the sea. So they replaced the emergency cots with beds and put better furniture in the enlarged building.

Now the lifesaving station became a popular gathering place for its members. They decorated it beautifully and filled it with exquisite furnishings, because they were now using it as sort of a club. Fewer members were interested in going to sea on lifesaving missions, so they hired professional lifeboat crews to do this work. The lifesaving motif still prevailed in the club's decorations, and a liturgical lifeboat was put in the room where the club initiations were held.

About this time, a large ship was wrecked off the coast. The hired crews brought in boatloads of cold, wet, and half-drowned people. They were dirty and sick. Some of them had black skin and some of them had yellow skin. The beautiful new club was in chaos. So the property committee immediately had a shower house built outside the club where victims of shipwrecks could be cleaned up before coming inside.

At the next meeting, there was a split in the club membership. Most of the members wanted to stop the club's lifesaving activities because they were unpleasant and a hindrance to the normal social life of the club. Some members insisted on lifesaving as their primary purpose and pointed out that they were still called a lifesaving station. But the latter group was finally voted down and told that if they wanted to save the lives of all the various kinds of people who were shipwrecked in those waters, they could begin their own lifesaving station down the coast. They did.

As the years went by, the new station experienced the same changes that had occurred in the old. It too evolved into a club, and yet another lifesaving station was founded. History continued to repeat itself, and if you visit that seacoast today, you will find a number of exclusive clubs along the shore. Shipwrecks are still frequent in those waters, but most of the people drown. This well-known and oft-repeated parable teaches us that over and over again, man forgets his purpose and true responsibility.

Too often, this lesson applies to Christians as much as to non-Christians. I would assume (I hope safely, but I know better, don't I?) that, as a Christian, you are a member of a local church. Let me ask you a question: "What is the true purpose of your church?"

Those who are longtime Presbyterians and know the Shorter Catechism would respond that man's purpose should be to "glorify God and enjoy him forever." But we must also add to this response to the next question of the catechism—that God has given us certain directions in how we may glorify and enjoy him. These directions come in the Word of God, the Bible. This applies, of course, not only to your church but to individual Christians everywhere. So your church, no matter how big or small, to truly be a church of the Lord Jesus, must have a purpose, just like any other church in the world. There must be a particular reason for the existence of every church.

You might ask where you go to find out exactly what the purpose of a church should be. We can't begin looking in the historical present (what is happening today), for we could easily be led astray, following a whim down a path to oblivion. Nor can we begin with the historical past (what happened in days gone by). It just isn't possible to pattern one church after some other church that may have been to some degree successful in the past. Times change. People change. Therefore, types of church ministry change.

Where we must begin, as in every part of the Christian life, is with the scriptural basis for the purpose of a church. Where in the Scriptures do we look for that basis? I guess the most common response would be the Great Commission in Matthew

28. Christ's twofold command contained there, to evangelize the lost and to edify the saints, is indeed the very best summary of the purpose of any church. These two main points must surely be included in the purpose of any church in one form or another.

But the Great Commission gives only very broad guidelines for the purpose of the church. It is almost too easy to say that we should be concerned with evangelization and with individual Christian growth. So just what do we mean by this? How does one go about doing these two?

Well, I think we can find the roots of the Great Commission throughout the ministry of Jesus before his resurrection. To me, the meaning is most clear and succinct in the final prayer that our Lord offered to God the night before he was taken from his disciples. The prayer is recorded for us in John 17.

As Jesus poured out his heart in prayer to God, he covered a multitude of ideas and thoughts. Let's concentrate our attention on those portions that speak directly to the work of Jesus on the cross of Calvary. Since we seek the roots of a church's purpose in Scripture, let's look closely at John 17:17– 19.

In these verses, we will see three things about the purpose of a church. First, we want to see how it begins at the cross. Second, we'll notice how it grows through the ministry of the Word of God. And finally, we will observe how it takes effect in the world around it. Let's see how the fact of Jesus' death will not permit a church to stop halfway in its purpose.

As Jesus prays in verse 19, " . . . *for their sake I consecrate myself,"* he is teaching us that his death on the cross is for our salvation (our justification before God). But he continues, *"that they also may be sanctified in truth."* So we see that his death was for both our salvation and our sanctification. When we consider our Lord's death, our first thoughts (as they should be) are turned to our sins, paid for completely through his death. His work went even deeper than that, however.

In writing his letter to the church at Rome, the Apostle Paul used the first five chapters to teach about justification by faith, about salvation. But in Romans 6, he turns his attention to the importance of the death and resurrection of Jesus for our sanctification. Beginning in verse 3, he writes:

> *Do you not know that all of us who have been baptized into Christ Jesus were baptized into his death? [4]We were buried therefore with him by baptism into death, in order that, just as Christ was raised from the dead by the glory of the Father, we too might walk in newness of life.*

Paul's not talking about the sacrament of baptism in this passage. He's talking about our sanctification, our Christian maturity; he's talking about our living out our new life. Just as the cost of our sins was not paid for us on the day we became a Christian (they were paid way back at Calvary), so also does our Christian maturity not start on the day of our salvation. It too began when Jesus' blood was shed on the cross, and it is rooted in his death.

Let me try to illustrate how to look at this. As we grow older and more experienced in the world, some might say that our human maturity began on the day we were born. But our human maturity did not begin on the day of our natural birth. For our human growth was to a great part determined through genes that were passed to us from our parents. The foundation of our human maturity goes back beyond our natural birth, even back beyond our nine months in the womb.

In the same way, our sanctification did not begin on the day of our re-birth. The foundation for our Christian maturity goes back all the way to Calvary. Since part of the purpose of any church is the "edification of the saints," we can see that this portion of its purpose has its roots at Calvary also. A church can never be interested solely in "getting people saved" and moving on to other potential converts once a person professes faith. Happily, there are very few congregations in the Presbyterian Church in America like that. It has always been the hallmark of Reformed churches to teach and train their people before and after the Lord saves them.

This is what Jesus is emphasizing in verse 17 of our text, as he prays to God: *"Sanctify them in the truth; your word is truth."* Jesus is making it crystal clear that the only source for our Christian maturity is the Word of God (the Bible). That is why every single sermon that is ever preached to you from any pulpit must be rooted in the Bible, not in knowledge found in the minds of men.

That is why the message of every single Sunday school lesson that is taught to you or by you must be rooted in the Bible or come from curriculum that you have confidence is based on biblical truth. It is also why every single psalm, hymn, or spiritual song sung in worship services finds its roots in the Bible and not just in the song of a man's heart. And, that is why every day of our lives we should show actions that are rooted in the Bible and not just in our mind's ideas and desires.

A precious passage in Acts 20 emphasizes this fact. Paul was meeting for what he believed was the last time with the elders of the Ephesian church. He called them to travel down to where he was staying at Miletus, on the southern coast of what is today Turkey. Paul gives them his final blessing in Acts 20:32, and it goes like this:

> *"And now I commend you to God and to the word of his grace, which is able to build you up and to give you the inheritance among all those who are sanctified."*

What a joyful thing to leave with them. In a very real sense, that is what I'm trying to leave with you today. For surely God's Word is able to build you up, to sanctify you, if you only apply it to your individual lives and to the life of your church. But beware! Be ready for results! For sanctification, personal growth and maturity, is not an end in itself. As you dig into the Word of God, you will be moved to take action on what you read and study.

So the third part of our examination of the scriptural roots of the purpose of a church is found in John 17:18. Jesus says, *"As you sent me into the world, so I have sent them into the world."* Do you see it, friends? We are commanded by Jesus to apply our sanctification in the world around us. He has sent us into the world for this purpose. Evangelization of the lost is the other half of the purpose of any church.

We see the force of this idea earlier in Chapter 17. There, as Jesus is praying not for himself, but for his disciples (actually, praying for all the elect (thosen chosen before the foundations of the World) of God, including us), he is aware that the elect are chosen for a purpose. That purpose is to be sent into the world. In verse 16, he identified us as *"not of the world,"* but we are certainly *in* it. No matter how we try to hide from this fact, no matter how much "otherworldliness" we try to coat ourselves with, we cannot deny the fact that we are in the world. And more importantly, we have been sent into this world as the elect of God for a purpose. It is most appropriate that this should be a substantial part of the purpose of any church.

Remember, our concern is to be sure we don't fall into the lapse of memory that beset those lifesaving clubs along that seacoast. We want to be careful not to forget that a primary purpose of a church is to save souls, as theirs was to save lives. So you must confront yourself with this important question: Is your church a congregation that fulfills its purpose of evangelizing the lost?

Let me repeat that question. It is so important. Will your church fulfill its purpose of evangelizing the lost? Before you answer that question, let's be sure of our discussion ground. We must define our terms. Your answer will vary according to these grounds.

What is evangelization? Simply put, evangelization results in the salvation of the lost. It is not social action. It is not personal sanctification. It is not personal testimony. It is not Bible studies. It is not any if these, or even teaching the Reformed faith, as important as all of these might be. Evangelization is synonymous with mission. It means taking the gospel to all those who are lost *for the express purpose of their possible salvation.* It means taking the gospel to your own family, your own neighbors, your own work associates, your entire community. Now, there is one question that must be answered as you decide whether you are to carry out the Great Commission in your church, in order to fulfill the purpose of the church: Are you going to take the gospel to the lost *for the express purpose of their possible salvation?*

In his first letter to the church at Corinth, Paul writes, *"For if I preach the gospel, that gives me no ground for boasting. For necessity is laid upon me. Woe to me if I do not preach the gospel! [17]For if I do this of my own will, I have a reward, but not of my own will, I am still entrusted with a stewardship"* (1 Corinthians 9:16–17).

I'm afraid that many people who say they hold to the Reformed faith hide out, or "cop out" if you will, behind a false interpretation of this verse. They say something like, "OK, if I fail to do my obvious duty to proclaim the gospel, I will still enjoy the bliss of heaven. Perhaps I'll get a lesser reward than my brother, Paul, who fulfills the Great Commission and proclaims the gospel (who evangelizes the lost)."

But don't you see it, my friends? Paul says, *"Woe to me if I do not preach the gospel!"* That word "woe" means death! It is the worst kind of heresy to say that you simply lose a reward. It gives you a false sense of security. The truth is that you may be slipping down the slick path to hell.

Many writers of biblical commentaries use mild-mannered, smooth writing so as not to ruffle feathers. As you are getting to know Don Clements, it should come as no surprise to you that I don't like those kinds of commentaries. Rather, I appreciate writers such as J. Oliver Buswell Jr., the now-in-heaven former dean of the faculty at Covenant Seminary, where I was trained for the ministry. Uncle Buz (as we referred to him behind his back) said this in his commentary on the verses we just looked at:

> To the person who holds the position that all you lose if you are not involved in evangelization of the lost is a reward, the true meaning of this passage of Scripture must be said. The correct interpretation of such Scripture indicates that if you do not show genuine concern for the salvation of the lost, there is in you no fruit of the Spirit, and the presumption is that you are still unregenerate. Woe to you!! Your pretended faith is spurious. Non-missionary Christianity is not genuine Christianity!

He doesn't pull punches, does he? What he is saying is that those who fail to carry out the command given in the Great Commission and here in John 17:18 may not be saved. If you fail to fulfill the portion of the purpose of the church to evangelize the lost, then the assumption is that you yourself are lost. For, as Paul writes in his other letter to the church at Corinth, it is the *"love of Christ that compels us."* It is a matter of simple logic to Paul. If you are saved, you are compelled to proclaim the gospel—you are compelled to be involved in evangelizing the lost.

Now do you see how important it is that you view the purpose of the church correctly? Do you see how absolutely interconnected the concepts of personal sanctification and evangelization are? We must see this if we are to be more than wedding crashers at the great marriage feast of Jesus and the church. We must be able to see that the death of Jesus on Calvary was not only for the payment of the debt for our sins, but also the root of our own sanctification. And it is the basis by which we are compelled to reach the lost with the gospel.

Through the Word of God, we can grow in our own personal sanctification and also go into the world with the good news of Christ. The Word compels us to go into our neighborhoods, towns, and cities as we have been commanded. This is not a light matter. It is worthy of your attention and prayers this very day.

Don't let your church become one of those lifesaving stations that dies and forgets its purpose. Don't become settled in your own little protected world—playing church, saying to yourselves in effect, "I'm saved, brother. I'll pray for you. I'll even put some money in the collection plate for missions. But I've got it made. I don't have to do anything else." You cannot ignore those people all around you who are dying spiritually, as those people were drowning in the troubled water of that rugged seacoast. You must open your ears and hear the lost crying out.

One of the places you frequently hear a lost man cry out is in his music. There are many powerful quotes in the lyrics from some of the current singers (such as Eminem). But I doubt whether my adult readers would recognize them. Paul Simon's classic song, "Bridge Over Troubled Water," is perhaps a good example. If you recall those words, then you can hear a lost man. He knows he is in troubled water. He knows he is not capable of navigating the water. He knows he cannot cross over that water by himself. He is crying out for the bridge to cross over!

You and I have that bridge with us right now! It is the cross of Jesus. Only through Jesus is there any crossing over the gulf that separates man from God. We say that we are Christians— that we have that bridge on which we have crossed over the troubled water. But we cannot just stand here clinging to the cross! We must take up that cross and go out into the community, using it as a bridge over the troubled water that faces those around us who are still lost.

Please recognize that your pastor cannot do this work for you. That is not his primary responsibility. You can't just hire professional lifeboat crews. A pastor's job is to lead *you*, to equip *you*, to encourage *you*, to exhort *you*.

Now that you understand the purpose of a church, it is time to fulfill it. Carry it out! My friends, every church must fulfill its purpose, or it too will surely die.

Chapter Twenty
Personal Conclusion – "Meeting Jesus,
Following Jesus"

(The material in this chapter is adapted from a sermon preached by David Feddes, speaker on the radio program "The Back to God Hour," and is used by permission.)

So far we have covered nineteen important things you should know about Jesus. But number twenty is probably the most important. It is your personal conclusion. After learning all of these important things about who Jesus is and what he has done, it's time to personalize all this information. It is time for you the reader to be sure you haven't missed the heart of this book about Jesus.

You may have noticed that most of the material in the first nineteen chapters centers on who Jesus is—his birth, what he did, especially his death on the cross and his resurrection afterward—and what all that means. What I have not done is cover a lot of the details of the three-plus years that he carried out his ministry on earth. It is during those years that people got to meet him, and many ended up following him.

It's time now for you to meet Jesus, and then to follow him. Meeting Jesus in person had a stunning effect on people. Even before Jesus became famous or did any miracles, those who met him in person were awestruck. It took just a few hours with him—sometimes just a few minutes—to realize that Jesus was like nobody they had ever met before. People quickly saw him as the key to everything they were looking for.

There is a passage in John 1:35–51 that is a classic illustration of this point. It's a relatively long section, but it's important to read it all the way through before we proceed:

The next day again John was standing with two of his disciples, [36]and he looked at Jesus as he walked by and said, "Behold, the Lamb of God!" [37]The two disciples heard him say this, and they followed Jesus. [38]Jesus turned and saw them following and said to them, "What are you seeking?" And they said to him, "Rabbi" (which means Teacher), "where are you staying?" [39]He said to them, "Come and you will see." So they came and saw where he was staying, and they stayed with him that day, for it was about the tenth hour. [40]One of the two who heard John speak and followed Jesus was Andrew, Simon Peter's brother. [41]He first found his own brother Simon and said to him, "We have found the Messiah" (which means Christ). [42]He brought him to Jesus. Jesus looked at him and said, "So you are Simon the son of John? You shall be called Cephas" (which means Peter).

[43]The next day Jesus decided to go to Galilee. He found Philip and said to him, "Follow me." [44]Now Philip was from Bethsaida, the city of Andrew and Peter. [45]Philip found Nathanael and said to him, "We have found him of whom Moses in the Law and also the prophets wrote, Jesus of Nazareth, the son of Joseph." [46]Nathanael said to him, "Can anything good come out of Nazareth?" Philip said to him, "Come and see." [47]Jesus saw Nathanael coming toward him and said of him, "Behold, an Israelite indeed, in whom there is no

deceit!" [48]Nathanael said to him, "How do you know me?" Jesus answered him, "Before Philip called you, when you were under the fig tree, I saw you." [49]Nathanael answered him, "Rabbi, you are the Son of God! You are the King of Israel!" [50]Jesus answered him, "Because I said to you, "I saw you under the fig tree," do you believe? You will see greater things than these." [51]And he said to him, "Truly, truly, I say to you, you will see heaven opened, and the angels of God ascending and descending on the Son of Man."

Here we read of two men who were told by Jesus' cousin, John the Baptizer, that Jesus was somebody special. Jesus wasn't yet well known and hadn't done anything spectacular, but the men decided to tag along behind him. Jesus turned and noticed them following and asked, "What do you want?"

Perhaps they weren't quite sure what they wanted or thought it would be too pushy to say that they wanted to get to know him, so they stammered, "Where are you staying?" "Come," he replied, "and you will see."

So they went and saw where he was staying and spent the rest of the day with him. It was already late in the afternoon, about four o'clock. That shot of time between four o'clock and bedtime was enough to amaze them and convince them to stick with Jesus and invite others to meet him.

One of the two men was named Andrew. The first thing Andrew did was to find his brother Simon and tell him, *"We have found the Messiah,"* the savior for whom God's people had been longing. Andrew brought Simon to Jesus. Jesus took one look at Simon and, without asking his name, said, *"You are Simon, son of John. You will be called Peter,"* which means "rock."

What sort of person knows your name without asking? What sort of person renames you "solid rock" when you're just a flighty fisherman? Simon Peter must have been puzzled, but like his brother Andrew, he was amazed and captivated by Jesus and decided to hang around with him.

The next day Jesus walked up to a man named Philip, who came from the same town as Andrew and Peter. *"Follow me,"* he told Philip. Now, if someone came to you and expected you to drop everything and go with him, what would you do? If someone ordinary told you to follow him, you might refuse. But Jesus' personality was so powerfully persuasive that when Jesus said, *"Follow me,"* Philip leapt at the chance. In fact, meeting Jesus was so exciting that Philip wanted someone else to meet him. Philip found his friend Nathaniel and told him, *"We have found the one Moses wrote about in the Law, and about whom the prophets also wrote—Jesus of Nazareth, the son of Joseph."*

Nathaniel, however, was not impressed, especially when he heard that Jesus came from Nazareth. Nazareth was a town with a poor reputation, a place for losers, and Nathaniel said so. There was nothing sneaky or subtle about Nathaniel. He didn't hide his feelings. He honestly said what was on his mind. "Nazareth," snorted Nathaniel. "Can anything good come from there?"

Philip didn't try to argue with Nathaniel. Philip simply answered, *"Come and see."* Philip was sure that meeting Jesus personally, even for a few minutes, would amaze Nathaniel and win him over despite his low opinion of Jesus' hometown. Nathaniel agreed to go. He had his prejudices and doubts, but he was still honestly willing to check Jesus out for himself.

When Jesus saw Nathaniel approaching, he said of him, *"Here is a true Israelite, in whom there is no deceit."* How did Nathaniel react? He may have liked the compliment. But what's a compliment really worth if it comes from someone you have never met before? How would this stranger know there was nothing phony about Nathaniel? Maybe Jesus was just trying to flatter Nathaniel. Instead of thanking Jesus for the compliment, Nathaniel shot back, *"How do you know me?"*

Jesus answered, *"I saw you while you were still under the fig tree before Philip called you."* At that, Nathaniel's doubts disappeared. This man whom he had never met before knew exactly where he had been and what he had been doing earlier that day and he also knew his character. Somehow, Jesus already knew him inside and out. Suddenly it dawned on Nathaniel who Jesus must be. *"Rabbi,"* he said, *"you are the Son of God. You are the King of Israel!"*

One after another, people who meet Jesus were amazed and gripped by his personality. This effect was evident even before Jesus had begun to do the things that would soon make him famous. Before long, Jesus would do mighty miracles and preach to enormous crowds who hung on his every word. Some folks would get caught up in the mood of excitement surrounding him, the way star-struck fans go into a frenzy over a celebrity superstar.

Andrew, Peter, Philip, and Nathaniel met Jesus at the beginning of his ministry, however, before he became famous and attracted huge crowds. So, it wasn't publicity or a general mood of excitement that made them marvel at Jesus. It was Jesus himself. He was so magnetic, so magnificent, that they sensed he must be the Messiah, the one promised by the prophets, the Son of God, their King. They still had a lot to learn, but one thing they knew: in meeting Jesus, they had met more than just another man.

In meeting him, they were getting to know God in a fresh, wonderful way, and were having their deepest longings satisfied. So, when they wanted to share their discovery with family, friends, and others whom they met, they didn't give a long speech. They just said, "Come and see. Check him out for yourself."

That's my invitation to you right now: come and see. Take a few minutes as you read this chapter to get to know Jesus on a personal basis. You've read all about him, who he is, and what he has done, but it is possible that you still believe all that is theory. I want you to get to know Jesus personally. Don't just go by hearsay or by what you happen to think of religion in general. Come and see Jesus, and meet him for yourself. Listen to what he has to say.

Would you like to meet Jesus—hear him speaking, see him in action, know him personally? Then go to a house where he's having dinner. Hop into a boat with him and his friends. Sit on a grassy hillside and listen to him tell stories. Walk with him down dusty roads and see how he relates to various people. Notice who it is who likes him, and why. Notice who hates him, and why. Come and see Jesus for yourself.

How can you do that? Do you need a magic machine to bring you to another time and place? No, you just need the New Testament Gospels written by Matthew, Mark, Luke, and John. Those inspired books have miraculous power to carry you across time and space and into contact with Jesus as he walked this earth long ago. As you go to meet him in that time and place, he will come to meet you in this time and place. As you enter his life, he enters your life. Come and see!

As the biblical Gospels carry you into contact with Jesus, one of the first things you notice is that Jesus is glad to see you and pleased that you want to meet him. You'll soon discover that Jesus welcomes anybody. It doesn't matter much who they are—man or woman, grandparent or child, fisherman or farmer, priest or prostitute, soldier or rebel, cop or criminal, ruler or slave, rich or poor, educated or uneducated, healthy or disabled, religious or rotten, sensible or demon-possessed. Jesus warmly welcomes anyone who wants to meet him and get to know him better. He never tells anyone that he is too important, or too busy, or too good for him or her.

As you're hanging around with Jesus, you'll see several young mothers with little kids and babies, wanting Jesus to touch their children and pray for them. Some of the people around Jesus might tell the women to go away. They'll say that Jesus can't be bothered with babies and housewives. But when Jesus sees women and children treated as though they don't count, it makes him mad. "Let the little children come to me," he says. "Don't hinder them. God's kingdom is for kids like these."

Later you'll be walking down the road behind Jesus, along with a crowd of others. Suddenly you'll hear a couple of loud-mouthed guys making a racket. "Lord, Son of David, have mercy on us." Two blind beggars, who are beside that road every day looking for handouts, have heard Jesus is going past. When they start yelling, the crowd scolds them and tells them to shut up. After all, Jesus is on the move; he's got big plans. Why should a couple of no-account freeloaders make a scene and interfere with his schedule? But the blind men won't give up. They'll yell all the louder, and Jesus doesn't mind at all. In fact, he seems pleased. He will stop and ask them what they want. They'll tell him they want to see. Jesus' face will be full of pity. He'll touch their eyes and suddenly they will be able to see. And they will join you and his other followers.

As you hang around with Jesus, you'll find out that he makes time not only for women, and children, and disabled people, but also for people who are downright bad. He will sit down for supper with crooks, and prostitutes, and riffraff of every kind. He'll accept invitations from almost anybody, and he'll even invite himself to their place if they feel unworthy to invite him.

Sometimes this will hurt his reputation among the more upstanding, religious members of society. They will think he has no standards. But Jesus will calmly tell them that the reason he came is to help sinners—and it seems to be working. Eating with crooks doesn't make Jesus go crooked. It helps crooks go straight. Welcoming prostitutes doesn't make Jesus sexually immoral. It helps prostitutes become sexually pure, and transforms them into wise, dignified women who stop selling their bodies and start serving God.

He even will meet people on their own terms. A rich, religious man named Nicodemus will want to see Jesus but won't want the public to see them together. He will want Jesus to have a secret meeting with him at night. Will Jesus refuse? No, he's friendly even with a man who is ashamed to be seen with him. When he sits down with Nicodemus, Jesus will inform him that he must be born again. He will tell Nicodemus that he must believe in him (Jesus) in order to be saved, and he will say that a saved person won't hide in the dark, but will live in God's light.

Jesus won't push anyone away, but he also won't pull any punches, either. He is willing to meet people on their terms, but they can only stay with him and follow him on Jesus' terms. He won't exclude anyone because of their past, but he won't include anyone who refuses to leave their past and entrust their future to him. There will be no one so bad that he or she cannot have him, but there will be no one so good that he or she doesn't need him. Jesus is willing to meet you where you are, but then you must be willing to follow wherever he leads.

In meeting Jesus, you will meet a combination of humility and authority you won't meet in anyone anywhere else; he possesses an astonishing union of tenderness and toughness. One moment he will be cuddling babies, the next moment he will be confronting rulers. One moment he will lie exhausted and asleep in a boat that's being rocked by a storm; the next moment he will order the storm around. One moment he will weep at the grave of his dead friend Lazarus; the next he will order death itself to release his friend. One moment he will be on his knees like a slave, washing other people's dirty feet; the next he will say he is their Lord and Master.

Jesus, you will see, feels the weakness, pain, and poverty of humanity; at the same time, he unleashes the power, healing, and abundance of God. He doesn't have even a small hut for a house; yet he strides through God's temple as though he owns the place. He doesn't have a penny to his name; yet he talks as though the whole world is his. Could even the least human be humbler and more vulnerable? Could even almighty God be greater and more powerful? What else can you think except that Jesus must be completely human and at the same time fully divine?

One thing is for sure: Jesus isn't boring. There will never be a dull moment when you're around him. When he speaks, you might feel confused. You might even get upset and angry over some of the things he says, but one thing you won't do is yawn. So much of what he says has an unexpected twist. He tells a story about a lousy crook and a respectable teacher. The punch line is that God accepts the crook and rejects the teacher.

Jesus tells another story, about a rotten kid who runs away from home, blows all his money, wrecks his life, damages his family's reputation, and when he hits bottom, stumbles back home. His dad welcomes him back with hugs and a big party. Meanwhile there's a well-behaved, older brother who seems to have done everything right and yet ends up feeling left out.

Jesus will say some things that seem like splendid common sense, but he also will say things that sound perplexing and outrageous. It will not always be easy to figure out what Jesus means. Still, his voice will ring with such authority that even if you can't understand him totally, you won't be able to ignore him.

He will feed thousands of hungry people with five loaves of bread and two fish. He will even raise the dead. A funeral procession will break up when Jesus brings the boy in the coffin to life, to the delight of his widowed mother. A girl lying dead on her bed will suddenly sit up in good health, thanks to a word from Jesus. It will be the greatest outburst of miracles anyone has ever seen—or will ever see.

The miracles will show Jesus' awesome power, and they will also show his love and compassion. Jesus won't just heal; he will also touch and talk with those he heals, restoring their spirits as well as their bodies. Sometimes he will declare their sins to be forgiven. You see, Jesus doesn't just cure problems; he cares about people.

Besides his power and compassion, you will also notice his personal purity. When you meet Jesus, you will find that he practices what he preaches. Even his enemies won't be able to come up with any scandal to discredit him. He will treat women with utmost respect, without a hint of lust. He will live one day at a time, trusting his heavenly Father, without using his fame to pile up money. There's nothing greedy about him.

He will be patient with people and never scold anyone unless it's for their own good. He can't be flattered, bribed, or seduced. You will see that he always uses his power for the good of others, never for his own convenience. Never has anyone been so perfectly in line with God's standards.

Still, you'll find that his perfect goodness isn't a grumpy, sour strictness. He will often speak of God's reign in terms of a great party, and almost everywhere he will go, people will throw parties for him. In fact, he will be involved in so many parties and the focus of so much fun that some folks will criticize him for not being stern and strict enough. They'll say he's got the wrong kind of friends, and that they are enjoying themselves far too much to suit the guardians of dour decency. But despite those complaints, Jesus will keep making new friends who will keep throwing parties for him.

You will soon know that Jesus himself is the life of the party. It will be impossible for his friends not to celebrate while he is with them. "I have come," he will explain, "that they may have life, and have it to the full." He will tell his friends that he embodies God's love to them. Why? "So that my joy," he will say, "may be in you and that your joy may be complete." Life to the full, complete joy—that's why there will be parties wherever he goes. People will never have been as happy as when they are with Jesus, and they will keep inviting others to come and see.

What about you? Now that you've met Jesus and had a few minutes to get acquainted, what do you think? Can you see what all the excitement is about? Can you see why so many people are convinced that he's the Son of God?

Would you like to know him better? Then don't stop here. Spend more time with him. Open your Bible to the Gospel accounts of Matthew, Mark, Luke, and John. Pray for the Holy Spirit to connect you with Jesus. Then read more and more of the inspired Gospel words, and brace yourself for the shock and wonder of being with Jesus.

If you will watch him in action, you'll see that no one ever did what Jesus does. If you will listen to him speak, you'll hear that no one has ever spoken the way he spoke. If you will get a sense of his character, you'll feel that no one ever lived the way he lives and that no one ever loved the way he loves.

Sometimes just hearing someone else talk about Jesus is enough to convince you that he's astonishing. That can be the first step in trusting him and having a personal relationship with him, but there's nothing better than getting to know him yourself.

In the Bible, there is a woman who goes through several failed marriages before she meets Jesus. Somehow, Jesus already knows all about her bad past, but he befriends her and says she can have eternal life in him. The woman is overjoyed. She rushes off to tell others in her village to come and see Jesus. Her testimony is so striking that many of the townspeople believe that Jesus must be the Messiah.

Do those townspeople stop with what the woman has told them? No, they go to meet Jesus for themselves and get to know him better. So they ask Jesus to stay with them awhile. Many who weren't convinced before soon become believers, and those who already believed what the woman said about

Jesus gain a more personal and powerful faith when they meet him firsthand. They tell the woman, "We no longer believe just because of what you said; now we have heard for ourselves, and we know that this man really is the Savior of the world."

I hope you'll have that same experience and believe him not just because of what is written here in this book, but because you've met Jesus for yourself and have a personal relationship with him, and know beyond a doubt that he really is the Savior of the world. (You can read my own testimony of how it was that Jesus came to be in my life in the Appendix.)

When Jesus says to you, "Follow me," do it. Only he can give you a life worth living. Only he can give you joy that lasts forever.

Appendix

My Testimony

In this appendix, I want to share with you my own testimony about my relationship with Jesus. I think it may be helpful because—perhaps very much like some of you reading this book—there was a long period in my life where I knew about Jesus (in fact, I probably knew quite a bit about Jesus), but I didn't really know him on a level to have a faith relationship with him.

As a young child growing up in Detroit, I attended Roman Catholic churches. My mother was Catholic and, as was the practice in those days, any child born to a Catholic had to be raised in the church. So we attended mass on a somewhat regular basis. I must admit I knew very little about what was going on. The only thing I could understand was that going to church had something to do with a God who had a son named Jesus and whose mother was named Mary.

During my early school years, I began attending weekly catechism classes. This was required in the Catholic Church as children approached two key milestones in their lives. One was called "First Communion," when it was determined that they knew enough to participate in the mass themselves. The second was called "Confirmation," when it was declared that the young person was now a full-fledged member of the church.

Of course, Catholics believed then—and still do today—that every child actually becomes a Christian at the moment of baptism as infants (that's why it is often called "Christening"), and the work of the church is simply to "confirm" that truth in their lives.

I went through the classes for First Communion, but sometime before my Confirmation, I made a unilateral decision to quit going to church. Needless to say, this caused much consternation in my home, especially with my maternal grandmother who was living with us at the time. But I quit, and ultimately both my parents quit going as well.

Some years later, when I started attending college in Detroit, still living at home, I began to attend a Lutheran church. In fact, it was my Dad's childhood church. The young pastor who started the congregation had lived next door to Dad's family, and they had all attended for some time growing up.

Again, during that period of almost two years I learned more things about Jesus. In fact, I believe that in preparing for membership in the church, I even learned about the great Lutheran doctrine of justification by faith. Whatever I learned, at least it was enough for me to become a member. Once again, however, as soon as I left home to join the Navy, I quit going to church.

I tell you all this background because it is important for you to know why I quit. It is the same reason for just about everyone who grows up in the church and then quits. It's also the same reason for anyone who attends a church for a period of time and then stops attending. I quit because what I knew about God, and what I knew about Jesus, made no difference in my life!

I knew a lot of things about Christianity. I knew that God was the Creator of the universe, and that he provided for his people. I knew that Jesus was his Son who died on a cross to pay the penalty for sins. I knew that the Bible taught that Christians were supposed to live good, moral lives. But at the same time, I also believed that virtually all Americans knew the same thing. Like most other Americans, I assumed that we were all going to heaven some day as long as we weren't too bad (you know, if we weren't murderers or something).

Through all the years I attended church, no one ever told me that knowing all these things about Jesus wasn't enough. Oh, some weird people would confront me and ask me whether I was saved, and try to get me to read tracts, but I just dismissed them as fools. For more than thirty years of my life, no one ever told me that knowing about Jesus was not enough. No one ever told me that what I needed—and what every one of you needs—is to know Jesus personally.

That finally happened in my life in 1969. Actually, the events leading up to that point started in 1967 when I married my wife, Esther. I knew she was a Presbyterian and that her parents were very religious. In fact, her Dad had been some kind of church leader. (I later discovered that he had been a longtime ruling elder in the church.)

I knew that Esther liked to go to church and I would go with her occasionally. I remember when we lived in Falls Church, Virginia, we went to a nearby Presbyterian church. I recall the pastor coming to visit us late one afternoon. Actually, he came about suppertime. Of course, we asked him to join us for our spaghetti dinner (which Esther was easily able to expand to fill one more plate), and boy, did he eat that spaghetti.

He also learned that I didn't know much about the Bible and, when I expressed some interest in learning more, he suggested I get a copy of a particular commentary, which I did. As I started reading in the commentary—of course, starting with Genesis (I always believe in starting books at the beginning)—I was confronted with so many contrary opinions and doubts about the truth of the Bible, I just quit reading. Why bother to read a religious book if nobody could agree? That certainly wouldn't make any difference in my life! So once again, I quit going to church.

In the fall of 1969, Esther and I moved from the Washington, D.C., area to the Philadelphia area, where I was assigned to a ship being rebuilt in the naval shipyard in South Philly. We found an apartment we could afford across the bridge, over in Cherry Hill, New Jersey, and moved in.

The first Sunday after we arrived was a pleasant September morning, so we decided to walk to church. About three blocks from our apartment was a relatively small, community church called Covenant Presbyterian Church. The small print on the sign read, "Reformed Presbyterian Church, Evangelical Synod." Even Esther had no idea what that meant (although she later confided in me that she figured it would be a conservative, Bible-believing congregation, unlike many of the so-called mainline Presbyterian churches).

Well, we started attending that church. At first, I did it for something to do. I knew Esther wanted to go to church; I figured we might make some friends; and besides, the pastor was different. He was passionate about what he said—as though it really was important to him. Interestingly enough, this pastor was not known in his congregation as one who did a lot of visiting. But he did make several attempts to visit us, and finally one night found us at home. He encouraged us to start attending a twenty-something Sunday school class made up mostly of young couples— some with and some without children. He also encouraged me to come by his office sometime to talk if I had any questions about the church.

One afternoon (this would probably be in late October), I got home from work early and decided to drop by his office. I probably had some weird question in my mind to ask him, although for the life of me I can't remember what it was. Anyway, we started discussing the Bible and Jesus, and he began drawing a diagram to show the relationship between God and man. I learned later that it was a classic presentation of the gospel as used by a Christian organization known as the Navigators.

The diagram showed God on one side, and man on the other, and a great gap separating them known as sin. The pastor was saying that the only way to cross that gap—in other words, the only way to have a right relationship with God—was through the bridge we know as the cross of Jesus Christ. I thought all of that was fine—I had heard that before—until he said something that I could not agree with. He said that the cross was the *only* way to have a right relationship with God. He said there was no other way in the world to have this right relationship with God except through Jesus.

Let me tell you, I was really shocked. I really liked this guy; I even enjoyed listening to his sermons. I really liked the Sunday school class. The young couples we were getting to know seemed really nice. In fact, they were the first people I had ever met who seemed to take religion seriously yet at the same time were also "normal." They enjoyed life; we did social events together. They were just regular people instead of the fools I had run into before who claimed to be Christians.

But when Howard Oakley (that was the pastor's name) said that Jesus was the *only way* to God, I got stubborn. That was impossible, I said. I'd been around the world for the past ten years, lived in four different countries, visited in at least twenty others, studied the philosophy of religion in college. I knew there were lots of religions who all believed pretty much the same thing, that people needed to have a religious, moral code by which to live and, as long as they lived their lives pretty much in accord with this moral code, they were OK with God. Certainly, there were lots of different bridges across to God, not just the one bridge of the cross of Jesus Christ.

In his maturity and wisdom, Howard figured out it wouldn't do much good to argue with me, so he asked me whether I had ever read the Bible. I told him I had tried once, but about the time I got to all the "begats" in Genesis, I had given up. He told me something I had never understood before, that the Bible was not simply one book, but rather a compendium of sixty-six different books. He said you didn't have to start with Genesis. He suggested that since my problem was with whether or not Jesus was the only way to have a right relationship with God, I probably should read about Jesus. And, he said, the best place to learn about Jesus was the Gospel of John.

He also asked whether I had a Bible. I, of course, lied, and said yes. That was good, he said, but just in case I ran across anything in my reading that I didn't understand, he lent me a copy of a small commentary on the Gospel of John written by a Presbyterian teacher named Charles Erdman. I knew Esther had a Bible, but I didn't want her to know that I was going to read it, so I went straight to a Christian bookstore on the corner and bought a Bible. In fact, I bought exactly the same Bible I had seen on Howard's desk that afternoon.

I brought the Bible and the little book home and put them in my bedroom, and quickly forgot all about them. Several weeks later, I took a bad case of the flu and stayed home from work for several days. We didn't have much around the apartment to read. We were using rented furniture since it was a temporary assignment and all our regular stuff was in storage. So I pulled the Bible and the little commentary out and began to read the Gospel of John.

You must understand that my whole purpose in beginning to read was to look for the loopholes. I wanted to find things I could use to argue with this preacher in order to show him that the Bible was just simply one more religious document like all the other religious documents in the world.

The first time through, I didn't see anything that seemed particularly new or different. Jesus was obviously upsetting to the religious authorities of his day and so he was executed by dying on a cross. I continued to assume (as I had assumed and believed for years) that most of this story, especially the part about the resurrection, was pretty much a myth. But it was a good myth. It was like all religious myths, which were simply different ways of telling the same story about how a person (no matter what their religion) could end up in heaven.

Since I didn't find the loopholes I was looking for, I decided to read the Gospel again, this time using the commentary. As I went through John's telling of the story of the life of Jesus, I began to see something different. I began to see that Jesus really believed that he was something more than just a religious prophet. Over and over again, he would describe who he was to his followers. *"I am the Bread of Life." "I am the Light of the World." "I am the Way, the Truth, and the Life."*

Well, over the course of those several days, I slowly began to realize that I was wrong and that Howard Oakley, the pastor of Covenant Presbyterian Church in Cherry Hill, New Jersey, was absolutely right. Jesus really was who he said he was. This story was no myth. It was truth. It was *true* truth. There really was a creator God. There really was a man called Jesus who was God's only, unique Son. And his death on that cross wasn't just an execution for being a troublemaker; it was the sacrifice of God's Son to pay the required penalty I deserved to pay for my own sins. There was, in fact, no other way to deal with the problem of my sins. I couldn't be good enough to earn my way to heaven. Only the finished work of Jesus, dying in my place, would qualify me for that eternal relationship and life with God. Jesus was the only bridge!

So finally, after I don't know how many readings of the book—five or ten, perhaps even more—I finally got to the section of John 20:31. As I once again read the words of that verse, it became totally clear to me. "These things are written that you might believe that Jesus is the Messiah (that he really is who he says he is) and that believing, you might have life in his name."

You see, friends, it's not enough to know about Jesus. In fact, it's not even enough to know who Jesus really is. James tells us in his epistle that even the demons believe that Jesus is the Son of God. That's not enough. What you believe about Jesus has to make a difference in your life. That is John's point when he writes ". . . that believing you might have life in his name."

Believing in Jesus has to make a difference in your life, in how you act, in what you do. That's exactly why three previous times in my life, I had attended churches, had learned about Jesus, had even understood quite a bit about God and sin and the cross. But every time I would quit attending church because what I had learned, what I had even believed, had made no real difference in my life.

Finally, in the fall of 1969, it *did* make a difference. My life changed. I not only believed, I trusted. I had true faith that Jesus was the only way to be in a right relationship with God. That faith brought about a change in me, so that I no longer was simply an American who culturally believed that I, like everyone else around me, was a Christian. I really became a follower and disciple of Jesus Christ.

That is exactly what I wish for every single one of you reading this book. I want you not only to know about Jesus, but to come to know him on a personal basis. I pray that you would see that who he is and what he has done have meaning and significance in your life, and that, as a result, your life also would change. I pray that you would stop doubting and confess that Jesus is indeed your Lord and your God!

About the Author

Dr. Clements was ordained in July of 1974 in the National Presbyterian Church (the original name of the PCA). After several years as a pastor in Central Georgia Presbytery, he returned to the U.S. Navy, where he had previously spent twelve years on active duty prior to entering seminary. Having left as an enlisted man (Chief Petty Officer), he returned as a Navy Chaplain.

Serving ten additional years on active duty on assignments with Destroyer Squadrons in San Diego; at the Naval Air Station in Pensacola; as Chaplain for a nuclear-powered guided missile cruiser and a submarine tender in Norfolk, and finally as Chaplain of the Naval Hospital, Newport, R.I., Don retired in 1985.

For the next eighteen years, he pastored two "turn-around" church revitalizations of small churches in Blacksburg and Narrows, Va. On January 1, 2003, he moved full-time into a ministry he had developed called *Metokos Ministries—Encouragement for Small Churches.* Affiliated with the Presbyterian Evangelistic Fellowship (PEF) as an evangelist, Don works with small churches (mostly under a hundred members) that need encouragement and resources to develop vision plans, go through pulpit transitions, and deal with other specific needs. (Visit his website at *www.metokos.org.*)

Don holds an M.Div. (with honors) from Covenant Theological Seminary in St. Louis, and a D.Min. (in Adult Education) from Gordon-Conwell Theological Seminary in South Hamilton, Mass. He and his wife, Esther, live with their cocker spaniel "Shadow" in their newly remodeled retirement home in the Appalachian Mountain town of Narrows, Virginia, and they spend lots of time visiting their three grown daughters, who live in Mississippi, South Dakota, and Virginia.